NOT GUILTY

MW00459580

THE UNLAWFUL PROSECUTION OF U.S. SENATOR TED STEVENS

BY ROB CARY

NACDL PRESS

™

THOMSON REUTERS™

For Customer Assistance Call 1-800-328-4880

Mat #41677241

"Thank goodness we don't have to rely upon the United States to give him a fair trial."

Emmet G. Sullivan
U.S. District Court Judge
October 8, 2008

AUTHOR'S NOTE

Brendan Sullivan asked me to join him in representing Senator Ted Stevens. Brendan is the most senior partner at Williams & Connolly LLP, the Washington, D.C. law firm where I have worked my entire career. Brendan practices law according to a set of rules he expects all Williams & Connolly lawyers to follow. One of his rules is this: "Do not speak publicly about a case outside the courtroom." What's more, Brendan practices what he preaches, and so do I.

In my 18 years as a Williams & Connolly lawyer, I had never spoken publicly about a case outside a courtroom. I agreed with Brendan's rule that "cases are to be won in the courtroom, not in the press." Clients are usually grateful that we stick to this rule, even after a case is over. They do not want to be reminded of a case that for most of them was a nightmare, even if they won.

So why have I decided to break our rule by writing a book about a case? There are three reasons.

First, the public must understand what happened to Senator Stevens. People need to know that it took the combined efforts of a dozen defense lawyers working around the clock – and the active presence of an exceptional federal judge – to prove that the prosecution itself was corrupt. Two investigations have resulted in over 1000 pages of reports that explain how the prosecution concealed evidence of innocence from the defense. But neither provides a narrative of the case from the defense perspective. This book tells the story as we lived it and explains how we would have used the evidence that was hidden from us.

Second, our criminal justice system is broken. It needs reform. *United States v. Stevens* is a textbook example of what can go wrong in a criminal case. If the government can conceal critical evidence from a U.S. Senator, it can conceal evidence from any citizen. I believe that what happened to Senator Stevens has happened more frequently than most of us could imagine. My hope is that this book will lead to reforms that will level the playing field for all citizens facing criminal prosecution – especially those with limited resources to defend themselves.

The third reason – equally important but more personal – is that Senator Stevens asked me to write this book. I tried to beg off. I recommended a best-selling author who wanted to do a book about the trial, but the Senator and his family said it had to be done by someone who had lived the case – before, during, and after. Ultimately, Catherine Stevens, the Senator's widow, delivered the clincher. She said, "Rob, Ted wanted this book to be written – and he wanted you to write it." So, with Catherine's encouragement – and Brendan's blessing – that is what I have done.

Rob Cary
Washington, D.C.
May 30, 2014

TABLE OF CONTENTS

Chapter
1

Arraignment

On the last day of July, 2008, moments after U.S. Marshals had parted a sea of photographers and television cameramen so Senator Ted Stevens could enter the courthouse, the defendant stood before United States District Court Judge Emmet G. Sullivan.

Wearing a summer suit, a light blue shirt, and a navy blue tie with a matching pocket handkerchief, the lawmaker was the picture of respectability. He stood, as always, as if at attention. An American flag pin adorned his lapel. Ted Stevens had been in the U.S. Senate for 40 years. In less than a month, he'd face an easy primary contest for re-election, but a hotly-contested general election was less than 100 days away.

The Senator's wife Catherine and daughter Beth sat in the front row of the packed courtroom. Down the hall, an overflow room with live camera feeds from the courtroom gave members of the media the ability to set up computers and type as they followed the proceedings.

The courtroom clerk asked Ted Stevens, "In criminal case number 08-231, you are charged with false statements. How do you wish to plead?"

"We plead not guilty, Your Honor," my senior partner, Brendan Sullivan, replied on behalf of the Senator.

Judge Emmet Sullivan (no relation to Brendan) said, "All right, how would you like to proceed, counsel?"

1

"Your Honor," Brendan replied, "there are a couple of things I want to bring to the Court's attention. The government, as you probably know, chose to indict this case 28 days before a primary election in Alaska, which is now scheduled for August 26th. The general election for Senator Ted Stevens is on November 4th, which will be 98 days after the indictment was returned, and I appear here today, not to ask for any special favors because he's a senator and served forty years in the Senate, but I do want to ask the Court to give consideration to the fact that he would like to clear his name before the general election, and to do that we respectfully request . . . if at all possible that the trial be in October so that he could clear his name before the general election."

* * * * *

Two days earlier, at the U.S. Department of Justice, seven blocks away, Acting Assistant Attorney General Matthew Friederich had held a televised press conference.

"Earlier today," he told the assembled reporters and his live CNN audience, "a federal grand jury, here in the District of Columbia, returned an indictment charging United States Senator Ted Stevens of Alaska with seven felony counts of making false statements. The charges relate to false statements that Senator Stevens is alleged to have made on his mandatory financial disclosure forms filed for calendar years 1999 through 2006.

"The indictment charges that while he was sitting as a United States Senator between 1999 and 2006, Senator Stevens accepted gifts from a privately held company known as VECO, its chief executive officer and others. VECO was an oilfield services company and operated on an international basis. VECO was one of the largest private employers in the state of Alaska.

"The gifts Senator Stevens is alleged to have received include substantial amounts of material and labor used in the renovation of a private residence which Senator Stevens and his wife owned located in the town of Girdwood, Alaska. These renovations are alleged to have included the addition of a new first floor with multiple bedrooms and a bathroom as well as a finished basement. VECO contractors and employees performed a significant portion of these renovations."

Friederich then added a bit of background. "As you may know, in about 2004, federal law enforcement agencies began an investigation into public corruption in the state of Alaska. The fact of this investigation became publicly known with the execution of search warrants at VECO and other locations in Alaska in August of 2006. To date, the investigation has resulted in seven convictions."

He went on to list a number of men who had been convicted, but as far as Ted Stevens and the criminal charges filed against him were concerned, the only significant name was that of Bill Allen, former CEO of VECO, once Ted Stevens' friend—and now his Judas.

* * * * *

Shortly after the press conference ended, a stunned Ted Stevens sat in my office. As a lawyer and a former prosecutor himself, he was having great difficulty trying to understand how he could have been indicted for, allegedly, not declaring as gifts the value of renovations to his Alaskan cabin when *he and his wife had paid over $160,000 for renovations that the tax assessor valued at $104,800 and a bank appraiser determined should have cost $124,000.* His temper rising, the Senator said. "We'll lose the election if I don't clear my name by November 4. I want the trial over before November."

My firm's practice is *not* to ask for speedy trials. Our founder, famed trial lawyer Edward Bennett Williams, used to say, "A continuance is as good as an acquittal, it just doesn't last as long."

I told the Senator that we never asked for a speedy trial, because we used the time to prepare.

"But I'm innocent!" he bellowed back at me. "The Constitution says I'm entitled to a speedy trial. I want a trial before the election."

The Senator was right about two things. First, he was innocent. I thought the government's case was frivolous. How could prosecu-

3

tors say that renovations were a gift if he paid more for them than they were worth? Second, he would probably lose the election if he didn't get exonerated quickly.

It was unheard of for a defendant in a white-collar case to go to trial so quickly. However, *this* defendant was 84 years old. And in the two years since he'd walked into our offices for the first time, I had become fond of him. He was a good man, and he deserved a speedy trial if he wanted one. Surely, if we had a fast trial, the truth would emerge.

I did some quick thinking and responded instinctively, "OK, so long as Brendan agrees. If he does, then we'll ask for a speedy trial."

Brendan was driving back from New England, having cut short his vacation after learning about the surprise indictment. When I reached Brendan on his cell phone, he told me he had already been thinking about whether we could try the case as quickly as the Senator would want. He and I agreed. "This is the one case in our careers where we need to ask for a speedy trial. This man deserves a trial before the election."

Senator Ted Stevens smiled as I reported the news. "But don't get your hopes up," I cautioned him. "Chances are almost 100 percent that Judge Sullivan will be too busy to give us a trial before the election."

* * * * *

At the arraignment two days later, after hearing Brendan's request for a speedy trial, Judge Sullivan addressed the Government's lead trial lawyer, Brenda Morris. "How realistic is it from the government's viewpoint that this case could be tried prior to November?"

Morris must have expected the question. "We can begin this case on September 22," she replied.

Judge Sullivan asked how long it would take the government to present its case. "Three weeks," Morris predicted.

That meant that if we could present our defense in two weeks, the trial would be completed by October 27, eight days before the general election.

Brendan told Judge Sullivan, "Usually we don't mind if a case is postponed two or three years." But this case was different. "I've never had a situation when the general election came 98 days after indictment," Brendan added. "I believe we can do it. We've thought about it and I'm happy to hear the government can do it, and if the Court can possibly find a way, we will do it."

Judge Sullivan took a recess to consult his calendar and see if there was a way.

* * * * *

In the meantime, my job was to take the Senator to the cellblock in the basement of the Courthouse for the routine booking of a criminal defendant: paperwork, fingerprinting, and mug shots. This was handled by the U.S. Marshals who seemed sorry that they were required to put a sitting U.S. Senator through the process.

I was not allowed to accompany the Senator into the cellblock, but the Marshals told me that they would take good care of him, and I believed them. They had done an exceptionally good job getting the Senator and his family into the courthouse safely. At trial, it would be our job—Brendan's and mine and that of the team we would need to assemble—to get him out just as safely.

* * * * *

Judge Sullivan returned to the courtroom. He had looked over his calendar and announced, to my great surprise, that he *could* accommodate our request for an early trial.

He then said, "The government is prepared to give you everything that the government believes is discoverable; is that right?"

Judge Sullivan was referring to discovery: the process by which the government and the defense are required to share information with each other. The most important type of discovery in a criminal case is *Brady* information, named after the 1963 case called *Brady v.*

Maryland, in which the Supreme Court made clear that the U.S. Constitution requires the government to provide "evidence that is favorable to the accused" and that is "material either to guilt or punishment." Interestingly, Judge Sullivan was raising the issue on the first day.

Brenda Morris replied, "The bulk of it, your Honor, next week. There will be some other matters that we just don't have available to give at this point, just because of the technical issues, but we will be able to give the bulk of it next week." In the days and weeks ahead, Morris would repeatedly pledge that all required information was being disclosed to the defense.

* * * * *

So began the case of *United States v. Stevens.* The Senator had pled not guilty. The trial would occur quickly and would most likely conclude before election day. And the lead prosecutor had pledged that all required information would be provided to the defense.

Chapter 2

Operation Polar Pen

It had all begun two years earlier, in early September, 2006. I was sitting in my office at Williams & Connolly in downtown Washington, DC, preparing for another trial. Getting ready for a trial is hard work, and over the years I've found I'm most comfortable and can do so best when I'm surrounded by reminders of what I love: photos of my wife and me on our wedding day; our daughters, then beginning the fifth and seventh grades; photos of my parents in Hannibal, Missouri, Mark Twain's hometown and mine; and framed drawings of the small-town courthouses where my late father, also a lawyer, had tried cases. There were photos of fishing trips, family reunions, and youth sports teams I had coached, plus photos of teams of lawyers with whom I'd worked on cases.

Williams & Connolly was founded by Edward Bennett Williams, the legendary trial lawyer who first brought respectability to the area of the law now known as white collar criminal defense. Williams died a quarter century ago—a month before I interviewed for a job at Williams & Connolly—but his influence is everywhere, especially in his many wise (and often also witty) observations that have been passed down through generations of the firm's lawyers. One aphorism attributed to Edward Bennett Williams is: "Every year in Washington they have a witch hunt. The key is not to be this year's witch." I was about to learn the truth of that statement.

My phone rang. It was Brendan Sullivan, our firm's most senior partner. "Rob," Brendan asked, "are you available to attend a meeting in my office with Senator Ted Stevens? He'll be here shortly."

I had little advance notice, and I had lots to do, but when Brendan Sullivan calls and asks you to attend a meeting with a sitting U.S. Senator, you say yes. I set aside what I was doing and headed straight to Brendan's office.

* * * * *

Brendan is a tall, thin man with white hair, a receding hairline, horn-rimmed glasses, blue eyes and a Rhode Island accent. He has a quick wit, a keen mind for strategy and an iron will. He works out of a large office in our firm with a conference table that seats eight to accommodate team meetings. I was introduced to the Senator and to a man named Bill Phillips. Bill had been the Senator's chief-of-staff in the 1980s (during which time Phillips earned a law degree by attending Georgetown Law School at night). Bill now had his own law firm and was a dear friend of Senator Stevens. Bill had brought the Senator to our firm.

Sitting side by side, Ted Stevens and Bill Phillips were quite a pair, and quite an obvious odd couple. The Senator was relatively short, just five feet seven inches in height, whereas Phillips was very tall, six foot seven in fact. The Senator had a tendency to frown (he was famous for being, or appearing to be, "grumpy") but Bill almost always had a smile on his face. The Senator was 82 years old; Bill Phillips was 51. Yet despite the dissimilarity in age and appearance, they were alike in several ways that counted. Both had eyes that twinkled; both were charming; and both had hearty laughs.

They were in Brendan's office because a group of the Senator's former staff members had determined that the Senator needed criminal defense counsel. They had asked Bill Phillips to lead the search. It wasn't that the former staffers thought Senator Stevens was guilty. (Everyone I met—and especially his staff and former staff—believed the Senator to be absolutely honest.) But the newspapers were reporting a possible scandal in the Senator's home state of

Alaska centered around VECO and Bill Allen. Former Stevens staffers were like a family, united by their love for the Senator, whom they called "the boss." They feared that because of the Senator's prominence, especially in the state of Alaska, the Senator might be drawn into the Bill Allen scandal. That's why they drafted Bill Phillips to find Senator Stevens a lawyer.

The word around Alaska was that prosecutors were going to claim that, thanks to Bill Allen, Senator Stevens and his wife paid less than full value for renovations to their cabin in their home state of Alaska. The Senator called it "the chalet"—somewhat facetiously—because of its steep, pitched roof. In truth it was no one's idea of a chalet. The cabin, the Senator's official residence in Alaska, was anything but fancy. I've been there several times, and my immediate thought upon seeing it was always the same: *this* is the official residence of a United States Senator?

It was a two bedroom home on a gravel road 40 miles from downtown Anchorage. There, all resemblance to a "chalet" ended. The main floor, which became the second floor post-renovation, was a medium-sized open room with little of what design magazines call "style". The furniture was older and distinctly un-modern. Most of it had been chosen by the Senator's first wife, Ann, who had died in the crash of a small plane in 1978. To the Senator, who rarely used the Girdwood residence, it was a place for comfortable solitude, a place where he could chop wood and enjoy the land he had nurtured to statehood.

In one corner of the garage there was a well-used punching bag normally found in gyms where boxers train. It would be a safe guess that very few chalets have a punching bag. In addition, there was a weight bench and weights, plus an exercise bike. Having seen this equipment with my own eyes on my first trip to the cabin, I was not surprised when the Senator told me, which he did not once but several times during the case, that he expected to live to be 120.

As they got older, the Senator and Mrs. Stevens decided it was time to add two more bedrooms so that their grandchildren could visit. Although the original cost estimate on the building permit was

$87,000, they ended up paying over $160,000 for the renovations. Because of the distance between Washington, D.C. and Girdwood, Alaska, the Senator accepted the suggestion of two friends, Bill Allen and Bob Persons (who owned a nearby restaurant) to keep an eye on the project.

When they took out a line of credit to pay for the project, the bank's appraiser found that the renovations should have cost about $124,000. The assessor for the City of Anchorage found that the renovations were worth even less: about $105,000. According to these unbiased real estate experts, the $160,000 that the Stevens family paid was *more than the renovations should have cost* and was *more than the renovations were actually worth*.

Significant gifts to U.S. Senators must be reported on financial disclosure forms provided by the Senate Ethics Committee. The Senator and Mrs. Stevens certainly didn't think that there was anything to report because they had paid for the renovations themselves. No complaint was ever filed with the Senate Ethics Committee.

Yet we heard persistent rumors that the Department of Justice was issuing grand jury subpoenas to every person who did any work on the cabin renovation, including some workers who also worked for Bill Allen at VECO. Federal prosecutors were apparently attempting to prove that the cabin renovations were worth more than the Senator had paid. We were being told third and fourth hand that the government would claim that by not disclosing that the renovations were worth *more* than the Senator and Mrs. Stevens paid for them, the Senator had lied by not disclosing the renovations as gifts.

As part of an investigation labeled Operation Polar Pen, the Feds were pursuing Allen and VECO, the very successful company he had founded. The Alaska press was reporting that the FBI had searched VECO's offices and the offices of a number of state lawmakers in Alaska for evidence that Bill Allen and his company had bribed them in exchange for legislative action on their behalf. All told, the FBI executed 20 search warrants in August of 2006.

Bill Phillips and the Senator's other former staffers knew that many prosecutors try to nail the highest-profile person they can. Bill Allen was a very big fish, but prosecutors were undoubtedly putting pressure on Bill Allen to buy his freedom by delivering a bigger fish. Rumor had it that the Feds had a strong case against Allen for bribing state legislators. With the leverage prosecutors had over Allen, he might say anything.

* * * * *

"Operation Polar Pen" was the FBI's code name for its investigation into whether the awarding of construction contracts for private prisons in Alaska was being done illegally. Federal investigations such as Operation Polar Pen are confidential. Thus we never learned when or how the investigation began, but much of what happened in the probe made its way into the newspapers, and by the time we met with Senator Stevens, the press was reporting that the FBI was investigating VECO.

VECO's founder, Bill Allen, was one of the most successful businessmen in Alaska. A large man with a folksy manner, Allen had dropped out of high school at 15, and found work in New Mexico where his family lived at the time. After stints in Texas, Louisiana, and California, in 1968 he moved to Alaska and began working as a welder on an offshore oil platform in the Cook Inlet of the Pacific Ocean. A good welder, young Bill Allen caught the eye of oil company executives who suggested he go into business himself.

Allen and a man named William Veltrie founded V-E Construction in 1969 which specialized in oil-related projects. They started with about a dozen employees. Just the previous year, oil had been discovered at Prudhoe Bay on Alaska's Arctic coast and it was about to become the biggest oil field in North America. V-E Construction was in the right place at the right time. Not long after they renamed the company VECO, Allen bought out Veltrie's share.

The Arab oil embargo of 1973 changed Alaska history. Before the embargo, many environmentalists and Alaska natives objected to building a pipeline to deliver oil from Alaska's North Slope down to shipping ports hundreds of miles to the south on environmental grounds. But the embargo changed attitudes overnight, as the actions of OPEC sent the price of oil skyrocketing. Americans realized that the United States needed Alaska's oil. Construction began in 1975. By the time the pipeline was completed in 1977, VECO had 1,500 employees.

In the 1980s, VECO's business experienced a downturn. It went through bankruptcy, but then Bill Allen got lucky. When the Exxon Valdez spill ocurred in 1989, Exxon chose VECO to be the lead contractor in the cleanup effort, and VECO became Alaska's largest employer. As VECO's founder and CEO, Bill Allen was making a fortune. By the year 2000, VECO had 4,000 employees.

Naturally VECO, like any company doing business in Alaska, had legitimate dealings with both the federal government and the Alaska congressional delegation. When Senator Stevens returned to Alaska, he sometimes saw Bill Allen and over time a friendship developed. Allen could be charming and in some ways was very impressive: a successful, self-made man with a down-home charm who appeared to many to be a model citizen.

But Bill Allen had a dark side which he had kept mostly hidden. Video surveillance conducted as a part of Operation Polar Pen revealed that Bill Allen was secretly paying cash to some Alaska state legislators. The FBI confronted Allen on August 30, 2006. What happened at this confrontation remains largely unknown; no meaningful record was made of the meeting (or, if one was made, it has never been disclosed).

Allen later admitted that the FBI threatened him with a 20 year sentence for what he had done. And Allen's son, Mark Allen, was in trouble too. Bill Allen and Mark Allen had been overheard on wiretaps talking about a scheme to kill Bill Allen's nephew, Dave Anderson (who will surface again later in this tale). Thus, Mark Allen faced a potential charge of conspiracy to commit murder. But if Allen provided "cooperation" to prosecutors, Allen could serve less that 20 years and his son (and other children who apparently had exposure to prosecution as well) would not be charged with crimes at all.

In addition to immunity from prosecution for his children, Allen was given time to sell his company. In fact, thanks to his "cooperation" with government prosecutors, Allen took advantage of the window they provided him to sell his company for $350 million. In addition, as part of his deal with the government, Allen's cooperation would be considered the same as VECO's, which meant that VECO would not be charged with crimes. This was critical, because Allen wanted to sell VECO, and if the company was charged with a crime, it would likely have been put out of business, and nobody would have paid any money for it.

Thanks to his cooperation, Allen was able to sell VECO to a company named CH2M Hill. But Allen's deal with the government had a kicker: CH2M Hill negotiated a special provision in the sales contract with Allen by which it held back $70 million of the purchase price to insure that Allen continued to cooperate with the government. That is, Allen and his family would not receive the additional $70 million if CH2M Hill suffered a loss because Allen did not cooperate fully with the government.

This deal made good sense from CH2M Hill's perspective, because if Allen angered the government and the government indicted VECO, VECO would probably be driven out of business. CH2M Hill would lose the hundreds of millions of dollars it had already invested in its purchase of VECO. So CH2M Hill made sure Allen cooperated.

What does "cooperation" mean? In theory, cooperation means telling the truth. But in far too many cases, cooperation has meant delivering the testimony the government wants to hear regardless of the truth.

Talk about incentives—Allen and his family would receive the last $70 million of the purchase price only if Allen kept the government happy. Allen would receive a reduced sentence. Allen's children would not be charged with any crimes. So Allen, of course, would cooperate—by delivering the testimony the government wanted to hear.

At the end of the day, prosecutors advised a federal judge in Alaska that Allen had cooperated and that his sentence should be reduced. Under the guidelines established by the U.S. Sentencing Commission, Allen's sentence would have been nine to eleven years. Theoretically he faced a maximum of 20 years in prison. However, based on the government's recommendation, Allen received a sentence of just three years of which, under the standard reductions available to him, he would serve less than two years.

All told, Allen's family received hundreds of millions of dollars from the sale of VECO, with each of the children receiving large chunks of money. Mark Allen, one of Bill Allen's sons, used some of his wealth to buy a racehorse named "Mine That Bird," which won the 2009 Kentucky Derby. On Derby Day, I watched on TV as Mark Allen celebrated in the winner's circle. As I thought of the deal his father had cut with our government, I was disgusted. Mark Allen had received immunity from prosecution and enough money to buy a Kentucky Derby winner.

* * * * *

After Allen began cooperating, articles appeared suggesting that VECO's CEO had another side that a jury would have despised: he sexually abused underage girls. After Senator Stevens' trial was over, an attorney from the Department of Justice's Child Exploitation and Obscenity Section working with the Anchorage Police Department investigated and recommended that charges be brought against Allen. Without any public explanation, the attorney's superiors at the Department of Justice rejected his recommendation.

Sergeant Kevin Vandegriff of the Anchorage Police Department, who had worked on the investigation, was upset at the Department's decision. "I think we put together a very solid case; we did a lot of work on it," he told the *Anchorage Daily News*. "It deserved to be indicted and heard before a jury." One of Allen's alleged victims called the DOJ's decision "devastating." Her primary reason for coming forward was "to get Bill to stop seeing young girls." To this day, the Department of Justice has not explained why it stopped the child exploitation case against Allen from going forward.

I do not know whether the government gave Allen a pass on child sex crimes as part of his deal. There is no direct evidence of it. I do know this: the possibility of a child sex abuse charge hanging over Allen like the sword of Damocles must have had an impact on him. It must have provided a strong incentive for him to please the government.

Regardless of what incentives the sex abuse allegations provided Allen, everybody admitted that he received extraordinary benefits in exchange for his testimony: a greatly reduced sentence; hundreds of millions of dollars; and a guaranty of freedom for his children. Many people would lie in order to reduce or eliminate the time they would otherwise have to spend in prison. Without a doubt, many people would lie for hundreds of millions of dollars. Almost all parents would lie to keep their children out of prison.

Prosecutors have a powerful set of inducements at their disposal, and they utilized this full arsenal of incentives to get Bill Allen to cooperate. Defense lawyers do not have the ability to incentivize witnesses. As Brendan says, "If a defense lawyer gave those sorts of benefits to a defense witness, that lawyer would be indicted and disbarred. But the government does it with impunity in many cases. The coin of the realm is freedom, for which the government gets the testimony it wants. The incentives the government provides to its witnesses in criminal cases is, in reality, legally sanctioned bribery."

* * * * *

By mid-September, 2006, multiple people had told Bill Phillips that if the Senator needed a lawyer, he should see Brendan Sullivan. Why? Perhaps because Brendan had been fighting (and shutting down) Washington witch hunts for decades. Brendan and a team of lawyers from our firm (before I arrived) successfully represented Lieutenant Colonel Oliver North in the Iran-Contra matter in the

1980s, fighting for him throughout Congressional hearings, an independent counsel investigation, and a criminal trial. After the four year battle, all charges against North were dismissed—a complete victory. Five years later, North won the Republican nomination in Virginia for the U.S. Senate. Today Oliver North is a successful author, television personality, and business person.

In the 1990s, Brendan and a team of lawyers from our firm successfully represented Department of Housing and Urban Development Secretary Henry Cisneros in another classic battle against government prosecutors with unlimited resources. The independent counsel spent tens of millions of dollars investigating whether Cisneros had properly disclosed payments to a girlfriend. Cisneros survived that legal attack, and went on to success in business, including a stint as President and Chief Operating Officer of Univision, the largest Spanish-speaking television network in the United States.

In the 2000s, Brendan and a number of my Williams & Connolly colleagues successfully represented New York Stock Exchange Chairman Richard Grasso against unfair charges brought by the Attorney General of New York. The Grasso team won a total victory in court.

Over the years, we've also represented many companies and individuals in cases that received little or no press attention. Nothing gives Brendan more satisfaction than achieving a quiet victory for a client with no media attention at all. I've seen it up close. Brendan does not like publicity, and he certainly does not seek it out. Brendan has turned down many high-profile, lucrative cases over the years because he was already committed to other cases that were not receiving any media attention at all.

Brendan's philosophy is that a commitment is a commitment. He is driven by a sense of duty. He worked as a lifeguard growing up in Rhode Island. He has told me many times that he learned from being a lifeguard that somebody's life may depend on your being where you're supposed to be. "Never abandon your post," he likes to say.

Most of all, Brendan is a fighter. He handled his first case as a lawyer while in the Army. Brendan was a Captain stationed at the Presidio in San Francisco during the Vietnam War after his graduation from Georgetown Law School.

The Army charged 27 soldiers with mutiny for singing "We Shall Overcome" in protest of the Vietnam War. Even though Brendan was not a Judge Advocate General's Corps attorney ("JAG Corps," as it is familiarly called) the word was out that he was the kind of officer who truly cared for his men and their welfare, and so he was asked to represent some of them. At first Brendan hesitated. He wasn't an Army lawyer, just a young transportation Captain who happened to have gone to law school. (In fact, he wanted to go into business after his Army service was completed and never intended to practice law.) But Brendan agreed, reluctantly, to represent the soldiers because he felt they were being treated unfairly.

As part of his defense, Brendan served a subpoena on a general to give testimony at trial. When he received the subpoena, the general did two things. First, he tore up the subpoena, and, second, he ordered Brendan Sullivan to Vietnam.

After newspaper headlines proclaimed "Army Captain Transferred to Vietnam for Defending His Client," the Army's retaliation against Brendan became a national news story. And then no less an American icon than Walter Cronkite picked up the story and mentioned it repeatedly on the CBS nightly news.

At that point, Congress intervened. An investigation determined that the general in question had ordered a "punitive transfer" because he was angered by Brendan's trial tactics, and in short order, Brendan's orders were cancelled and he returned to the military courtroom. The three-star general didn't fare so well. He soon retired and lost one star for his misconduct.

Struck by Brendan's courage, one of his former professors at Georgetown Law School, Assistant Dean Richard Allen Gordon, told Brendan that he wanted to set him up with an interview with the legendary Edward Bennett Williams. Despite the fact that his first response was, "Are you crazy?" Brendan agreed. After meeting Brendan, Williams said, "OK kid, I'll give you a shot." That was 1969, and Brendan has been working at our firm ever since and is now Williams & Connolly's senior partner.

* * * * *

While Bill Phillips and the Senator's other former staffers were worried that they were about to witness a witch hunt, the Senator was not worried. The Senator knew he was not a criminal. He believed to his core that he had not done anything wrong. He was 84 years old and had lived his life well. He knew that investigations are a way of life in Washington. He had been investigated before and cleared.

In fact, after one investigation of Senator Stevens, the FBI actually apologized to him. During that investigation, the Senator had opened his office to the FBI. He wanted to do the same thing this time and told me he was confident that this investigation would end the same way. I wasn't so sure. What I had seen in other cases made me deeply skeptical of the government, especially when they were providing benefits to a snitch witness like Bill Allen.

The first thing we wanted to impress upon the Senator was that he should not meet with the prosecutors and tell them his side of the story, which he wanted to do. He thought that if only he could meet with them, he could convince them he had done nothing wrong. We disagreed, fearing that if he did so the government would simply have Bill Allen revise his testimony. A snitch always knows what to do.

There was an additional danger. What we knew, and the Senator probably did not, was that modern legal history is replete with examples of criminal defendants who did themselves grave harm by speaking to investigators before knowing all the facts. These defendants were not necessarily guilty of the potential crime for which they were being investigated in the first place, but, because they spoke to government investigators before they understood the facts, they were found guilty of obstruction of justice or of making a false statement to the government.

One of the most famous examples is Scooter Libby, the former Chief of Staff to then Vice-President Dick Cheney. Libby was found guilty of making false statements to government prosecutors investigating media leaks regarding a CIA agent. Libby was not charged with—much less found guilty of—the underlying offense of actually leaking classified information. But he was found guilty of making false statements to investigators. If Libby hadn't spoken to investigators, he never would have been charged with any crime.

Another well-known example is the home decorating media star Martha Stewart. She was being investigated for insider trading. She did not engage in insider trading, but like Libby, she made statements to government investigators which turned out to be wrong. She was convicted of making false statements—not of insider trading—and went to jail. In fact, Stewart wasn't even *charged* with insider trading. Like Libby, if she hadn't spoken to investigators, she never would have been charged with any crime.

Still another example of a completely avoidable obstruction of justice charge was the case against the accounting firm Arthur Andersen. At trial, Andersen was found guilty of obstructing the government's investigation of financial reporting of the Enron Corporation. Again, Andersen was not charged with participating in improper financial reporting at Enron. Rather, Andersen was charged with obstructing the government's investigation of that financial reporting, because a few Andersen employees destroyed potentially relevant documents. The Andersen conviction for obstruction of justice was eventually overturned by the U.S. Supreme Court—but not before Andersen went out of business and 85,000 employees lost their jobs.

What are the lessons from the Libby, Stewart, and Andersen cases? First, don't let the target of a criminal investigation make statements to government investigators—because you generally do not know everything that the government knows or, for that matter, everything that the government can get someone to say. And you do not know what prosecutors will later claim was a "false" statement. Second, when an investigation is under way, do not do anything that prosecutors could possibly say obstructed the investigation. Preserve all evidence. Do not throw out any documents. Leave everything the government wants exactly where it was when the investigation began. Do not delete emails. In other words, when prosecutors are looking for this year's witch to burn at the stake, don't help them stack the wood.

Chapter
3

Alaskan of the Century

Aside from a few rumblings and a lot of rumors out of Alaska, we heard little or nothing from the U.S. Government for months and months. But, on May 9, 2007, Bill Welch, the Chief of the Justice Department's Public Integrity Section called. He told me that Senator Stevens needed to sign a "tolling agreement" before the close of business that same day.

A tolling agreement is an agreement to extend (or "toll") the time limit, also known as the statute of limitations, that normally applies to the government's decision to bring charges. In most cases, the federal government has five years in which to bring a criminal case. Welch wanted Senator Stevens to sign the tolling agreement, which would extend that deadline, voluntarily.

"Why would—why *should*—the Senator agree to extend the statute of limitations on a day's notice?" I asked.

"Because if he doesn't," replied Welch, "we will indict him tomorrow—in the District of Columbia—for tax evasion and for making false statements on his financial disclosure forms."

* * * * *

My first thought was instinctive: if Ted Stevens, a high-profile Republican, did not sign immediately, he would be indicted in Washington D.C., a city with roughly ten times as many Democrats as Republicans. Alaska, by contrast, where prosecutors could have decided to bring a case against Senator Stevens, has more Republicans than Democrats, though the numbers are not nearly so lopsided.

Welch broke into my silence by telling me that I needed to track the Senator down and get him to sign the agreement immediately.

With Bill Phillips's help, I found the Senator, and when confronted with what was actually a non-choice, he decided that rather than be indicted the next day, he would sign the agreement.

* * * * *

What really bothered me—in addition to the government's arrogant behavior—was that they could treat *this man* so callously. First and foremost, Ted Stevens was an American citizen, and all American citizens are entitled to fair treatment from their government. From one persective, that is all anyone should need to know. But Ted Stevens had led an extraordinary life and some background on that life provides additional perspective and may explain why some DOJ lawyers were hell-bent to get him.

It is a sad fact that our culture encourages the destruction of those who have accomplished the most. This is especially true in Washington, D.C., where public officials are especially susceptible to this phenomenon. The higher they've climbed, the more Washington relishes their fall.

Ted Stevens was a towering figure in Washington. He had served more than 40 years in the Senate. He was the longest-serving Republican Senator in American history. Moreover, he came from an era in the Senate when bipartisanship was valued more than it is today. Many of his good friends over the years were Democrats.

From 2003-2007, Ted Stevens served as President Pro Tem of the Senate, a position that put him third in line of succession to the presidency (behind the Vice-President and the Speaker-of-the-House) should something happen to the President. The longest serving President Pro Tem in American history was Senator Robert C. Byrd, a Democrat of West Virginia. Here is what Senator Byrd said about his friend Ted Stevens:

I have always known Senator Ted Stevens to be an outstanding Senator, a great colleague, and a trusted friend. Oh, I realize, he may grumble every now and then. He is getting a little bit grumbly. But you can forgive him for that. You never have to be concerned about turning your back on him. He is honest. He is straightforward. And his word is his bond. Over the years we have had our spats, but never once did I doubt our friendship, our admiration for this country, its flag, each other, and our ability to work together.

Ted Stevens' best friend in the Senate was Democratic Senator Daniel Inouye of Hawaii. Senator Inouye, a rather formal speaker, described his friendship with Senator Stevens as "a very special one. When it came to policy, we disagreed more often than we agreed, but we were never disagreeable with each other. We were always positive and forthright." When he was being less formal, he called Senator Stevens his "brother." Ted Stevens and Daniel Inouye loved each other. Stevens, a Republican, campaigned for Inouye, and Inouye, a Democrat, campaigned for Stevens.

Senator Stevens was also a legendary figure back home. He helped write the legislation that granted Alaska statehood. He made the grueling 12 hour flight home to Alaska as often as possible, and he had a rule in his office: he would always meet with any Alaskan who came to Washington. He was a tireless and unapologetic advocate for all Alaskans. His motto was, "To hell with politics, just do what's right for Alaska. . .." And though some have argued that too many federal dollars were spent in Alaska, I learned from Senator Stevens that there are at least two characteristics that distinguish Alaska from other states and in his view made this appropriate. First, 62 percent of the land in Alaska is owned by the federal government. No other state is even close. It takes federal dollars to preserve and maintain that land. Second, there is appalling poverty in parts of Alaska. The work done by Ted Stevens and others alleveated much of that poverty, but there are still parts of Alaska that lack basics such as running water. As the Senator said, "we ask for special consideration because no one else is that far away, no one else has the problems that we have or the potential that we have, and no one else deals with the federal government day in and day out the way we do."

Ted Stevens was so revered in Alaska that in 2000, the state legislature named him "Alaskan of the Century," the highest honor possible for a state that was still in its first century as a state. They also named the Anchorage Airport after him, a rare honor for somebody still alive. According to the *Almanac of American Politics'* entry for Senator Stevens during his final years as Alaska's Senior Senator: "No other Senator fills so central a place in a state's public and economic life as Ted Stevens of Alaska; quite possibly no other Senator ever has."

Senator Stevens loved Alaska and could be a ferocious advocate for the state he loved. He was not a large man, yet he earned the nickname "the Incredible Hulk," because he liked to think he'd transform into a hulk-like figure when advocating for legislation in which he believed. He even had an Incredible Hulk necktie he would often wear when debating legislation on the Senate floor.

While Senator Stevens could get angry quickly, especially when he thought somebody was showing disrespect for Alaskans, those who knew him well understood that his temper was usually a tool he used to help Alaska. When asked once whether he had a bad habit of losing his temper, Senator Stevens quipped, "I never lose my temper. I always know just where to find it."

* * * * *

Ted Stevens had a unique role in American history, and he lived through some of the most pivotal events of the last century. He was born in 1923 in Indianapolis. Right after the stock market crashed in 1929, his parents divorced. Neither of his parents could afford to feed and clothe the six year-old boy, so they sent him to live with his grandparents. When his grandfather died, young Ted and his grandmother went to live with an aunt in California.

Like many others during the Great Depression, Ted Stevens worked multiple jobs while in high school. He worked at a bakery before school, delivered newspapers after school and worked at a movie theater on the weekends.

Ted was 18 years old when Japan bombed Pearl Harbor. Like many in the "Greatest Generation," he wanted to enlist that very day. But his aunt intervened, and got a promise out of him that he would not enlist until his nineteenth birthday. So on that day, November 18, 1942, 19 year-old Ted Stevens attempted to enlist in the Marine Corps to be a pilot. He failed the eye examination, but rather than sit out the war as he could have, he found an eye doctor who offered a program of eye exercises to improve his eyesight. After two months of these exercises, he tried the Army. He passed the Army eye exam and enlisted in the Army Air Corps. (The Army Air Corps would later become the Air Force.)

Soon he was flying C-46 and C-47 supply planes in Asia for the Fourteenth Air Force of the Army Air Corps, also known as the Flying Tigers. The Flying Tigers were led by another legend—General Claire Chennault. Many times, First Lieutenant Stevens' missions took him behind enemy lines. All told, he flew 228 combat missions. The planes he flew were slower and more vulnerable to attack than today's aircraft. Half of his colleagues were killed. He told me once that he could navigate his route during daylight by the reflections of the sun off the wrecked aircraft on the ground. The pilots called it "the aluminum trail." The Army awarded him two Distinguished Flying Crosses for his service.

After the War, Ted Stevens finished college at UCLA and then enrolled at Harvard Law School. He graduated from law school in 1950 and worked for a few years at a law firm in Washington, D.C. known as Northcutt Ely, where he represented the State of California in water rights cases. He met Ann Cherrington in Washington in 1952, and they were soon married. That same year, Ted Stevens got a job practicing law in Fairbanks, Alaska, and he and Ann couldn't pack their bags fast enough.

Like so many of the post-World War II generation, Ted Stevens and his family sought opportunity and adventure in the American West.

But what set young Ted Stevens apart was that he not only headed west, but he also headed north.

Ted Stevens quickly became one of Alaska's most noted lawyers and was asked to be the top federal prosecutor—known as the U.S. Attorney—for one of three districts in the territory of Alaska. After serving with distinction in that post, Ted Stevens was appointed to be a lawyer at the U.S. Department of the Interior in Washington, D.C. Because the vast majority of the land in Alaska was (and still is) owned by the federal government, the Department of the Interior had jurisdiction over the territory of Alaska.

When Ted Stevens arrived in Washington, President Eisenhower opposed statehood. (Interestingly, the President was concerned that Alaska would send a Democratic congressional deligation to Washington if granted statehood.) Ted Stevens' nickname at the Department of the Interior was "Mr. Alaska," because he argued the cause of Alaskan statehood every chance he got. He even had a sign on his door that read "Alaskan Headquarters." Ted Stevens was a relentless advocate, and the tide eventually turned. Alaska became a state in 1958, and Ted Stevens worked on the legislation that made it the 49th state.

After working at the Department of the Interior, Ted Stevens moved back to private practice in Anchorage, because there was more legal work for him there than in Fairbanks. One of the first cases he worked on was a case for the Native Alaskan people of Minto. Ted Stevens defended them from the Federal Bureau of Land Management, the Federal Bureau of Indian Affairs and the State of Alaska, all of which were trying to claim land the Native Alaskans thought was rightly theirs. He did not charge the Native Alaskans for his work. This marked the beginning of a lifetime of siding with indigenous people in disputes with government authorities.

In 1964, Ted Stevens ran for, and won, a seat in the relatively new Alaska House of Representatives. In the next term, he was elected Majority Leader. Ted Stevens ran for the Republican nomination for a U.S. Senate seat in 1968, but was defeated in the primary.

Later that year, when Bob Bartlett, the Senator holding the other Alaska seat in the U.S. Senate, died in office, Governor Walter Hickel appointed 44 year-old Ted Stevens to be the next U.S. Senator from Alaska. After being appointed to the office, Senator Stevens won a special election in 1970 and was re-elected six times—in 1972, 1978, 1984, 1990, 1996 and 2002. None of the elections were close.

During his forty years in the Senate, Stevens was instrumental in the passage of many pieces of landmark legislation, including bills settling Native Alaskan land claims, creating the Trans Alaska Pipeline and protecting fisheries from exploitation.

The Senator took a special interest in athletics. He was the architect of the Ted Stevens Amateur and Olympic Sports Act, which promoted the American Olympic movement and he championed funding for the World Anti-Doping Agency to prevent abuse of performance enhancing drugs by international athletes. I did not know until after his death when he was elected to the U.S. Olympic Hall of Fame, that Ted Stevens had been an outspoken critic of President Carter's boycott of the 1980 Moscow Olympic Games. Senator Stevens didn't think it was fair to the athletes to make them pawns in a political battle.

Senator Stevens was also a champion of Title IX of the Education Act of 1972, which is best known for providing equal opportunities to female athletes. When I asked Senator Stevens what prompted him to support this literally game-changing legislation, he told me, "My daughter was a very good baseball player, and she thought it was unfair that she could not play little league baseball. I thought she had a point, so I joined my friend Birch Bayh in supporting legislation to make sure that women would have equal opportunities." (Birch Bayh was a Democrat, but that didn't stop Ted Stevens from doing the right thing.)

Title IX was attacked many times over the years, and when it was, Ted Stevens was its most stalwart defender. Donna de Varona, the Olympic gold medal swimmer and one of America's first female television sportscasters, described one of these attacks:

The biggest challenge came in 1984 when the U. S. Supreme Court ruled that Title IX applied only to programs that directly received federal funds, which left women's sports opportunities unprotected. Stevens responded by co-sponsoring a National Girls and Women in Sports Day. Female gold medalists at the 1984 Los Angeles Olympics toured Capitol Hill to remind legislators that the accomplishments were a direct result of the opportunities paved for them by Title IX.

In 1988, after intense lobbying on Capitol Hill, Stevens helped pass the Civil Rights Restoration Act, which corrected the Supreme Court ruling by extending Title IX to all programs run by a school that receives any federal aid.

Though well-known for its role in athletics, Title IX actually requires equal opportunities for women in all facets of education. Title IX changed the world for future generations of women, including my daughters.

* * * * *

Senator Stevens was also known for looking after federal employees. In the 1980s, as chair of the Senate subcommittee responsible for civil servants, he was a key player in the creation of the Federal Employees Retirement System and the Thrift Savings Program, which allowed federal employees to direct their own retirement savings into a number of investment packages, just as many private sector employees can do.

It is politically popular today to stereotype and ridicule federal employees. Ted Stevens did not believe in that. He was demanding of federal employees, but thought that they should be treated fairly if they did good work—whether that was politically popular or not. While a strong supporter of all federal workers, Ted Stevens' highest priority was the men and women who served, as he had, in our Armed Forces.

* * * * *

In short, Ted Stevens was an American hero among a generation of heroes. His integrity among those who knew him best was beyond dispute. His staff loved him. He was respected by Senators on both sides of the aisle. It was shocking to me—and to those who knew him long before I did—that federal prosecutors would attack him so viciously.

* * * * *

On May 10, 2007, having been summoned the previous day, I went to the Department of Justice. When I arrived, I was met by Mr. Welch and escorted, personally, to a conference room to meet with a team of Department of Justice lawyers.

On the way to the conference room, I passed a bulletin board covered with newspaper articles about a state representative in Alaska whom the Feds had recently arrested. The bulletin board reminded me of the trophy case at my high school. I don't know if they walked me past their "trophy collection" on purpose or not— but if they did it to intimidate me, their strategy backfired. Instead, I was repulsed.

A prosecutor's job is to enforce the law, not to gloat. Watergate prosecutor Jim Neal once told a jury, "It is not fun casting stones. But to keep society going, stones must be cast. People must be called to account." Calling lawbreakers to account is a prosecutor's legitimate job. Posting newspaper articles like souvenirs is not.

Upon doing a bit of research, I found that the state representative was still awaiting trial. I was offended that the government was clipping *and posting* newspaper articles about a citizen presumed innocent under the law.

* * * * *

Chief Welch brought me to a conference room where Brenda Morris, Deputy Chief of the Public Integrity Section, and Edward Sullivan, a more junior attorney in the Public Integrity Section, were waiting. (Eventually there were three men named Sullivan in the Stevens case: Brendan, Edward, and the judge, Emmet G. Sullivan.)

29

William Welch, a large man with a receding hairline, had played football at Princeton. He had a disarming, work-a-day manner which made him a likable guy. In the legal community, he was known as a very aggressive and tough prosecutor.

I had not had a previous case against him. Despite his threats to get the Senator to sign the tolling agreement, I wanted to like him.

I had encountered Brenda Morris at a legal conference a few months earlier where she'd spoken on public corruption. She was quick on her feet and made a positive first impression. She exuded supreme confidence.

When someone from the audience asked her for advice on dealing with her office, her answer was, "Don't be an asshole." She went on to give examples of lawyers who had tried to explain to her that their clients were innocent, when she believed they were guilty. "Don't try that with me," was the message. Unaware that she soon would be our opponent, I remembered thinking then that she would be a difficult courtroom adversary.

At the meeting, Brenda Morris did most of the talking. First, she said that the government wanted Senator Stevens to consent to searches of his "cabin" in Alaska and his townhouse in Washington. Then she moved on to her real agenda.

Morris said that she and the other prosecutors were willing to talk about the potential charges and discuss a resolution of their investigation so long as the Senator would agree to plead guilty to some sort of *criminal* conduct. Morris emphasized the word "criminal."

In other words, the deal she offered was this: We'll tell you what the Senator did and lay out what evidence we have if, and only if, the Senator agrees *in advance* that he committed a crime; you admit up-front that you are guilty, and *then* we'll tell you what crime you are guilty of and how we will prove it. Some deal.

What a way, I thought to myself, to treat a World War II veteran, a member of what Tom Brokaw calls "the Greatest Generation," who had flown combat missions over China with the Flying Tigers, a man who'd survived and returned to serve his country for forty years in the United States Senate. Ted Stevens had earned our respect. He didn't deserve this. No citizen, no matter what, deserves this kind of treatment.

As defense lawyers, we are ethically obligated to report a plea offer to our clients, even if we don't like the proposal. Because what Morris had laid out was technically a plea offer, we were duty-bound to report it to the Senator.

Bill Phillips set up a meeting with the Senator, and he and I went to meet with him that day in his office.

Senior U.S. Senators usually have two offices on Capitol Hill. The main office is a large suite in one of the Senate office buildings, which are connected to the Capitol by a series of tunnels and an underground trolley. The second office, called the "hideaway office," is located in the Capitol building itself. Because he was in the Senate leadership, Ted Stevens had one of the best hideaway offices— small, but with expansive westward views of the Washington Monument, the Lincoln Memorial, and, in the distance across the river, Arlington National Cemetery, where so many American war heroes are buried, some of whom had served with Senator Stevens. Bill and I went to the hideaway office to meet with the Senator. As we arrived, the sun was beginning to set.

In this beautiful and majestic setting I broke the news of the prosecutors' demand that he agree to plead guilty to criminal charges. Instantly, the atmosphere in the office turned surreal. The Senator shook his head, gazing out the window, as if he couldn't believe this was happening. When I was done, he turned his full gaze on me.

"No, absolutely not!"

With that, Ted Stevens categorically rejected the idea that he would plead guilty to anything. He was adamant that he had not committed any crime.

Now it was my turn to look out the window. As I looked out at the beautiful green landscape where many of his fallen comrades were buried, I thought what I would think many times during this course of Senator Stevens' ordeal: this man does not deserve this.

There were never any plea negotiations. Any thought that this 40-year veteran of the U.S. Senate who had risked his life for his country was going to allow himself to be branded a criminal was absurd. I called the prosecutors and told them, "The Senator will not plead to anything."

* * * * *

Two weeks later, with the DOJ's ultimatums still ringing in Ted Stevens' ears, the President of the United States, George W. Bush, held a dinner at the White House in Senator Stevens' honor. As the Senator was well aware, the event presented some problems, at least potentially. Prior to the event, he was worried that if news of the possibility of his indictment leaked—*always* a danger in Washington—it might embarrass the White House and President Bush. But if he declined, that in itself could create its own buzz. In addition, if Senator Stevens told the White House he was reluctant to go through with the dinner in light of the investigation, it might appear he was trying to influence the Department of Justice by way of the President. And if that charge surfaced, it could conceivably lead to an allegation of obstruction of justice—or a devastating political fire storm.

In the end, we decided to say or do nothing, and just go ahead with the event. After all, Ted Stevens *did* deserve to be honored as the longest-serving Republican in the Senate.

* * * * *

As I said, we never engaged in any plea negotiations, but over the ensuing months, we had extensive discussions with the Public Integrity lawyers over access to the Senator's documents. The government wanted the Senator to consent to a search. To be specific, they had the temerity to ask that the Senator waive all of his rights under the Constitution so their agents could rifle through all of his files.

This created a dilemma for the defense. While the Senator had nothing to hide, and by nature was inclined to give his consent, doing so would trigger several other problems.

For one thing, we had to be concerned about what would happen when the press learned of an FBI search of the Senator's office. Even if he consented to it, a search reported on and, worse still, filmed by the media would undoubtedly have negative political consequences for the Senator. People would assume that he must be *guilty* or else the government would not be searching. (Unfortunately, many Americans no longer believe in the notion that a citizen is innocent until proven guilty.)

Secondly, the United States Constitution has a provision known as the "Speech or Debate Clause" which prevents the Executive Branch from questioning what any member of the legislative branch does in fulfilling his or her legislative duties. Under the Constitution, the Executive Branch cannot seize any documents having to do with legislation. This is an important Constitutional separation-of-powers principle, and to agree to a search would compromise that principle and set a bad precedent for other members of Congress.

We proposed that instead of an invasive search, the Department of Justice serve on the Senator a reasonable subpoena for documents, a subpoena in which a court would order exactly which documents would be provided by the office. We could then assure that the Department of Justice was receiving only what it was supposed to receive, namely, documents related to the specific investigation.

Legislative documents to which the Executive Branch was not entitled could be separated out and listed on a log, and the court could later determine if they were protected by the Speech or Debate Clause. The Senator would cooperate; the institutional prerogatives of the United States Congress would be protected and preserved; and so long as there were no leaks, we would avoid a media frenzy.

The Department of Justice never did serve a subpoena for documents. They had something else in mind.

* * * * *

While we were waiting for the DOJ's next move, we learned of an additional complication, this one in far-away Alaska.

It came to our attention that at the tail end of the renovations to the cabin, Bill Allen—who had the habit of acting as if the cabin were his—had put some Christmas lights on a large tree on the lot. The Senator had not asked for them, and as for Mrs. Stevens, she absolutely hated them. By the summer of 2007, the Stevenses were both concerned that the Christmas lights were killing the tree.

The Senator was hesitant to take them down because of the investigation. He remembered that Rule Number One is to do no harm. And that, as I mentioned, meant leaving everything exactly as it was when the investigation began.

But the tree was dying. And the Senator thought that as long as the Christmas lights were preserved, surely the government would not claim that taking them down to save the tree was interfering with the investigation. So the Senator reluctantly asked that they be taken down (and saved). A worker arrived to remove the lights, and as he was untangling the wires from the branches, out of nowhere a man appeared in the yard. It was an FBI agent, who apparently had been watching the whole time.

Now prosecutors had what they needed, an excuse to search the cabin, and within days, the government had executed a search warrant on the cabin. The media apparently received a tip, and television cameras suddenly appeared, 40 miles from Anchorage. The FBI "raid" of the Stevens' cabin made the national news.

It was just as we feared: most people assume that the government doesn't raid homes (especially homes of U.S. Senators) unless the homeowner is guilty. Especially when the homeowner is a politician. And talking heads immediately said as much on television.

When the government raided the Senator's home in Alaska, I was waiting for a jury verdict in another case thousands of miles away. But that didn't really matter. Once it starts, there is nothing a defense lawyer can do to stop a government raid.

* * * * *

The government's next step after raiding the chalet was to request that we provide emails from the Senate computers. Again, we asked that the Constitution's Speech or Debate Clause be honored. That is, we requested the ability to withhold internal Senate emails related to legislation, because they are protected by the Constitution.

Surprisingly, the government agreed to that condition, giving us a list of emails that they wanted, most of which contained specific words or were addressed to specific recipients. Working with the Senate Sergeant at Arms, who is responsible for the Senate's computers, we produced some 9,000 emails from the Senate server.

* * * * *

Next, the government requested that we comply with a burdensome request for hard copies of documents from the Senator's office. The Senator originally declined. Enough was enough—tracking down all of the documents would divert time, energy and staff from his legislative work, and there was plenty of day-to-day legislative work to be done. But, if he didn't, the government might search his Washington, D. C. home as well as his Capitol Hill office. In my opinion, searching his office on Capitol Hill would unquestionably violate the Speech or Debate Clause, something I doubted they would do.

But what if they did? They'd already raided the cabin, and in a media center like Washington, D.C., raids on his home or office would be yet another national news story. That would be an even greater distraction to the Senator's official duties than devoting the resources necessary to comply with the prosecutors' request. So the

Senator reconsidered and agreed, in lieu of a search of his office or even a subpoena for documents, to produce all the documents that the government requested—over 70,000 pages in all. As with the emails, we segregated the Speech or Debate Clause materials and listed them on a log. My younger colleague Simon Latcovich did the lion's share of the work. One set of documents Simon logged as speech or debate materials was Senators Stevens' original copy of the Pentagon Papers circulated by fellow Alaskan Senator Gravel in the 1970s.

* * * * *

Among the hard copy documents that we provided to the prosecutors was a note (written after the main renovations had been done) from Senator Stevens to Bill Allen. The note read:

10/6/02

Dear Bill:

When I think of the ways in which you make my life easier I lose count!

Thanks for all the work on the chalet. You owe me a bill. Remember Torricelli my friend. Friendship is one thing. Compliance with these ethics rules entirely different. I asked Bob P [Bob Persons, a personal friend of the Senator's and a Girdwood neighbor] to talk to you about this so don't get P. O.'d at him—it just has to be done right.

Hope to see you soon.

My best,

Ted

Brendan and I recognized immediately that this note was a remarkable piece of evidence. The Senator was trying to make sure he paid for everything he got. It was, we thought, a snapshot into the mind of an innocent man. How could the government possibly say that Ted Stevens was trying to get something for nothing? He asked for a bill, and he paid more than the renovations were worth.

* * * * *

On February 28, 2008, we were again summoned to the Department of Justice. This time I counted six prosecutors and three FBI agents in the room. "I am not bluffing," Deputy Chief Brenda Morris told us. "We will obtain an indictment of Senator Stevens," she threatened, but she added, as if she were about to bestow a great favor upon the Senator, "if he agrees to plead guilty, I will make sure he will not have to serve any jail time."

We had a meeting with Ted Stevens and Bill Phillips. It was our duty to report the government's proposed deal. "No way," the Senator responded. "I didn't commit any crimes, and I'm not pleading guilty to anything. Tell them, no way." He then became angrier: "Tell them they can shove their plea deal up their asses," he told us.

* * * * *

Later that Spring, Public Integrity Section Chief William Welch called Brendan and told him we should ask for an appointment with the Attorney General.

Why? Because if a decision were made to obtain an indictment, we would want to request that the Attorney General himself consider overruling the decision. Michael Mukasey, the new Attorney General was so busy, Welch said, that we needed to get on his schedule well in advance.

So Brendan wrote to the Attorney General requesting a face-to-face meeting. He did not receive a reply. In fact, we did not hear back until mid-July, when the *Deputy* Attorney General's office called for a meeting.

The Deputy Attorney General, the second-in-command at Justice, was Mark Filip, a star lawyer who had been appointed to be a federal judge at the very young age of 38. He had given up a lifetime appointment as a federal judge to serve the Justice Department. A political conservative, Filip had been a faculty member with Barack Obama at the University of Chicago. By all accounts, he was brilliant and fair.

When Brendan met with the Deputy Attorney General on July 22, 2008, Filip confessed that he had not yet read the materials provided by the Public Integrity lawyers. On one hand, this was not particularly surprising, given the breadth of his responsibilities and the tendency of subordinates to provide overly lengthy written materials to busy top officials. On the other hand, the meeting concerned whether or not to indict a sitting U.S. Senator.

Brendan reported to me that the Deputy Attorney General was friendly, appeared to be reasonable, and had listened to his arguments against indicting the Senator. We hoped that good judgment would carry the day. We were now four months out from Election Day in Alaska when Senator Stevens would make his eighth bid for re-election.

It was the Justice Department's stated policy, one reiterated by Attorney General Michael Mukasey, that the Department would not interfere with any election. At his confirmation hearing in October 2007, the nominee for Attorney General was asked by Patrick Leahy, Chair of the Senate Judiciary Committee, for assurances that the Justice Department would not bring criminal charges against candidates on the eve of an election.

Here's how nominee Mukasey responded: "Obviously, the closer you get to an election, whether there is a charge that either deals with a candidate or deals with an issue that can affect the outcome, the higher and higher has to be the standard and the greater and greater has to be the necessity for bringing the charge at the particular time in order to justify it."

This seemed to satisfy Senator Leahy. And it sounded pretty good to me too. Thus, based on the Attorney General's own words, none of us believed the Department of Justice would interfere with the election in Alaska.

* * * * *

The Department of Justice is supposed to operate above politics. Decisions about the enforcement of our laws—especially our criminal laws—are too important to be influenced by politics. As a result, there are only a small number of political positions at the Department of Justice set aside for appointment by the President. Most of these presidential appointees must be confirmed by the Senate, which also serves as a check on the President's power. But once these appointees are on the job, they are supposed to make decisions without considering the political consequences.

The vast majority of positions at the Justice Department are known as career civil service positions, and those jobs are not political at all. In fact, it is illegal to consider politics when hiring for civil service positions. This is true at all federal agencies, but it is especially important at an agency with the power of the Department of Justice.

Unfortunately, during the administration of President George W. Bush, the Justice Department had developed a reputation for being very political. A great controversy erupted over the firing of U.S. Attorneys who were considered soft on Democrats, meaning that they were supposedly not indicting Democrats as often and as quickly as certain of their more politically-minded higher-ups in the Department would have preferred.

The Office of the Inspector General, an independent watchdog within the Department of Justice, eventually found that senior Department officials had acted legally in firing the U.S. Attorneys, but the public perception was that in *this* Department of Justice it mattered whether one was a Democrat or a Republican.

The Inspector General did find (on July 2, 2008) that the Department had improperly taken politics into account when deciding whom to hire for entry level attorney positions in the Civil Rights Division. What appeared to be the final straw occurred on July 28, 2008, when the Inspector General issued another report finding that the Department had repeatedly used political criteria to hire civil service employees. The next day, the *Washington Post* ran a front-page story about this practice. It featured a photograph of a high-ranking Justice Department political appointee who regularly asked civil service applicants, "What is it about George W. Bush that makes you want to serve him?"

In a thinly-veiled effort to weed out job-seekers who were not Republicans, the official had asked many people that question. The *Post* reported the Inspector General's conclusion that a senior official had violated federal law by considering political affiliations in selecting civil service employees. The message was clear: the Justice Department had inappropriately favored Republicans.

Unfortunately for our client, issuance of the Inspector General's report gave the Public Integrity Section lawyers, who so badly wanted to catch the biggest fish in Alaska, the perfect opportunity to make their move. In this environment, any action by senior Presidentially appointed Justice Department officials seen to favor a Republican—such as turning down a request from lower-level DOJ prosecutors to indict the longest-serving Republican senator in history—would, if leaked to the press, add fuel to the fire. And the chances were that turning down an indictment of a Republican Senator would have leaked to the press.

Given this atmosphere, there was no way that the leadership of the Justice Department could veto a request from hard-charging lower-level prosecutors to indict a prominent Republican.

In fact, indicting a Republican Senator would help rebut the charge that the Department was favoring Republicans.

More wood was being stacked.

Chapter
4

Indictment

The July 29, 2008 edition of the *Washington Post*, with its lead headline about bias at the Justice Department, was still sitting on my desk when Bill Welch called and told me that a D.C. grand jury had returned an indictment of Senator Stevens that morning.

The grand jury system, conceived by our nation's founders as a protection against unfair criminal charges, has evolved into nothing more than a tool for prosecutors to gather evidence. Prosecutors have the authority to issue subpoenas for all manner of documents and data, such as computer records. And a prosecutor can issue a subpoena requiring any citizen to testify before the grand jury. There are few limits on a prosecutor's power to use the grand jury other than an individual citizen's Fifth Amendment privilege to decline to testify.

Defense lawyers cannot cross-examine witnesses or present exculpatory evidence to a grand jury. Defense lawyers are not allowed, in fact are expressly forbidden, in the grand jury room. Prosecutors can present an entirely one-side version of events to a grand jury; there is no requirement to present both sides of the issue. It is an entirely lop-sided affair, and it only requires a vote of a majority of the grand jurors to indict.

When Welch told me the grand jury had returned an indictment, I asked him to send me a copy of the indictment. Welch said that he would, but he never did. Actually, there was no need: several news organizations had immediately posted it on their website, and CNN was carrying DOJ's press conference on live television.

The next day, the story of the Senator's indictment was on the front page of the *Washington Post*. It read: "Senator Stevens Indicted on Seven Corruption Counts: Longest-Serving GOP Senator Is Accused of Making False Statements About Money from Alaska Oil Firm." The Stevens indictment was everywhere. The story of Republican bias at the Department of Justice was long gone.

The 28-page indictment alleged that the Senator had failed to disclose gifts for six years. (There was a separate count for each year, and an overall count alleging what the government called a "scheme".) The principal charge was that the Senator had failed to report the value of more than $250,000 of improvements to his cabin. It also alleged that over several years the Senator had engaged in a scheme to lie to the American people about these so-called gifts.

That Ted Stevens had schemed to lie to the American people was unthinkable to those who knew him. But we would learn that it was not unthinkable to many members of the public, who seem to believe that public officials are by definition corrupt. The witch hunt had reached its peak, and the Department of Justice was leading the charge.

* * * * *

Bill Phillips brought the Senator to my office as soon as he could, just barely beating a swarm of cameras posted outside in hopes of catching footage of the Senator coming to (or going from) our office. The image of a senator arriving or departing his lawyer's office would have been treasured by cable and broadcast news producers. One producer kept a camera crew in the lobby of our busy building, and refused to leave until the Senator or one of his lawyers agreed to appear on camera.

I wanted to go and ask him to leave. Politely, of course. Bill told me that was not a very good idea, and he was right; my polite request would have made the news as well. The cameraman left that evening when we closed.

Mitch Rose, another former member of the Senator's staff who had volunteered to help the Senator during his time of need, arrived at our office and helped the Senator prepare a brief statement for the press denying the allegations, which we sent to members of the media who had sought a comment from us. Mitch was new to me, but he had a great reputation as a top notch professional. And he had the wonderful habit of showing up, usually unannounced, to help the Senator and his family when they needed it the most. Mitch, like all of the Senator's former staffers, was not a fair-weather friend.

* * * * *

The Senator called Senator Kay Bailey Hutchison of Texas to tell her that he would resign his position as ranking member of the Senate Commerce Committee. She was next in line in terms of seniority, and Senator Stevens thought stepping aside was the right thing to do. He would not resign his seat in the Senate representing Alaska and he could continue to vote his conscience, but he would resign his leadership positions so that the stature of the Senate would not be diminished. Senator Stevens loved the Senate and never would have done anything to hurt it.

When Senator Hutchison learned that she would assume his leadership position on the Commerce Committee, she told Senator Stevens she knew that he would be cleared and that she would return his position to him as soon as that happened. She also gave him, based on her own experience in being cleared of frivolous, politically-motivated criminal charges in Texas, two pieces of advice.

First, she said, get to trial as soon as possible. Second, she told him that when the cameras were pointed at him—which would be most of the time—it was best *not* to be filmed with your lawyers. Better to be filmed with a family member, preferably a beautiful woman.

I agreed especially with the advice about not being phographed with your lawyers. Many lawyers cherish the publicity of being photographed with their clients during trials. Not us. We would follow Senator Hutchison's guidance. From then on, family went first with the Senator when cameras were present.

The reaction of Senator Stevens' colleagues to his indictment provided me with a glimpse into their personalities. Some, like Senator Hutchison, reacted with grace, loyalty, and fairness. Others tried to take advantage of the situation. The breakdown had nothing to do with party affiliation. Some Democrats were fair while others were not; some Republicans were fair while others were not.

* * * * *

The indictment also gave me a window into Ted Stevens' personality. Before the indictment, my relationship with the Senator was somewhat strained. He was often angry. I had seen traces of his famous grumpy moods several times during the investigation. He couldn't believe that the government would seriously consider indicting him. He didn't believe that the system could be so unjust. Bill Phillips, Brendan Sullivan and I thought otherwise and had to deliver that news to him, which caused some tension in our relationship with the Senator.

The criminal justice system was more unfair than he had ever imagined. He did not understand when we would tell him that a witch hunt was afoot. He would react angrily, because he simply could not believe that prosecutors would be so unfair. But we were proven right. And once the indictment was returned and the Senator realized that we were correct, he was never grumpy with us again.

* * * * *

The idea that our criminal justice system is fair is deeply engrained in the American psyche. Perhaps not surprisingly, this is particularly true among former prosecutors (like Ted Stevens) and judges who should be more skeptical of what government prosecutors represent to them. Many times, judges who were prosecutors remember that when they were in the office they acted properly and lawfully. It's difficult for them to think that others don't.

Three years before I joined Williams & Connolly, in a case before Federal Judge Walter Black in Baltimore, Brendan and Williams & Connolly partner Barry Simon caught government agents lying and creating backdated documents. (Brendan and Barry researched the manufacturing process and proved that the particular type of paper on which the original backdated documents were printed did not exist as of the date the government put on the documents.) The judge's initial reaction to their allegations was in substance to say, "If you are coming in here and telling me that the government is lying and acting improperly, then you are in the wrong courtroom because I used to be a prosecutor myself."

Of course, the judge had not been a prosecutor for many years. However, after 28 days of hearings, he was so stunned by what Brendan and Barry proved that he wrote a 25 page opinion calling the government's misconduct the worst he had ever seen.

* * * * *

Most courthouses have more than one judge. In the District of Columbia, where the government had chosen to charge Senator Stevens, there are 18 active federal trial judges. The process of being assigned to a judge is called "drawing a judge off the wheel."

The expression comes from a time when judges' names were picked from a spinning wooden drum, with a small door on one of its sides, similar to the kind used for bingo games in church halls—a completely impartial, blind system for selecting which judge will preside over a case. Even though it resembles a small barrel, lawyers call it "the wheel," and one is still used in a few federal courts. The federal court in the District of Columbia, like most courts, now uses a computer to choose randomly a judge. But lawyers still call the process drawing a judge off the wheel.

We drew Emmet G. Sullivan off the wheel. Judge Sullivan was born and raised in Washington, D. C. After earning his undergraduate and law degrees from Howard University, he received a prestigious fellowship which enabled him to use his law degree in a Washington, D. C. neighborhood whose disadvantaged residents did not have access to lawyers. After that, he served as a law clerk for a judge. He spent 11 years in private practice before beginning an impressive 17-year career as a judge in the local and federal courts of the District of Columbia. He had received presidential appointments from Republican George H.W. Bush and Democrat Bill Clinton.

* * * * *

Any lawyer—prosecutor or defense lawyer—should have considered Judge Sullivan a good draw because of his reputation for impartiality. One could hardly imagine a case where judicial independence was more important than the Stevens case. After all, Executive Branch officials were bringing charges against one of the Legislative Branch's most senior members. This case called for a judge with a lifetime appointment—that is, a federal judge—an independent member of our nation's third branch of government. Judge Sullivan would prove himself to be very independent, just as the founders envisioned.

Chapter
5

Discovery

Lawyers are required to share information and documents with the other side in a case. This is called discovery. In civil cases (which have comprised half of my case load over the years) as opposed to criminal ones—there is a lot of discovery. In a typical civil lawsuit, there are few limits on discovery, and so the plaintiff and defendant share vast amounts of information, often reaching into the millions of documents in corporate cases.

Most people are surprised to learn that our system of criminal justice operates quite differently. In criminal court, there are limits on what information must be shared.

That is not to say that the government does not have ample opportunity to obtain evidence. Before indictment, prosecutors are able to obtain information through the use of grand jury subpoenas—issuing broad subpoenas that require citizens and companies to provide documents and evidence, as well as compel them to appear in court to testify before a grand jury. There are almost no limits on what can be asked, and, as mentioned, witnesses are not allowed to have their lawyers in the grand jury room. Indeed, neither witnesses nor the citizens who are the targets of the grand jury are allowed to have lawyers in the room.

The government also has other ways to get information, such as rewarding informants. The government can offer benefits such as reduced jail time (or no jail time at all) to witnesses who may have committed crimes themselves or who are at risk of being charged with a crime. The government can pay witnesses. Prosecutors can obtain search warrants that allow their investigators to rifle through people's homes and records. The government can intercept phone calls and subpoena emails and text messages. Prosecutors have the agents of the Federal Bureau of Investigation available to interview witnesses at taxpayer expense. And, when FBI agents come knocking—usually early in the morning—most people, understandably, talk to them. The government may even deceive witnesses to convince them to cooperate.

By contrast, as a defense lawyer, I could be imprisoned if I offered anything of value in exchange for testimony from a fact witness, rifled through a citizens' files, intercepted phone calls, or purposely misled witnesses to obtain favorable testimony.

Defense lawyers start with a disadvantage in criminal cases because they do not have the same tools to obtain information that prosecutors have. What defense lawyers do have is the ability to ask the government for discovery after an indictment has been returned.

The government's primary obligations to provide discovery fall into three categories.

First, under the Rules of Criminal Procedure, the government is required to provide the evidence it intends to use in its case and any items (usually documents) that are material (or relevant) to the defense.

Second, under a Supreme Court decision in the 1950s called *Jencks v. United States*, the government is required to provide verbatim statements its witnesses have made. Most often, these are transcripts of grand jury testimony. However, under a law passed by Congress and added to the Federal Rules of Criminal Procedure in the aftermath of the *Jencks* decision, the government does not have to provide such statements until *after* the witnesses have testified in open court.

As a result, often the first time the defense hears what a prosecution witness has to say is when he or she is on the stand. Upon saying "no further questions," the prosecutor then hands the defense a stack of grand jury testimony for the first time—and defense lawyers race through the transcripts on the spot as they begin their cross-examination. Sometimes prosecutors keep their witnesses away from the grand jury so that they do not create a verbatim transcript that needs to be produced under the *Jencks* decision. (Oftentimes, a federal judge will encourage the prosecution to provide witness statements in advance, stating that he, the judge, will grant a continuance in the middle of a trial if it is provided for the first time. But the law does not permit a judge to *order* advance production.)

Third and finally, under the case of *Brady v. Maryland*, decided by the Supreme Court in 1963, the government must provide "evidence that is favorable to an accused" and that is "material to guilt or punishment." The Supreme Court ruled that the due process clause of the Fifth Amendment to the Constitution requires this.

To most of us, this seems like common sense, especially when one considers the investigative advantage that the government has. If juries are supposed to decide guilt and innocence, they need access to information in order to do so. The *Brady* decision applies to all favorable information, whether government agents have written it down or not.

* * * * *

As noted earlier, Judge Sullivan raised the issue of providing discovery on the first day. And so did we.

At arraignment, we asked for the discovery materials to which we were entitled. "The government's been investigating this case I believe at least a couple of years," Brendan said. "We request that we be provided discovery as immediately as possible. We were hoping to get some today."

Deputy Chief Morris responded, "As far as discovery, your Honor, we do have discovery that is all ready for the defendant. We would ask that the defendant provide us with a 500-gigabyte hard drive so that we can copy that material and then provide it to him. The bulk of it can be provided next week."

The government had undoubtedly spent millions of dollars on the investigation, but now wanted us to furnish a relatively inexpensive 500-gigabyte hard drive as a precondition to receiving evidence. Unbelievable.

We purchased the requested hard drive and immediately sent it to the government. The next day, I followed up with a letter asking for all the evidence the government intended to use, the evidence material to the defense and any information favorable to the defense.

* * * * *

Once the government has provided the discovery it is obligated to provide, then the rules require the defense to disclose the evidence it intends to use in its case. Because the defendant is presumed innocent until proven guilty and the prosecution bears the burden of proof, the defense needs to see the government's evidence of guilt before it can respond with its defense. That is why the government must disclose its evidence first.

Senator Stevens had already voluntarily complied with all of the government's requests before the government had even charged him, providing everything that he had that was relevant to the case. And the government had already used its full arsenal of weapons to gather information in its investigation: search warrants, grand jury subpoenas, wiretaps, paid informants and immunity deals.

Not satisfied, the prosecutors demanded discovery from Senator Stevens before disclosing a single piece of evidence to us. The government had it backwards. It reminded me of something out of *Alice in Wonderland*. The Stevens prosecutors hammered relentlessly for the defense to provide discovery first, implying that we were engaged in dishonest tactics when we told them that the Senator—unlike the government—had already disclosed all of his relevant documents. But they wanted more.

What was going on? I suspected a tactic I'd seen in other cases: prosecutors sometimes want to see all the defense evidence first so that that they can adjust their story to meet it. There's a good reason when that happens. It means the prosecution has lost confidence in its own case.

Prosecutor Morris promised the hard drive containing the "bulk of discovery" by the end of the second week after indictment. (Apparently it wasn't "all ready" after all.) On the afternoon of Friday, August 7, at the last possible hour, they provided a hard drive of data that they called "discovery."

We called it a mess. It contained days and days of recordings of audio and video surveillance from Operation Polar Pen that appeared to have minimal relevance, if any, to our case. There were no transcripts and no index.

When we asked for an index of the recordings so that we could review them efficiently, the prosecutors refused. They essentially said, "Here is a bunch of junk. Knock yourselves out and see if you can find anything relevant." If we had one lawyer start listening to the recordings beginning on the day we received the recordings, it would have taken that lawyer the rest of the year to review them. But we didn't have until the end of the year. The trial was now less than six weeks away.

We asked Judge Sullivan to order the prosecutors to give us an index. Only then did they agree to do so. But when we got our index, it came with a caveat: "We must stress. . .that you should not rely on the index as your sole source of who was captured on the audio or video tapes. There is no substitution for reviewing the materials yourself." Oh well.

Fortunately we had some eager law students our firm had hired for the summer who were ready to help. In the days they had left before returning to school, they began by collecting voice samples, trying to figure out who was who on the tapes. They then camped out in a conference room with computers and head phones. Fueled by pizza, soda and coffee, after several days, they got through them all. None of the recordings were of more than marginal relevance.

The process made me wonder once again: what happens to defendants without the resources of a firm that can afford to hire law students for the summer? Even in our law firm, what if this hadn't been summer? Our other lawyers were busy on other cases for other clients. It costs a lot of money to have lawyers review tapes. Why couldn't the government provide us with a simple accurate index?

The hard drive also contained pages and pages and pages of electronic copies of documents which were also a mess. It was impossible to tell what pages belonged together, or where one document started and another ended. One series of copies was lumped together into one long electronic document of 67,000 continuous pages without a break. There was no way to find an isolated page within that document without toggling through all 67,000 pages. If one were to stack 67,000 pages of documents, the stack would be about 30 feet tall—all without a single staple or paper clip.

The government had provided its documents without what are known as "load files"—the electronic form of a staple or paperclip or file folder. Without them, the reader has to guess when one document stops and another one starts, which makes reviewing the document almost impossible. We were in a race against the clock to try to save the Senator's career, and the government was jerking us around.

By contrast, the materials that we had provided—voluntarily—before indictment were stamped, numbered and well-organized. When we saw how disorganized the Government's electronic documents were, we pointed out that we had done it the right way. But they never did organize their documents. Their response was essentially: *We are the U.S. Department of Justice. How dare you question us?*

* * * * *

The hard drive also contained photographs of the interior of the chalet, apparently taken during the search. But when we looked at many of the photographs, we were surprised. Something was out of whack. In the government's photos, the interior of the home appeared to be much larger than we knew it to be. (By this time, some of us on the team had been to the cabin and seen it with our own eyes.) It occurred to us that perhaps the FBI had used wide-angle lenses to make the chalet look larger than it was.

We hired one of the country's leading crime scene photographers, Professor Edward Robinson of George Washington University, who literally wrote the book on crime scene photography. Professor Robinson told us that the photographs were likely digital photographs and that digital photographs contain electronic codes known as "metadata" imbedded in the electronic record of the photographs. The metadata would tell us whether wide-angle lenses were used.

However, Professor Robinson told us it appeared that before loading them onto the hard drive they'd given us, the government had stripped the meta-data from the photographs. We asked the prosecutors for the metadata. They refused to provide it, so we flew Professor Robinson from Washington, D.C., to Alaska, to observe the rooms and take appropriate comparison photographs.

We then told the government that we were going to have him testify before Judge Sullivan as to why we needed the metadata. Only when we brought Professor Robinson to a hearing and threatened to have him demonstrate the deceptive tactics did the prosecutors relent—but not by handing over the metadata. Instead, they informed us that they would not be using the photographs we had questioned.

We ultimately prevailed on this issue, but why did we have to go to all that trouble and expense in the first place? And what about a defendant without the resources to hire his own crime scene photography expert and fly him to Alaska? In a sense, the government won—because fighting the government's deceptive tactics was a huge distraction for us, taking us away from preparing for trial.

* * * * *

The Federal Rules of Evidence provide that "evidence of other crimes, wrongs or acts is *not* admissible" to show that a defendant is essentially a bad person, and therefore must have committed the crime for which he is being tried. The rules also provide, however, that "evidence of other crimes, wrongs or acts may be admissible for other purposes, such as proof of motive, opportunity, intent, preparation, plan, knowledge, identity or absence of mistake or accident." If the government wants to offer evidence for one of those purposes, it is required to give "reasonable notice in advance of trial" to the defense.

This confusing series of rules needs some explanation. Take a murder case, for example. As a general rule, prosecutors cannot use the fact that the defendant killed another person in the past to prove that the defendant is the type of person who would commit murder. However, if the method of committing the murder was exactly the same—say poison with a rare substance—prosecutors might be able to use the facts of the other killing to show that the defendant's preparation and planning was the same for both. If prosecutors want to use such evidence, they need to notify the defense in advance of trial so that the defense may consider, before trial, whether the evidence is admissible.

Prosecutors usually send a letter to the defense giving notice of the "other crimes, wrongs or acts" they intend to use. That is the ordinary practice. But not for the Stevens prosecutors. They filed a notice on the court's website listing the otherwise inadmissible evidence they hoped to use. By filing it on the public website, notification was automatically sent to all major news organizations.

Among the acts they wanted to use was evidence that the Senator had entered into a contract to purchase a condominium in Florida for $360,000 and then sold it before moving into it for $515,000. After paying taxes on it, the Senator made a profit of just over $100,000. The transaction was disclosed on his ethics form and tax return. Prosecutor Nicholas Marsh argued that there was a period of time that the Senator had not paid the full deposit due and for that period of time he should have disclosed that he had an interest free loan. It was confusing and crazy.

Marsh, who was tall, trim and dressed as if he were a senior partner at a Wall Street law firm, was obviously very intelligent, and his arguments were always creative, though sometimes hard to follow logically. He appeared to have a lot of intellectual firepower but little or no judgment. His overly-complicated arguments often made little sense to me.

I thought that his argument about the condo was just an excuse to smear the Senator as a privileged person who made an investment that yielded a profit in a short period of time.

The truth is that the Senator, who was considering spending time in Florida, had changed his mind about moving into the condo. The real estate market was going up. He made a nice return, but there was nothing more to it than that. But these prosecutors apparently didn't care about the truth; all they wanted to do was to suggest impropriety and illegality.

The press loved the story, and his political opponents in the re-election campaign exploited it, all thanks to the prosecution's having posted it publicly.

We filed legal papers arguing that the evidence was irrelevant and that the government was engaged in an unfair "smear job." The press also loved that—"smear job" being just the sort of expression reporters adore. When the story hit the local press I was in Alaska interviewing witnesses, and several Alaskans congratulated me on calling the government's tactics a smear job. Our intention was not to have the words "smear job" picked up in the press. We were just trying to inform Judge Sullivan of what we saw.

In the end, the prosecution introduced some of the documents about the real estate investment, but did not really argue to the jury about it. They could not explain why there was anything wrong with the condominium transaction. Because there wasn't.

* * * * *

Judges usually require the government and the defense to disclose their exhibits in advance of trial. Judge Sullivan ordered all exhibits disclosed in advance of trial, and then gave each side two days to make objections. When the day came for us to disclose our exhibits, we provided an organized list to the government, as well as both a paper and electronic copy of each document so that the prosecutors could quickly and conveniently review our proposed exhibits and make their objections. The prosecutors gave us a list of documents—but no paper copies of documents. They told us we could go hunting for the exhibits in the hopelessly disorganized hard drive—without load files—they had provided us.

When we asked for the same courtesy we had provided them, they reacted with the same arrogance we had seen earlier. We had to go to Judge Sullivan, who ordered them to provide us with copies of their exhibits. But once again, we were distracted from trial preparation by their inappropriate gamesmanship.

* * * * *

The most important discovery in a criminal case is *Brady* information. Every defense lawyer wants to know what the government with its vast investigative resources has uncovered that could be helpful to the defense. The practice at our firm is to push and push and push for *Brady* information. (We should not have to push at all. It is, after all, the law that this information be provided.) We were concerned that this prosecution team did not appear to be providing anything that they considered *Brady* information. We raised our concerns in a series of letters.

On August 21, 2008, exactly one month before jury selection was to begin, the government responded to our requests for favorable evidence with this statement signed by Deputy Chief Brenda Morris: "We understand our obligations and we will continue to provide you information pursuant to these obligations." In other words, we the prosecutors will decide what we think is favorable to the defense. If we don't think evidence meets our definition of "favorable to the defense," we won't be sending it over. And, it soon became clear, they didn't think that much of anything was favorable to the defense.

We continued to push for what the FBI had learned in its witness interviews, and the government finally claimed to comply by writing us a letter on September 9, the night before we were supposed to be in court to argue again for *Brady* information, and just two weeks before the trial was to start. The letter purported to summarize all of the *Brady* information from witnesses of whom the government was aware. They argued in court that they did not have to turn over the interview memos themselves because they had helpfully gone through the memos and summarized everything that was favorable to the defense. They seemed to be saying, *Stop complaining, you've now got everything you're entitled to.* (They didn't address why we had to file a motion to get them to do this the night before we were to appear in court or why they hadn't given us the letter back on July 31 when almost all of the discovery was "all ready.")

We pressed on. We wanted the actual interview memos. If any of the government's witnesses' testimony was inconsistent with what he or she had previously told the government in an interview, we needed the interview memorandum to confront the witness and, if necessary, to call the interviewing FBI agent to the witness stand to verify the original statement and contradict the court testimony. These memos are prepared on what the FBI calls a Form 302 and thus are called 302s. We needed the 302s.

Not only did the government resist turning over the 302s, but they mocked us for asking. When I was arguing for access to the interviews, Brenda Morris said, "Every time they call, they expect me to drink out of a fire hose just because the defendant has 'U.S. Senator' in front of his name." This clever (if obnoxious) line made it into the newspaper. The government's cynicism and arrogance was escalating.

Judge Sullivan ordered the government to give the defense those portions of the interview memos that contained *Brady* information to the defense. The government did so, but redacted the interview memos—striking through lines of text with a thick black magic marker or covering them with opaque white tape—to hide any portion of the memo they felt did not contain *Brady* information . . . which was most of the memo.

This is a practice the government uses properly in cases where there is a legitimate concern for the safety of witnesses who testify for the government, such as in dangerous cases where citizens are testifying against drug kingpins or Mafia hit men. Most prosecutors would realize there is no legitimate rationale for redacting testimony in a case against an 84 year-old World War II war hero and long-serving member of the U.S. Senate.

But this group of prosecutors was different. They weren't concerned with witness safety. They were too busy preparing an ambush.

Chapter 6

Motions

I assembled a team of Williams & Connolly colleagues to prepare pre-trial motions which would set the rules of the road for the upcoming trial. Most came to Brendan or me and volunteered because they heard we only had six weeks to get ready for trial. Soon, in addition to Brendan and me, the team was comprised of partners Craig Singer, Alex Romain, and Joe Terry, along with six associates.

Craig Singer was my first recruit. Craig had a great intellect and was a tremendous writer. I wanted him to be the principle editor of the papers we would be filing with Judge Sullivan. Craig was a graduate of Wesleyan University and the University of Chicago Law School and a former law clerk to John Paul Stevens of the Supreme Court. A man of many varied interests, Craig, a fan of Philadelphia sports teams and authentic American music, owns thousands of vinyl record albums. We called him The Professor, a nickname Senator Stevens loved.

Brendan and I also recruited Alex Romain, with whom we had worked on several cases. Alex was a graduate of Yale University and the University of Michigan Law School, who had clerked for two distinguished judges in Massachusetts. The son of Hatian-American immigrants, Alex speaks French and Creole fluently, and was trained as a classical pianist. A meticulous lawyer, Alex was very charming, which masked his toughness. Alex's job would be to hound the government for discovery and handle witnesses at trial.

Joe Terry volunteered for the case, and I accepted his offer. Highly-articulate, Joe was a national champion debater at Northwestern. After graduating from law school at the University of Chicago, he clerked for a federal appeals judge in Louisiana. Before he and his charming Aussie wife had children, Joe climbed mountains in his spare time. He has an office that looks like the set of "Mad Men" and enjoys vintage automobiles. The son of a fisheries economist, Joe was born in Fairbanks, Alaska. We needed somebody on the team who knew his way around the state. We sent Joe to Alaska to find witnesses.

The associates on the brief-writing and factual development team were crackerjack young lawyers who'd all graduated from the top law schools: Steve Cady, Amy Davis, and Simon Latcovich of Georgetown; Beth Stewart of Harvard; Ed Kilpela of Michigan; and Neelum Wadhwani of Texas.

Simon was the first associate to join our team. A graduate of the Naval Academy, Simon drove a destroyer in combat during the Iraq War. Brendan recruited him to come to the firm after a presentation by the Dean of Admissions at Georgetown on students who had turned down Harvard and Yale Law Schools to attend Georgetown. Simon did so because Georgetown offered him a full ride scholarship and his helicopter pilot wife, who also graduated from Annapolis, was based in Washington. Simon worked more hours on the case than anybody else on the team. He provided discovery to the government, dealt with the Senator and his staff, and prepared motions for Court.

Beth Stewart was from Columbus, Georgia. She attended Harvard College, where she was President of the Student Body, and then Harvard Law School. A political conservative, she worked briefly for the Senate Judiciary Committee where she assisted in the confirmation hearings of Chief Justice John Roberts. Charismatic and charming, she would also handle witnesses at trial.

Ed Kilpela was a student leader at Penn State before attending Michigan Law School. He volunteered for the case and worked on legal papers for the judge. At trial, he coordinated all of the witnesses, making sure that they were properly served with subpoenas. He made sure that every witness had transportation and lodging and showed up for court at the right time ready to testify. He tried to schedule their testimony at a time which would minimize their inconvenience. That was a big job, which required good organization and diplomacy.

Amy Davis and Steve Cady volunteered to help after the case was under way. Amy was a cheerleader at Harvard before attending Georgetown Law School. In addition to a razor sharp intellect, she had an infectious personality and unbridled enthusiasm. She drafted motions and kept the factual presentation organized.

Steve Cady had been a paralegal at our firm, working on an antitrust case against Microsoft. He worked in our library while attending Georgetown law school at night. Nicknamed "Superman" because of the amount of work he generated, Steve became a member of the team simply by sending unsolicited useful work product to the team during trial based on what he was reading in the media. He quickly became a full-fledged member of the team.

Neelum Wadhwani worked tirelessly on the jury instructions and legal research projects. She taught Rhetoric and Composition and founded her own website development company before attending law school at the University of Texas. She stayed up all night several times making sure that we prepared first-rate legal briefs and were always prepared for legal arguments in court.

I had participated in the hiring of each of these lawyers as a member and chair of our firm's hiring committee. They were all brilliant. To the surprise of many (but not me, because I hired them), they were also very nice people. They were enthusiastic, but they were also fairly young and all newly-minted. They had learned nothing about corrupt prosecutions in law school. They all matured greatly over the next several months.

* * * * *

We filed dozens of motions—written requests for Judge Sullivan to take legal action such as dismissing the case or ordering that evidence be provided. I would lead brainstorming sessions to come up with ideas for motions. We would develop a plan, which I would then run by Brendan. Once he approved of the plan, the younger lawyers would start writing the motions. Craig, Alex, and Joe would edit and redraft portions of them. Bill Phillips, the Senator's friend and former Chief of Staff, would review them for historical accuracy and political sensitivity. I would make the last edits to them, usually focusing on the introduction, themes and main legal arguments.

* * * * *

Our first motion asked the court to transfer the case to Alaska. The law allows a federal case to be transferred "for the convenience of the parties and the witnesses and in the interest of justice." Because convenience of the witnesses is an important factor, the first step was to find out how many of the government's witnesses would be from Alaska versus Washington, D.C., so the day after the Senator was arraigned, I wrote a short letter to prosecutor Nick Marsh: "Please advise me by the close of business today your best estimate of how many witnesses the government intends to call in its case-in-chief and the number of those witnesses who reside in each state."

Here was his response: "Although we do not believe we are required to provide you with a final, comprehensive witness list at this time, we can represent to you that we believe the government's trial evidence will include testimony from multiple witnesses who reside in Alaska, multiple witnesses who reside in the D.C. area, and multiple witnesses who reside in other jurisdictions. Those categories have been listed in order of anticipated numerical size."

Not very helpful. In fact, it was like another scene out of *Alice in Wonderland,* but this time we faced the Mad Hatter, who only spoke in riddles.

We estimated that over 90 percent of the witnesses would be from Alaska. We suggested that Judge Sullivan and his staff could travel to Alaska for the case. We also argued that the Senator needed to campaign during the evening. After all, the election was less than 100 days away. We argued that the case was about a cabin in Alaska, and the jury should be able to see it.

The prosecution team argued that, in legal terms, "its choice of forum was entitled to great deference," that is, that the United States government's choice of where to try the case should matter more than ours. Unfortunately, for us, that is a position with a great deal of legal precedent supporting it.

The prosecution had raided his cabin in Alaska, but argued that the trial should take place in Washington, D.C. because the Senator had voluntarily provided documents to the prosecution in the District of Columbia. The prosecution argued—despite the fact that Marsh had chosen not to tell us the specific number of witnesses from Alaska, much less who those witnesses would be—that our motion must fail because we could not prove how many potential witnesses would be from Alaska.

The prosecution claimed it would be unfair to the government to hold the trial where the Senator was campaigning for election, even though they had indicted a Republican Senator in Washington, D.C., a jurisdiction where Democrats outnumber Republicans by a margin of ten-to-one.

We were concerned with the burden and expense of flying witnesses from Alaska to Washington, D.C. for the trial. Under the rules, if a defendant subpoenas a witness to testify, he must pay for the witness's travel and hotel expenses. The only realistic way to transport a witness from Alaska is to buy them a plane ticket. We spent thousands of dollars per witness getting them to Washington, D.C.

In order to illustrate how inconvenient it would be for the witnesses to travel to D.C., we arrived at the court with a map of the United States showing the true distance between the lower 48 states and Alaska. The map had originally been commissioned by Senator Stevens and Senator Inouye, the long-time Democratic Senator from Hawaii, who were frustrated that most maps of the United

States presented Alaska and Hawaii as if they were just off the coast of California.

Our prediction on the number of witnesses would turn out to be very close: 42 of the 48 fact witnesses had to make the long, non-direct trip from Alaska to Washington, D.C., to testify. We were right about that. But the government was right about the law. The government's choice of forum—like many things—was entitled to deference, and thus the case stayed in Washington, D.C.

* * * * *

The Stevens' indictment never alleged that the Senator was bribed; it only charged him with failing to disclose so-called gifts.

Bribery is defined as an agreement to exchange one thing for another, and, in the law, there must be a "quid pro quo," which in Latin means "this for that." The Justice Department never argued that Senator Stevens traded his vote for any benefits or gifts.

In fact, on the day of the indictment, at the press conference at the Justice Department, a reporter asked Acting Assistant Attorney General Friedrich if this was a bribery case. The Assistant Attorney General answered, "The indictment does not allege a quid pro quo." In other words, the government was not saying that the Senator accepted bribes. Anybody who really knew Ted Stevens would tell you that the Senator would do just about anything that was proper to help the people of the state of Alaska. That did not include accepting bribes. And not even the richly-rewarded Bill Allen ever said that he bribed Senator Stevens.

But when it came time to go to court, the prosecutors alleged that some of Stevens' actions in the Senate benefited Bill Allen's huge petroleum services firm and Alaska's biggest employer, VECO. They claimed that this gave the Senator a motive to falsify his disclosure forms. Of course, any action that benefitted Alaskan business generally—especially the petroleum industry—benefitted VECO. And Senator Stevens had taken lots of action over the years that benefitted the state's biggest industries, of which the petroleum industry is the largest. While not actually saying it, prosecutors were insinuating a quid pro quo.

It was unfair. Stevens' job was to serve Alaska's citizens and enact legislation that would help the Alaskan economy. To use this against him did not seem right. There was no quid pro quo, and the prosecutors knew it. Yet they were happy to hint that perhaps there was some bribery.

We filed a motion asking that this suggested "motivation" be stricken and kept out of the trial. I argued to Judge Sullivan that the prosecution wanted to "taint the courtroom with suggestion of a quid pro quo" when it knew full well that no such thing had taken place.

At one point, prosecutor Joseph Bottini argued that when people considered the benefits Stevens allegedly received and the fact that he did take action that benefited VECO, "they would say, 'Ah ha!'" That was my point exactly, that jurors would make the ah-ha connection between alleged benefits and actions, which was not the charge. Bottini quickly backtracked, realizing he'd been caught arguing a link that the government had to concede did not exist.

In the end, Judge Sullivan ruled that evidence of actions the Senator took that benefitted VECO would be admitted, but that he would instruct the jury that nobody was suggesting that there was a link.

Trial lawyers are often skeptical about jury instructions; we wonder whether juries understand them and abide by them. But the law presumes that juries follow the instructions they are given, and our jurors were told to disregard any suggestion of bribery.

* * * * *

The Constitution of the United States states that only the U. S. Senate can discipline its own members for violating the rules of the Senate. Article I, Section 5, Clause 2 of the Constitution of the United States provides that each House of Congress, and only each House of Congress, has the authority to "determine the Rules of its Proceedings, punish its members for disorderly behavior, and, with the concurrence of two thirds, expel members." Neither the Senate Ethics Committee nor the full Senate had disciplined Senator Stevens for any non-disclosure of gifts, which they would have had the right—and obligation—to do if they believed there was significant wrongdoing.

We filed a motion saying that the Department of Justice had no constitutional basis for prosecuting a Senator for an alleged violation of the Senate's rules regarding disclosure obligations. We argued that the Executive branch was unconstitutionally seeking punishment of a member of the Legislative branch, for an alleged breach of the legislature's rules.

Article I, Section 5, Clause 2 is there for a reason, and it is called the separation of powers. Yet this wasn't the first time the Executive branch had overreached when it came to the Legislative branch. Senator Stevens told me that he knew a number of U.S. Senators who have felt harassed by the Department of Justice.

This was too weighty an issue of constitutional law to address right before the trial, and Judge Sullivan denied our motion. But it is an important issue, and I believed, would have been a powerful issue on appeal if we ended up in the federal appellate court.

* * * * *

The prosecution also put forth motions of its own, many of which were technical. One stood out above all others. Prosecutors filed a motion seeking to prevent us from cross-examining government witnesses Dave Anderson, Rocky Williams, and Bill Allen regarding "rumored personal vices." The government argued that "rumored personal vices" were off limits.

What were those rumored personal vices? For Rocky Williams and Dave Anderson, two workers who purportedly spent a lot of time working on the cabin, it was "rumored" that they were alcoholics. The government suggested that these rumors were unsubstantiated, and that we should not be able to raise questions about them in court. We argued that their alcohol use affected their ability to remember things and their ability to work efficiently on the cabin. Judge Sullivan deferred ruling on that until the witnesses actually testified.

As for Bill Allen, I mentioned earlier that newspapers had reported that Allen had been under state investigation for statutory rape. There was a rumor that the federal government had put an end to that investigation. The government represented to the court that there had been an investigation in 2004, that it ended then, and that the government did not stop it on account of Allen's status as a witness in our case. Indeed, the government argued, accurately, that the Polar Pen investigation was not underway in 2004.

We knew that Bill Allen had been investigated by state police several years earlier for statutory rape for having sex with an underaged girl—and that that investigation had closed without any charges being filed. However, we later learned that once Allen's cooperation in the current corruption investigation of the Alaska legislature was in the headlines, a young prostitute made charges against him, and state officials opened a new investigation.

When the government filed their motion to stop us from raising these "rumored matters" (on cross-examination), we didn't know about that second investigation. We thought the investigation regarding Bill Allen that prosecutors didn't want us to ask about in court was the one from years ago. The prosecutors had filed their motion under seal to keep it out of public view. We disagreed, arguing that this motion should have been filed on the public record; it went directly to the credibility of the government's star witness.

Typically, the government had posted its notice about an irrelevant real estate transaction of the Senator's in Florida on the court's public website, yet when it came to their witness, they wanted that far-more-damaging information kept under seal.

We pushed for information about the sex investigation of Bill Allen. The government argued that we were off-base. They also stated there had been a suggestion that Bill Allen had asked an underaged female to lie for him. But, they said, they had conducted a "thorough investigation" and found no evidence of that. They said that they knew nothing else.

Judge Sullivan ruled that we could cross-examine Allen about the fact that there had been a state investigation, but nothing more. We could not mention statutory rape or child prostitutes. This would have been a reasonable decision *if* the government had been telling the truth.

* * * * *

Judge Sullivan ordered that all pretrial motions needed to be filed five weeks before trial, a normal deadline for a judge to set as a trial approaches. It gives both sides the opportunity to see the other side's motions, and to file a written brief arguing why the request should be denied. It also gives the judge plenty of time to issue rulings before the action begins.

It is also normal for either the prosecution or the defense to ask permission to file additional motions after the pre-trial deadline has passed, should any new issues arise. At this point, because we had only possessed the government's disorganized 500-gigabyte hard drive for less than a week, we filed a motion to reserve the right to deal with any new discovery issues that turned up.

The prosecution opposed this standard motion, saying that "additional discovery motions are unnecessary." Their argument essentially was: *A deadline is a deadline, whether we have violated the Constitution or not. You have no more rights. Sit down and shut up.*

Judge Sullivan disagreed with the government, and granted our request to allow us to file more motions if the government's actions required it.

Chapter 7

Jury Selection

Trial lawyers have input into who sits on their juries. Many believe that picking the jury is the most important part of a trial. Edward Bennett Williams, however, thought picking a jury was overrated. He used to say that he would just as soon try his case before the first 12 people pulled off the street than spend a lot of time on jury selection.

The jury selection process began with the clerk of the court sending notices to potential jurors that they were required to report to the courthouse for jury duty. Anyone who has ever received a notice for jury duty knows that once you arrive at the courthouse, you're going to be asked a lot of questions. This is usually done in the courtroom. The process of asking questions of potential jurors is called "voir dire," from the French "to see and to speak," because judges and lawyers get a chance to size up jurors by seeing them speak. Sometimes only the judge asks questions during voir dire. Sometimes the lawyers ask questions as well.

In some cases, especially those that have received publicity before trial, the potential jurors are also asked to complete a written questionnaire. The purpose of the questionnaire is to obtain information from potential jurors without taking a lot of time in court and without the pressure of having to answer in front of others. Many lawyers believe that a questionnaire reveals the most useful information about a juror because he or she can answer it candidly and in private.

69

Potential jurors who have some reason that they should not be on the jury—such as a medical condition or an admitted bias—are stricken (removed or excused) "for cause." After potential jurors are stricken for cause, the lawyers get to "pick" the jury from those who are left. They do so through the use of "preemptory challenges." When a lawyer uses a preemptory challenge, he or she can ask that the juror be removed for almost any reason whatsoever. The only limit is that a preemptory challenge cannot be used for an inappropriately discriminatory purpose such as race, gender or religion. Otherwise, a lawyer can have an otherwise qualified juror removed based on any reason at all, including the lawyer's mere hunch about how that juror might decide the case.

The defense typically gets more preemptory challenges than the government. This is an acknowledgement that jurors are more likely to be biased in favor of the government. In our case, we were given twelve preemptory strikes and the government was given eight.

After removing some potential jurors for cause, we were left with 36 potential jurors placed, by the clerk's office, in a random numerical order. While those 36 jurors sat in the courtroom (with nothing to do but watch us), we were given a sheet of paper on which to list the twelve people whom we wanted to strike using our preemptory challenges. At the same time, the government was given a sheet of paper upon which to list its eight preemptory challenges. That would leave 16 jurors. The first 12 in numerical order would be the jury. The next four would be alternates. If something happened to one of the first 12 during trial, an alternate would take his or her place.

* * * * *

Jury consultants are specialists who sell their services to lawyers and their clients who want to select the best jury possible for their case. These consultants are usually psychologists, sociologists, public opinion experts or others who claim to have extraordinary insight into who is or is not going to make a good (or bad) juror for your side.

The government hired a jury consultant to assist them in picking jurors who would be most likely to find Senator Stevens guilty. The government spent our taxpayer dollars on Dr. Jo-Ellan Dimitrius, the same expert used by O.J. Simpson's defense team to help pick the Los Angeles jury that acquitted Simpson of murder charges. Dr. Dimitrius, the author of "Reading People: How to Understand People and Predict Their Behavior—Anytime, Anyplace," which I had on my bookshelf, is one of America's best known jury consultants.

For our part, we chose not to hire a jury consultant. I have worked with jury consultants in other cases. They were quite good, and expensive. In this case, we did not have the resources—including the time—to hire and work with a jury consultant. We would have to go with our ability to pick the best possible jury in our hometown of Washington, D.C.

During jury selection, I could see that the government, assisted by Dr. Dimitrius, had fancy charts they were using to analyze each juror. I wondered if the jurors figured out that they were being analyzed by O.J. Simpson's jury consultant.

$$* \quad * \quad * \quad * \quad *$$

When the government suggested that juror questionnaires be used, we agreed, and so did Judge Sullivan. The case was all over the news, and it was important to try to figure out who had read or heard about the Senator and who had not, and who was biased or not. This was a case that might engender bias.

One question that was, properly I thought, not on the questionnaire was: do you consider yourself a Democrat or a Republican? It is well-known that most citizens of the District of Columbia are Democrats, and we did not need a questionnaire to tell us that. Asking them to state their political affiliation in open court would have given the government the opportunity to use their strikes to eliminate any Republicans who found their way into the final group of 36. We were aware of no law preventing that.

The answers to the juror questionnaires are confidential, as are the jurors' identities. I cannot disclose how they answered their questionnaires, but what they said in follow-up questions in open court is part of the public record. I only recall one potential juror whom we knew, according to his questionnaire, was a Republican. Lead prosecutor Morris disclosed that fact in open court in arguing after voir dire that he should be excused for cause.

That potential juror was struck for cause, because he expressed some doubt when asked whether he could be fair to both sides. He said he could be fair, but his doubt was enough to get him excused for cause. The prosecutors did not even need to use up their preemptory challenges to get rid of the one known Republican in our pool of potential jurors.

There was another potential juror whom I recall quite clearly. In open court, she stated that a family member had a bad encounter with the criminal justice system. As she described the case, it became clear to me that her family member was a co-defendant in a case which Brendan and I had tried. In that trial, her family member was found guilty. (It was a hung jury as to our client.) She thought that the trial was unfair. But she assured Judge Sullivan that she could be fair to both sides in our case. The government, of course, used a peremptory strike to get rid of her.

Since we had a limited number of preemptory challenges to use, I wanted to predict how the government would use their challenges. If I wanted to get rid of somebody, there was no sense in burning a challenge on somebody whom the government was going to strike. I wrote down the eight names I thought the government would strike. I turned out to be right about all but one. At the end of the process, we had 16 citizens left sitting in the jury box: twelve actual jurors and four alternates.

Here is how Matt Apuzzo of the Associated Press described it: "By the time the jury box was full . . . , it was clear the Senate's longest-serving Republican was a long way from home. Stevens failed in his bid to transfer the trial to Alaska, where he has been a figure in politics for generations and where he is known fondly as 'Uncle Ted.'

Instead, he will face trial in Washington, where one juror after another said they knew nothing of Stevens or the FBI investigation that has swirled around him for more than a year.

Rather than standing trial in one of the nation's most reliably Republican states, Stevens saw the 11 women and five men jurors and alternates selected from a heavily Democratic district."

* * * * *

I did not know whether a single juror was a Democrat or Republican, but I did know that the government had gotten rid of all potential jurors whom I suspected had positive feelings about Senator Stevens. Most jurors favor the government until you give them a reason not to. Nothing personal against the men and women serving on the jury, but I agreed with Edward Bennett Williams. I would just as soon have had the first twelve citizens off the street.

Chapter
8

"This Case Is About Concealment"

The following article, entitled "The Ill-Timed Trial of Senator Stevens of Alaska," appeared in *The New York Times* on the Saturday before the trial was set to begin.

WASHINGTON—In a year of mesmerizing political scenes, one of the most remarkable will begin to play out next week just down Constitution Avenue from the Capitol.

Senator Ted Stevens of Alaska, who as the longest serving Republican senator has prowled the corridors of Congress since 1968, will go on trial in federal court on charges of failing to disclose $250,000 in gifts and home renovations from a politically connected oil services company.

What makes the proceedings so astounding is not just that Mr. Stevens is a figure of outsize proportions in Alaska and the Senate. Or that the gifts came from a company headed by a longtime friend of Mr. Stevens at a time when the relationship between federal officials and the oil industry is under scrutiny. Or that his state, usually an afterthought in national elections, is now at the center of America's political conversation because of the selection of Alaska's little-known governor for the Republican presidential ticket. . .

No, on top of all that, the criminal proceedings will start about 40 days before Alaska's voters must decide whether Mr. Stevens, 84, merits a seventh full term. His trial, near enough to the Senate so that he can excuse himself from the defense table to go cast votes if necessary, will substitute for his campaign in the closing weeks of the race.

"The verdict will essentially be the election," said Jennifer Duffy, a nonpartisan analyst for the Cook Political Report. In the view of Ms. Duffy and other experts on congressional elections, Mr. Stevens, who is locked in a very competitive race with Mark Begich, his Democratic opponent, can still prevail if he is able to win the case, which is scheduled to begin on Wednesday. A guilty verdict could end his rather amazing political career. . . .

* * * * *

At 9:27 on the morning of Thursday, September 25, 2008, the fourth day of *United States v. Stevens,* the jury had been selected, the pre-trial motions had been ruled upon and opposing counsel were ready with their opening statements.

Seated at two large tables in front of Judge Emmet G. Sullivan were the prosecution and the defense teams. For the government were Brenda Morris, Nicholas Marsh, Joseph Bottini and FBI Special Agent Mary Beth Kepner. The four Williams & Connolly lawyers were Brendan Sullivan, Alex Romain, Beth Stewart, and me. Senator Stevens sat with us.

The government, as is the custom, opened first. Brenda Morris stood at a podium facing the jury and began to read from a type-written script. She lost no time in getting to what she must have considered the heart of the matter, stating, in an authoritative tone, "This is a simple case about a public official who took hundreds of thousands of dollars' worth of free financial benefits and then took away the public's right to know that information."

Gesturing toward the Senator, she continued, her attitude and her tone becoming increasingly sarcastic, ". . . he took away the pub-lic's right to know this information by repeated false statements he made on his public financial disclosure forms filed year after year after year with the United States Senate. The public, this pub-

75

lic official, the defendant, did these things so that the free financial benefits that he was receiving would not have stopped and the public would never have to know."

Continuing to read her script, she said:

> Ladies and gentlemen, this case is about concealment. It's about the defendant hiding things from the public, valuable things, a few thousand dollars here, a couple hundred thousand dollars there, things that the defendant received from friends and benefactors who were the powerful. The defendant hid these things so that the public wouldn't know that he had gotten them, and, more importantly, so the public wouldn't know who he had gotten them from. It's about this defendant's knowing and intentional decision to conceal that information, that one of the heads of the largest companies in Alaska, as well as other prominent friends, gave the defendant more than a quarter-million dollars' worth of financial benefits that the defendant never paid for, and that the defendant decided the public just didn't have to know. . . The public had a right to know this, but the defendant said no, and instead he decided to violate the law.

> Now, the indictment charges the defendant with seven separate counts. You'll hear more specifics about each of those counts at the end of the trial, but to sum it up, the indictment charges that the defendant had a scheme to conceal from the public the valuables he received and that the defendant knowingly and repeatedly omitted and falsely represented valuables he received on six different financial disclosure forms, one a year, from 2000 through 2006. Each form is filed with the United States Senate, and each, he swore, was accurate and true.

Morris continued to read:

"The defendant is a career politician," she said, making the last two words sound like a crime. "He has been a member of the United States Senate for over forty years representing the state of Alaska."

That was another dig, but it was what she said next that infuriated me.

Ladies and gentlemen, you do not survive as a politician in this town for that long without being very, very smart, very, very deliberate, very, very forceful, and at the same time knowing how to fly under the radar. . .

The government's evidence will demonstrate that the defendant clearly knows how to get things done with little said. He can be very subtle. The defendant trusts few, and the evidence will show that those he trusts are very, very loyal to him. They know how to get things done for the senator subtlety. That's the way he wanted it.

Now, during this case, ladies and gentlemen, I'm going to tell you what the government will prove that defendant received, then . . . I'm going to tell you how the defendant concealed the receipt of all these things from the public.

First, the unpaid financial benefit. In this trial you will see proof of a lot of benefits that the defendant received from multiple separate and independent sources, including companies and personal friends. Now, the biggest unpaid financial benefit, not just in terms of dollar value but just in sheer extravagance, is the major assistance the defendant received to complete and transform his house in Girdwood, Alaska.

Brenda Morris spoke for another half an hour or so. She painted a picture of a corrupt politician who schemed to use his office to receive gifts that he then hid from the public. Morris referred to Ted Stevens as "the defendant" 145 times, because that made him sound guilty. She only called him Senator Stevens 11 times. She closed by saying, "At the conclusion of this case, ladies and gentlemen, I will come back to you and I will ask you to find the defendant, Ted Stevens, guilty of a scheme to hide the truth through repeated false statements . . . because as you will see, he made a choice. He made the choice to repeatedly violate the law, and that's simply why we're here, ladies and gentlemen."

* * * * *

Following a fifteen minute break, Brendan gave the opening statement for the defense. He began by thanking the jurors for their service—and for not trying to get out of jury duty—and by explaining to the jurors why he had to wear a microphone clipped to his jacket lapel (so he could be heard by the people in the overflow courtroom). And then he got down to business, in his characteristic common sense, professional way.

> At the end of the day I'm going to ask you for a verdict of not guilty because the evidence will show he is not guilty. Our effort here today is to give you a little preview of the evidence, and as you can imagine, sometimes people's view of the evidence differs dramatically.

> We've seen that in our own lives. If anyone has been around children, you hear one story from one child and you hear another story from another child that's so different. I'm going to tell you a different story. I'm going to tell you the story that the evidence actually shows that Ted Stevens had no intent to violate the law, he had no intent to make any false statements. He intended to file accurate statements, and he did file accurate statements to the best of his knowledge.

> Why all of a sudden in his eighty-fifth year of life on this earth did he decide all of a sudden to go out and become a criminal and file false statements? The evidence will show he did not file false statements. And the evidence of intent, which is what you'll be looking for here, is found in many, many ways.

For the next half hour or so, Brendan carefully listed those ways, but the heart of his opening was the Torricelli note—the note that said, "It just has to be done right," the note that we thought was so helpful to the defense.

Brendan quoted it word for word. He said, "It jumps off the page and grabs you by the throat to show you what the intent of Ted Stevens was." Everybody in the courtroom must have known that we thought it was the most important evidence in the case.

He ended by saying, simply: "At the end of the case, I'm going to come back here—I have one more time to talk to you, fellow citizens, one more time—and I'm going to ask you to free him from this burden, send him right out that door, because there's no evidence by which the government can convince beyond a reasonable doubt that he intended to commit a crime. . .

And that is exactly what should have happened, except for one thing. The government broke the rules.

* * * * *

The government's first witness was a VECO engineer named John Hess. Although Hess was not a licensed architect, Allen had asked him to prepare some simple plans for the cabin on computer software and then to have lunch with Stevens to discuss them.

Hess testified that the purpose of the renovation was to create some space for the grandchildren and that Catherine Stevens was the "driver of the project." Hess also testified that local restaurateur Bob Persons was going to be involved, because the Senator himself was too busy. Hess further told the jury that the Senator had sent him a note after lunch asking for a bill for his work and emphasizing the importance of complying with the Senate ethics rules.

Mr. Hess testified further that he believed the note was "a real attempt to abide by the Senate rules and do the right thing." The Senator, for his part, asked for a bill for the drawings. He believed that the cost of the drawings were included in the total of more than $160,000 that he and Catherine paid. John Hess might as well have been our witness.

Prosecutors then called five workers who had spent time at the cabin. One was employed by the contractor—Christensen Builders—whom Bill Allen had arranged to do work, and others were employed by VECO. Not one of these workers ever met Senator Stevens. Only one—an employee of Christensen Builders—met Mrs. Stevens. How? He met her on a day she brought muffins by for the workers. It was the only day he ever saw her there.

There was nothing these initial witnesses said that indicated the Stevenses believed they were getting something for nothing, as the government had alleged in its opening.

The government's seventh and next witness was a woman named Cheryl Boomershine, a bookkeeper at VECO, who testified that internal records at VECO were authentic and reflected amounts of time spent by VECO workers, the costs of which were not passed on to Ted Stevens. According to the records, one of the workers, named Rocky Williams, worked full-time "and then some" at the cabin.

According to the records, in September of 2000, Williams supposedly had averaged over 10 hours per workday at the cabin, and often worked at least one day on the weekends. In all, he supposedly spent 246.5 hours that month working on the cabin (if he had worked an eight hour day every workday of the month, he would have spent 160 hours at the chalet. Hmm.)

In October, Rocky Williams supposedly worked even more— 284 hours—and in November, he (allegedly) worked 281.5 hours. In December, he slacked off a bit, purportedly working only 278 hours. In January, according to the records, Mr. Williams worked 250 hours at the chalet, an average of 50 hours a week.

These records were presented with great flair by government prosecutor Nicholas Marsh. He put them on an overhead projector for the jury, and circled the numbers. All told, the records indicated that VECO workers spent $188,000 worth of time working on the cabin.

I cross-examined Ms. Boomershine, but not aggressively, as she was simply a bookkeeper testifying about the records. The law allows for the use of business records at trial even though records are normally considered hearsay. Hearsay is defined by the Rules of Evidence as an out-of-court statement offered for the truth of the matter asserted in the statement. A statement in a document is created out of court and therefore is usually hearsay unless an exception applies. There is an exception for business records kept in the ordinary course of business, which are considered to be accurate and reliable. As long as somebody familiar with the records comes in and testifies that they are authentic, believed to be accurate, and maintained and kept in the ordinary course of business, what is stated in business records is not considered hearsay.

I pointed out that Bill Allen had approved all of the time records, and she agreed with me that she was relying on Bill Allen's approval of the records. Her testimony closed down the first week of trial.

* * * * *

That weekend, out of the Alaskan blue, we caught a break. I heard from Rocky Williams. He told me he had not worked nearly as many hours as the records indicated. In fact, Rocky told us that he rarely if ever spent a full work day renovating the Girdwood residence.

Rocky told us—Simon Latcovich and me—that during that same time period he often worked on other matters, such as servicing Bill Allen's camper, boats, snow machines, and fishing lodge equipment, all of which were kept at a warehouse Allen called his "Toy Box". Rocky revealed that he often spent time keeping inventory at a place VECO used for long-term file and desk storage. And even while at the cabin, he spent a lot of his time on his cell phone coordinating other activities.

He assumed that VECO would allocate his time amongst all the various projects on which he spent time, not just the cabin. He was wrong. Rocky also told us that the Senator himself showed almost no interest in the renovation project. According to Rocky, the Senator was only interested in two things: keeping Mrs. Stevens happy and having a place where he could chop and burn wood.

Rocky said the government had flown him from Alaska to Washington to testify and that he had worked with the prosecutors to get ready to testify. But he also told us that the prosecutors had suddenly reversed course and decided to send him back to Alaska. Rocky said that he had told the government and the grand jury the same things he had just told us.

We were stunned. What Rocky was telling us was clearly *Brady* information, evidence of innocence, which the government must share with the defense. We immediately requested Rocky's grand jury testimony from the government. (As discussed earlier, as surprising as it is to many people, the government does not have to provide previous statements of witnesses unless they contain favorable information or until after they have testified.)

Prosecutor Marsh refused. But when Brenda Morris heard of our request, she overruled him and disgorged it. The grand jury transcript confirmed that Rocky had told the government what he told us.

We mobilized our team and within a matter of hours had prepared a motion asking Judge Sullivan to dismiss the case. If he wasn't willing to dismiss the case, we asked that a mistrial be granted.

Craig Singer led the writing team. Our motion, which we filed just before midnight, began like this:

> The defense believed that Rocky Williams was a key government witness. The government apparently thought so too. For the better part of the past two weeks, the government has had Mr. Williams in Washington, D. C., interviewing him and preparing him to testify. Apparently, government counsel did not like what they heard. They sent him back to Alaska last Thursday, the day of opening statements.

> Shortly after indictment, defense counsel contacted Mr. Williams and requested an interview. Mr. Williams declined. But on Friday evening Mr. Williams called defense counsel, and today defense counsel were able to interview him for the first time. In three telephone conversations today, Mr. Williams disclosed highly exculpatory information to defense counsel that apparently has been known to the government for years. Among other things, Mr. Williams informed defense counsel that he spent nowhere near 8 hours per day, 6-7 days per week, on the Girdwood home renovation project—in direct contrast to the timesheets that the government has placed in evidence to

support its central theory that the unpaid cost of the project to VECO was $188,000. This new information gravely undercuts the government's case as described in its opening statement and as presented by government witnesses to date. Yet the government never disclosed this information to defense counsel pursuant to its unquestionable *Brady* obligations. Worse yet, the government has presented evidence at trial that, in light of the information now disclosed to defense counsel by Mr. Williams, can charitably be described as grossly misleading.

The government's decision to withhold this information has prejudiced the defense. Had it been disclosed, the exculpatory evidence would have been a significant theme of defense counsel's opening statement, and it could have been used effectively to cross-examine the government's witnesses. In particular, this evidence was directly relevant to the testimony of government witness Cheryl Boomershine, who testified about Mr. William's billing entries on VECO timesheets, which inaccurately suggest that he worked full days, 6-7 days a week, with substantial overtime, on the Girdwood [renovation] project.

We pointed out additional *Brady* evidence that had not been disclosed, including the Senator's lack of involvement in the renovation. We reminded the Court that we had asked for *Brady* information over and over again and had been assured by the prosecutors over and over again that they were in full compliance.

When we arrived the next morning, Judge Sullivan had read our motion. He said he was "disturbed about the contents" of our papers.

Marsh explained for the government: "We've worked with Mr. Williams for a very long time, since 2006, before he came to Washington, D.C., about a month, three weeks ago. The agents that had been working with him gave us fair notice that he was much different. In fact, he was almost unrecognizable. He's a chronic alcoholic, and he's lost about 60, 70 pounds, we estimate. He actually looked to be a much different person.

We found out that right around the time of our interviews in Alaska, he had to undergo a procedure to have fluid drained off of his stomach because he couldn't breathe. He was having trouble getting around. He had a yellowish tint to his body, and had lost a ton of weight from his face. We brought him here early because in part we wanted to work with him. We will provide the Court with his grand jury testimony. As the Court will see, he's a very good witness for us. We had him here, we worked with him trying to get his body to stabilize.

I thought to myself what the government had said was Williams's "rumored personal vice" of alcohol abuse was more than a rumor.

Brenda Morris injected, "We brought him here early because of his health so that he could be settled before."

Marsh continued, "We then continued to work with him over the days, and all the agents and prosecutors, none of us are doctors, but we noted a severely marked deterioration in his health. He was having trouble breathing and turning. . ."

Morris interjected again, "Light green"

. . . Marsh continued, "-light green to gray."

Again Morris jumped in, "He was getting doctors' calls when we were interviewing him where he was breaking appointments to be with us."

Marsh then continued, uninterrupted this time: "Where we made this determination that we had a bigger problem was when we were debriefing him probably about a week-and-a-half ago, a week ago maybe. Your Honor, I'm sorry, the days are running together. We were debriefing him on the matters. He got a call from his doctors while in the debriefing and finished up and he told the attorneys, the agent, 'That was my doctor. I'm two weeks late on my tests. They think there's something wrong with my liver.'

At that point we thought about it. We took stock of our case. We realized we could proceed with this case without Mr. Williams, and that we're generally concerned about his health . . . we sent him back, told him to get his tests. He's under subpoena from Williams & Connolly for October 6th. We told him to make sure he contacted them once he got back to let them know he was no longer in D.C."

The hospital at Johns Hopkins University, for two decades the top-ranked hospital in the world, is only 45 miles from the federal courthouse in downtown Washington, and there are several excellent hospitals in Washington that are even closer, including the hospitals affiliated with Georgetown University and George Washington University. Alaska has no comparable hospitals, and many Alaskans come to the lower 48 states when they have especially challenging medical conditions. The notion that Rocky Williams had to get on a 12 hour non-direct flight to Alaska because of a desperate medical condition was not credible.

I did not doubt that he had a medical condition, but I didn't think for a minute that was the reason they had sent him away from our world class hospitals to Alaska.

Marsh then argued something we would hear over and over again: "It doesn't matter if these costs billed to VECO were $188,000 or $295,000 or $85,000. What matters is, were they more than $265?" (Gifts over $265 were supposed to be reported on Senate disclosure forms.)

I responded for the defense: "The clear implication of Ms. Boomershine's testimony and the accounting records that they put in as reliable business records was that Mr. Williams was there working . . . in the month of December 278 hours, all on the Girdwood residence; November, 281 hours. Every day except for Thanksgiving, and the government's case is that those numbers overwhelm any inference that the $160,000 that Senator Stevens paid was a fair price for these renovations. The case that they presented in opening and they presented through all these witnesses is that there was so much work done that he could not have missed it, that he must have known that VECO was doing a substantial amount of work. Our defense is that he paid a fair price, and Mrs. Stevens paid a fair price.

. . . They put on testimony, the last witness on Friday, presenting Mr. Williams' time records as unimpeachable, reliable business records, suggesting that he worked such a large amount of hours on this project it overwhelmed any defense that Senator Stevens' family paid enough, and we stand by our position that this case ought to be dismissed, or, in the alternative, there ought to be a mistrial. It's not fair."

I argued that we got lucky that this information was disclosed to us—that if we hadn't gotten that call from Rocky Williams, it never would have been disclosed to us. I argued that the government clearly has "a very different conception of what *Brady* is than we do" and that they ought to be producing for us all of the interview memos.

Marsh responded that the government had gone to great lengths to provide *Brady* material, adding "We're distressed that we're being accused of this. We believe that we disclosed exactly what we needed to do." They filed papers accusing us of "win at all costs tactics." They said, "This time, defendant has gone too far, accusing the government of *Brady* violations and of proffering misleading evidence at trial. Nothing could be further from the truth. . . ."

Once again, their arrogance was just stunning.

* * * * *

Judge Sullivan was upset that the government had unilaterally sent a witness under subpoena back to Alaska. "It would have been better if government counsel had picked the phone up before they unilaterally decided to put him on a plane and send him back to Alaska and tell the man to call you when he gets to Alaska. That doesn't make any sense at all. I'm flabbergasted that was the decision.

Do you want to take one more crack and give me a reason why that was done? When you arrive back here, here's a witness who is subpoenaed, the government knows this witness is subpoenaed, there are compelling reasons why the government has decided not to call him, put him back on a plane, send him back to Alaska, and tell him, by the way, when you land, call the defense attorneys. . ."

Marsh attempted to defend his team's actions: "We never tried to hide him."

Judge Sullivan continued: "What gave the government authority to tell a subpoenaed witness, who has a federal subpoena in his hand, you can leave this jurisdiction because the United States says you can? What gives the United States authority to do that? Why wasn't I consulted about that before the United States made a unilateral decision? Now I'm peeved about that. . . It's a federal subpoena to appear in my court. . . By the way, we're not going to tell the judge either. You knew defense counsel had subpoenaed him. You didn't pick up the phone and say, look—No one thought to call the Court and say, 'Judge, notwithstanding your subpoena, we're going to send this man back.' Who gives the United States the authority to do that? . . .He's under subpoena to appear in this court. You basically told him go on back home, and when you get there don't bother about calling the judge, call defense counsel if you want to, but we're not going to tell anyone, as we drive you to the airport. . .

"The government better start opening its eyes."

*****

At the end of the day, we were allowed to recall Cheryl Boomershine as a witness. She had been sightseeing in Washington, and I felt rather silly bringing her back to court in her tourist clothes. What had happened was not really her fault—after all, she was simply a bookkeeper who had put down on the company's books information that others had told her.

I established that she did not know whether or not Williams worked the hundreds of hours the government's exhibit said he worked. I asked her if she had met with the government before testifying. She had. Wanting to show the jury that the government had not been straight with Ms. Boomershine or the jury, I then asked her if anybody from the government had told her that Rocky did not work nearly as many hours as his records indicated.

This drew an objection from Marsh, and Judge Sullivan sustained the objection. That may have been the technically correct ruling, as it was probably hearsay. According to legal theory, I needed to get that information from Rocky Williams himself. But the government had sent him back to Alaska, and now he was too sick to travel.

In later filings, we called the government's shifty maneuver "the Rocky Williams caper." This sounded like a keystone cops episode, and it drew some laughs. I laughed, too, because I believe it's appropriate (and healthy) to find humor in difficult circumstances, but the fact remained that what these prosecutors had done was very serious.

* * * * *

Prosecutors called several more workers. Few had any interaction with Senator Stevens, and among those who did speak with Ted or Catherine no one testified that either of them acted like they were getting the free services alleged by the government.

* * * * *

After a couple of mini witnesses, the government called Bill Allen to the stand. Everybody agreed that he was the most important witness in the case, and his testimony was much anticipated. Prosecutor Joseph Bottini, a large man with a bushy mustache, waited for Allen to take the oath and swear to tell the truth, the whole truth, and nothing but the truth.

Under Bottini's questioning, Allen testified that he did not send bills for time spent by VECO workers at the cabin. Not surprisingly, the government did not have him address the fact that the Senator and Catherine had paid $160,000 for work worth far less. Nor did Bottini ask Allen what he thought the renovations were worth. Nor did the government attempt to elicit any testimony to indicate that Allen and the Stevenses had any sort of agreement that they would not be billed what the renovations were worth.

The "it has to be done right" note was a problem for the government. Right before the morning break on October 1, 2008, Prosecutor Bottini introduced it. This was a common tactic trial lawyers call "taking the teeth out" of a point of evidence. By introducing it on direct examination rather than waiting for it to come out on cross-examination, it gives the impression that you are not afraid of it. I expected this from the government. Bottini pointed out to Allen that the note asked for a bill. And he pointed out to Allen that the note said that Bob Persons was going to talk to Allen about it.

But then Bottini went further than I ever would have imagined. He asked Allen the following questions and received the following answers:

Q: Did you send Senator Stevens a bill or an invoice after you received this note from him?

A: No.

Q: Mr. Allen, do you remember having a conversation with Mr. Persons after you got the note from Senator Stevens?

A: Yes.

Q: What did Mr. Persons tell you?

A: He said, oh, Bill, don't worry about getting a bill. He said, Ted is just covering his ass.

* * * * *

This was a bombshell. With one fell swoop, Bottini and Allen turned our best evidence on its head. Allen's testimony transformed favorable evidence for Senator Stevens into evidence of a scheme to avoid payment. We had never heard this before, and we immediately concluded that it was a lie, concocted to eliminate the value of the "it just has to be done right" note. It simply didn't sound like the Ted Stevens we had come to know and love. It didn't sound like Bob Persons either. It had the ring of a lie and though some lawyers might have decided to argue that it was just Bob Persons saying something to Bill Allen without authority from Ted Stevens, we decided to take it on as a lie. We felt in our bones that it was a lie. The question was "how to prove it to be a lie?"

One of the techniques trial lawyers are taught is to save your best material until right before a break. Jurors are more likely to remember the last thing they heard, and it will linger in jurors' minds during the break. Most trial lawyers know this. Bottini used this technique perfectly. This bombshell broke immediately before the break.

After the break, we returned for a bit more testimony, but then one of the jurors got sick and Judge Sullivan had to adjourn the trial until the next day. As it turned out, the trial was put off for another four days—with "covering his ass" lingering in the juror's minds all the while. The government had played it just right.

Another technique trial lawyers are taught is to pick a theme and emphasize that theme. The government now had a theme: Ted Stevens was "covering his ass." Prosecutors used this testimony to argue that the "it just has to be done right" note was not evidence of good faith at all, but rather was evidence of an evil intent. And this testimony was their proof. Unless we could prove that the testimony was a lie, it was a disaster for the defense.

90

Chapter 9

No Harm, No Foul

October 1st, the day Allen delivered the "covering his ass" bomb-shell, was a rough day for us. In a moment, the tide took a strong turn in favor of the government. The prosecutors now had testimony that corroborated jurors' likely cynicism about Members of Congress. On our side of the courtroom, we knew that Bill Allen was lying—but proving that he was lying would be difficult. We were behind.

Just before midnight, as I was getting ready to go home, I noticed an email from Brenda Morris. It had been sent at 11:29 p.m., and attached was a letter signed by her.

Dear Mr. Cary,

As we are all aware, the government is under a continuing duty to provide the defendant with information in the government's possession, custody, or control that is "favorable" to the defense. This obligation includes, among other things, the production of information that could reasonably be used to impeach a government witness.

In connection with the ongoing trial testimony of Bill J. Allen, this evening we undertook a re-review of, among other information, all memoranda of interviews between federal law enforcement agents and Mr. Allen. During the course of that re-review, we have located two memoranda that, out of an abundance of caution, we are providing to you in redacted form. The unredacted portions of these memoranda could arguably

91

constitute cumulative *Brady* material that was provided in summary fashion in our August 25 and September 9 letters but was not provided to you in redacted format . . . .

We have also reviewed, again, all of the interviews of Mr. Allen to insure that no other reports pertain to this matter.

Very truly yours,

Brenda K. Morris

* * * * *

It was late, and I had not had much sleep for weeks. I stared at the convoluted letter. I then turned to the attached "redacted memoranda." One said that Bill Allen had told the government that he "believes that Stevens would have paid an invoice if he had received one for the work done by John Hess." The second memo said that Allen had told the government that the Senator and his wife "would have paid the bill" for the work of Rocky Williams or Dave Anderson if they had received one.

I was stunned. That was the Ted Stevens I knew. But it was exactly the opposite of what the government was arguing and exactly the opposite of what the government had told us in their September 9th letter, which purported to summarize all information from witnesses interviews favorable to the defense and which the government did not deliver until the night before we were supposed to be in court arguing for *Brady* information.

Here's what the government's September 9th letter said about the Senator paying bills: "Allen stated that he believed that defendant would *not* have paid the actual costs incurred by VECO, even if Allen had sent defendant an invoice, because defendant would not have wanted to pay that high a bill."

Now, in the middle of trial, we learned from the October 1 letter that Allen had said just the opposite.

* * * * *

I went home and collapsed into bed. During trial, I usually work myself to exhaustion and fall immediately to sleep. But on this night my sleep was so fitful that after a few hours of tossing and turning I got up, showered and dressed, and returned to the office where I stared at the pages again. What I had seen at midnight was not a dream.

When Brendan arrived, I went into his office and showed him the letter and memos. After he'd read them, Brendan looked up and said, "I'll handle this one."

I sent an email to Judge Sullivan and the prosecutors telling them that we had a "major matter" we needed to raise before the jury took the box. I knew the government had sent the Court a copy of its letter to me, and I had a strong hunch Judge Sullivan was going to raise it whether or not we did. I was right: when we arrived, the judge was on the bench, ready to go.

Brendan stepped to the podium: "I have been a member of this court for almost forty years. I was sworn in right here, and I can't do my duty to defend this citizen or any citizen if the government of the United States does not abide by the instructions of the court to present *Brady*. If the government does not abide by the law, I cannot do it. I'm incapable of defending. . .

"The integrity of the process has been breached. It must stop. The testimony that was elicited from Mr. Allen with some flair at the break, like skillful lawyers do, to leave lingering in the minds of the juror the impact of the testimony. The testimony was elicited about the, quote, cover your ass, end of quote, an explanation apparently that this witness presented to this jury based on a statement Bob Persons made to him. Of course, we contend that that statement is an absolute lie.

"Had we had this kind of exculpatory information, my opening would have addressed that kind of an issue, because I opened about intent, the Stevens' intent, that they paid the bills, that they were honorable. But for the unusual circumstance of a continuance yesterday afternoon for a couple of hours, I would have been into my cross-examination an hour. I've never seen anything like it. I ask that the Court dismiss this case for *Brady* violations; in the alternative, that it grant a mistrial. There is no other remedy. We can't go back. You've tried, I've tried. I'm not even saying it's intentional on the part of the government. I don't know whether it's intentional. It doesn't matter whether it's intentional. The integrity of the proceedings has been breached and I ask for the Court to remedy this problem now with the power that it has to do justice. That's what we're here about. That's what you give your life to and that's what I've given my life to in these courts but I can't do it under these circumstances."

Brendan wasn't the only person upset. Judge Sullivan was also upset, and justifiably so. Like Brendan, he spoke extemporaneously— and eloquently—about the importance of what was happening.

Judge Sullivan began: "I've been talking about *Brady* from day one. [The defense] raised it on day one. And I've been reminding the government of its ongoing obligations and the government is aware of its ongoing obligations. It's very troubling. If the government is the gate-keeper . . . for favorable information for the defendant, it's the prosecutor's responsibility. The prosecutor has an obligation to turn it over to the defendant.

"This is not about prosecution by any means necessary. This is not about hiding the ball. The government has an obligation to turn this information over. And do you know what? If prosecutors don't want to do that, they ought to resign . . . because the integrity of our system of justice depends upon fair-minded prosecutors abiding by the oath they've taken to apply the law and to follow the law.

Judge Sullivan continued: "This is the government's chief witness, everyone agreed. I find it unbelievable . . . that this was just an error. It strikes me that this was probably intentional. I know I'm getting out there on a limb by saying that. I find it unbelievable this was just an error. This is the government's chief witness."

Brenda Morris responded for the government. She claimed that her team's failure to disclose this information was not intentional. And she said, "By the luck of God Mr. Allen is still on the stand. They can still cross-examine Mr. Allen on this and cross-examination hasn't happened." She said, "There is no harm here." In other words, no harm, no foul.

Brendan replied, "I can't believe this is rectifiable. You can't undo what's been done here. I can't say I defended this man with my whole heart and soul with the oath I took to defend zealously. I'll never believe if we proceed that can happen, no matter how much you do, how you try to do it. I can't. My heart's beating twice as fast as it should be for a 66 year-old man from the moment I saw that. This can't happen in a court. They've said, 'We know our responsibility.' How many times have they said 'We know our responsibility.' Let them step up to bat. Come back up here and dismiss this case. Dismiss it!"

Brenda Morris quickly shot back: "I'll come back up and ask you, Mr. Sullivan, how are you prejudiced?"

The judge interjected, "Wait, wait. Let's focus on me." Lawyers are supposed to address their arguments to the judge, not to each other.

Morris argued, "He's getting a fair trial." She turned back to Brendan and directed her comment to him, "Believe me, you're getting a fair trial."

Judge Sullivan did not like that. He erupted, "He's getting a fair trial because I'm here. That's the only reason he's getting a fair trial, because I'm ensuring that he gets his fair day in court. Thank goodness we don't have to rely on the United States to give him a fair trial."

Judge Sullivan then posed a question to the government. "Suppose after trial the government realized it had not complied with the Court's order? What's the remedy then?"

The ensuing dialogue was breathtaking:

Morris: Well, again, Judge, we thought about that because I think—

95

Judge Sullivan: You thought about what?

Morris: We thought that whether or not about the judge's order, whether or not—what would happen, and that's just it. In thinking of it in just the—

Judge Sullivan: I'm sorry, I don't understand.

Morris: In thinking of it in the box of just *Brady*, it's not an issue. [In other words, Morris was arguing that this information did not need to be disclosed under the *Brady* decision.] In thinking of it outside the box of it being *Brady* in the Court's order in addition to the *Brady* to turn over the 302s, that's where we said we got a problem. It doesn't matter whether or not they still had the information. It doesn't matter whether or not they had the information in a letter or other bits and portions and pieces of 302s. This is part of what the judge ordered us to do with this 302.

So far, Morris had not answered the question. So Judge Sullivan tried again:

Judge Sullivan: What's the remedy after trial when the government realizes it's not complied with—

Morris: Judge, I don't know whether or not, to be quite honest, we would have ever realized it but for getting prepared and that came across yesterday, us getting prepared. We looked at it and said wait a minute—

Judge Sullivan: Getting prepared for?

Morris: For turning over information to the defense with regard to other witnesses, and that's what we looked at it for, and that's how we found it.

Judge Sullivan: The review should have taken place before Allen testified, right?

Morris: No, no, no. That review—our review, initial review for the *Brady* did, Judge, and that information has been provided to them.

Judge Sullivan: So someone went down meticulously and looked through all of this information that was just turned over?

Morris: In that particular 302, what happened is [FBI Special Agent] Michelle Pluta's name was on it. We knew Michelle Pluta was on one of the 302s, and in turning over Michelle Pluta's—because we were going to turn the 302 over to the defense as her *Jencks,* because remember we had discussed that the 302s would be *Jencks* for the agents, and so in looking over the 302 for Michelle Pluta, that's when it was realized, whoa, did we turn this part over? We looked at the redacted 302 that was turned over, because a portion of that 302 was turned over, but that information wasn't there, but they still had the information, so that portion had been redacted, but it was in other parts, but still, according to your order, that shouldn't have been redacted, it should have been given over. So that's where it came up. And that is as honest as I can tell you, Judge.

* * * * *

Ah ha! Now, I understood. Morris never did answer Judge Sullivan's question, but I now understand why the government had produced the 302. They were planning on using Agent Michelle Pluta, an FBI agent as a summary witness. The rules allow both sides to call a summary witness in a complicated case to summarize documentary evidence. Usually the government picks an FBI agent who has not been that involved in the case. That way they are less vulnerable on cross-examination to giving up information about the case. And an agent who knows very little about the case is not so likely to have witness statements to turn over as required by the *Jencks* Act.

We had an agreement with the prosecution that they would fulfill their *Jencks* obligation by turning over witness statements 24 hours before any witness testified, and we would also turn over any witness statements we had 24 hours before the witness testifies, so the 302s written by Agent Pluta had to be turned over as *Jencks*. She hadn't written many 302s, but when the government looked at this 302 of hers they were about to turn over in its *entirety* as *Jencks*, they had seen it contained favorable information for the defense that should have been turned over as *Brady*.

The prosecutors realized we would have gone nuts when we got it, and that we were going to catch them. So they were trying to beat us to the punch.

But their letter had said, "This evening we undertook a re-review of, among other information, all memoranda of interviews between federal law enforcement agents and Mr. Allen." They had made it sound like they were undertaking an ordinary review in an abundance of caution. But now we knew that they gave it to us because they had to under the *Jencks* Act. They were about to get caught.

97

* * * * *

Judge Sullivan gave us a few hours to put together a brief. Again Craig Singer, who normally edits our briefs, was pressed into service, and, still at the courthouse, he sat down at a laptop computer in the "War Room," a tiny space down the hall from the courtroom that we'd filled with equipment, files and supplies.

From the beginning of the trial until the end, the War Room—festooned with an Alaska state flag provided by Catherine Stevens and redolent of peanut butter and jelly sandwiches—was the scene of frenetic activity. The associates, Simon Latcovich, Beth Stewart, Neelum Wadhwani, Amy Davis, Ed Kilpela and Steve Cady—plus paralegals David Gerkin and John Holton—were knocking themselves out, driven by the twin forces of professional duty and professional shock at seeing, first hand, government prosecutors dealing from the bottom of the deck, a lesson definitely not taught in law school.

Their diligence was not lost on our client. Senator Stevens, a legendary hard-worker himself, mentioned several times how impressed he was by the dedication of the team that was laboring on his behalf. Each one of them got at least two personal, handwritten notes from him thanking them for their hard work and dedication.

Interestingly, for the most part the Senator saw only the daylight half of it. For my part, I saw most of their hard work and dedication, but not all of it. I learned later from Beth Stewart, that, in addition to working very hard individually, they had one another's back. As Beth told me, "Among the associates, when any of us was getting ready to go home, generally close to or after midnight, we would still call the others to see if they needed any help. . . . Bottom line is that in those crazy sleepless weeks, I do not remember anyone *ever* having a cross word with anyone else."

* * * * *

Craig and the war room team cranked out a fine brief in just a few hours.

"Before trial," it began, "the government told defense counsel that Mr. Allen had told the government that he believed Senator Stevens would *not* pay an invoice if one had been sent for work by VECO employees. Now, after weeks of preparation, after opening statements, and after most of the government's case has been presented to the jury, the defense learns for the first time that Mr. Allen told the government, on at least two different occasions, that he believed that the Stevens family *would have paid* invoices if they had been sent.

"Late last night, with Bill Allen's direct testimony almost completed and cross-examination scheduled to begin today, the government provided for the first time this crucial *Brady* . . . information that it was ordered to produce . . .

"Enough is enough. The Court should dismiss the indictment. In the alternative, the Court should immediately declare a mistrial, because no lesser sanction could possibly cure the prejudice caused by the government's pattern of severe *Brady* violations. The new information goes to the core of this case—Senator Stevens' state of mind. It is impossible at this point to have a fair trial.

"This is the sort of information defense counsel would have used to maximum effect in opening statement. It would have shaped all aspects of the defense. In short, it is not sufficient now, on the eve of the government's case resting, to say 'no harm no foul'."

* * * * *

The government responded a few hours later with a brief of its own, arguing that what they had provided the night before was "merely cumulative." In other words, they claimed that they had already provided the information to us (but they had redacted portions of material that should have been left in).

Again, they pointed to a disclosure they made from Bill Allen's first interview with the government in which he told them Senator Stevens wanted to pay for everything he got. And, they argued, no harm had taken place because cross-examination had not yet begun, and we were free to cross-examine Allen all we wanted.

* * * * *

Late in the afternoon of this incredible day, the court held a hearing at which I argued that the case should be dismissed. At the very least, I said, Judge Sullivan should grant a mistrial and start the trial over. Not having had anything to eat since breakfast, I was running on fumes, but this was no time to feel sorry for myself. When I stood up to speak I noticed there were a lot more reporters in court than there had been previously. Clearly, the word had spread that something big might happen. (Indeed, one well-known journalist had already predicted on the elevator that the case would be dismissed.)

I stood at the podium and faced Judge Sullivan. "Through nobody's fault but the government, the playing field in this case is not even, and no penalty imposed by this Court can even the playing field at this point. . . . We asked for *Brady* material the day after the indictment in this case. It should have been produced promptly. This investigation had been going on for two years. They resisted and resisted, and we came to court at least four times on *Brady* issues. They finally sent us a letter on September 9th purporting to summarize what was in the interview memos.

"We, then, at 11:30 last night, [October 1, 2008] get two 302s that are absolutely 100 percent opposite. One says: If Rocky Williams or Dave Anderson had invoiced Ted and Catherine Stevens for VECO's work, Bill Allen believes they would have paid the bill. And another one, a 302 from February 28th 2007: Bill Allen did not invoice Stevens for the work that had been performed. However, [Allen] believes that Stevens would have paid an invoice if he had received one.

"Now Your Honor, what's all the more remarkable is we had to push and push and push to get the 302s in this case, and finally, Your Honor ordered them produced—and lo and behold—they affirmatively redacted *Brady* material. They took the affirmative act of redacting *Brady* material out of those 302s. One of the 302s that they produced last night is one that we had previously gotten in redacted form."

Something was very odd about how this all went down. The government had sent us a letter on September 9 that told us that Bill Allen did not believe that Ted Stevens would have paid a bill. Then, on September 17, after we pushed and pushed, they sent us redacted 302s. One of the 302s was dated September 16, but purported to be of an interview dated September 9."

If I was confused, then so was Judge Sullivan, who said, "Now, coincidentally—I don't understand the significance of this coincidence, but it is a coincidence—but apparently. . . Allen was interviewed by the FBI agent the same day I believe. I'm not sure I understand that. And the last debriefing was when, September the 9th?"

Morris responded, "No. No. No. September 9 is when the government turned over its. . . *Brady* letter to the defense."

The Judge asked again, "Was Allen interviewed that day?"

"No. No," Morris responded. "He was not interviewed that day."

I noticed that Ms. Morris spoke with great conviction and certainty. (After all, she represented the United States Government.) She even submitted an affidavit stating that the September 9 letter was based on 302s that had already been prepared. But great conviction or no great conviction, what Brenda Morris said was simply not true.

Judge Sullivan suggested that a continuance would be appropriate so that the defense could have time to figure out how to weave the new information into the defense and retool the cross-examination of Allen.

I argued that that would not work: "Through no fault of the Court or the defense, [the 'covering his ass' testimony] is lingering in the jury's mind while we take this break that's been necessitated by the government's own misconduct. The letter that was sent to us and the Court last night suggested that this was part of an ongoing review of materials in connection with Bill Allen's testimony. In fact, we learned this morning upon questioning from the Court that it was finally produced because [FBI agent] Michelle Pluta is going to be a summary witness at the end of the case. Her 302s are going to be *Jencks* in this case [and] that's how this was uncovered. They were going to have to give us those 302s as *Jencks*.

"Your Honor, we just got lucky again—just like we did with Rocky Williams and the $188,000 VECO bills. . . We didn't know about it until Mr. Williams was back in Alaska. We were deprived of the information as we formulated our case. This important information . . . goes right to the heart of it, especially given the government's theory that there was some sort of conspiracy or joint venture or combined conduct between Mr. Allen and the Senator."

Judge Sullivan interjected: "Let me ask you this. In focusing on an appropriate sanction and/or remedy, assuming the Court finds a *Brady* violation, should the Court also take into consideration the Williams series of events?"

"Yes," I responded, "Your Honor, it should."

Judge Sullivan asked "Why?"

"Because that was *Brady* information that we got, once again, because we were lucky. It was not disclosed to us. It wasn't until we were able to talk to Mr. Williams on a Sunday when he was back in Alaska that we learned this *Brady* information for the first time. We got lucky once. We got lucky again. And we may find that when all the 302s are produced, maybe we're going to get lucky a lot more, but we think there's a pattern, especially given the great resistance that the government gave to giving us this information in the first place, there's a pattern of *Brady* violations.

"And the trial, Your Honor, in our view is broken, and it can't be fixed. It's . . . been played on an unlevel playing field. We're well through it, and we were entitled to this information before the trial started, ... Your Honor, we've been trying one case, and now we find information that should have been produced right after indictment that wasn't, and now we've got to try a different case. . ."

"It's fundamental," I said, "it goes to the heart of the case . . . [my] point is this is a recurring pattern. [In] the September 9th letter from the prosecution, we did not have all the *Brady* material in it. We finally get the 302s. They affirmatively redact out *Brady* material, and it's only because we got lucky—because Special Agent Pluta was going to be a summary witness, and they looked at their *Jencks* material there and they've got to turn it over. Then, lo and behold, we get it."

Brenda Morris tried to interrupt, but Judge Sullivan asked her, "What about that *Brady* information that someone took the time to blacken out?"

Morris: Judge, again, it's my understanding -

Judge Sullivan: That's favorable information, right?

Morris: Yes.

Judge Sullivan: It's shaded. It was kept from the defendant.

Morris: I—yes, Judge.

Judge Sullivan: And the question is why?

Morris: Your Honor, my understanding is that the information was believed to have been given to the defense and that this was new in this—the part that hadn't been shaded was new or different in that that kind of information had been given before like in that statement where—

Judge Sullivan: Wait. Wait.

Morris: It says Mr. Stevens agreed to pay for everything.

Judge Sullivan: Wait. Wait a minute. What you're telling me is that someone recognized it was favorable information, but shaded it because that person thought the favorable information had previously been disclosed to the defendant?

Morris: I don't want to misrepresent it because I'm not a hundred percent sure.

Judge Sullivan: I just want an answer as to why someone sat down with a black felt pen. . .

Morris: It was a mistake.

Judge Sullivan: . . .and struck through favorable information.

Morris: Judge, it was a mistake. Again, if it was in any way intentional, we could have explained this away or rationalized it away as to why it didn't have to be turned over, and that's not—no, it was a mistake, but again—

Judge Sullivan: That goes to whether or not the government is taking its obligations as the gatekeeper very seriously.

Morris: I understand that.

Judge Sullivan: I mean the government does have an obligation—

Morris: I understand that.

Judge Sullivan: —otherwise, favorable information is never disclosed to defense attorneys.

Morris: You're absolutely correct.

Judge Sullivan: And someone took—[it's] you know, very easy to get a black felt tip pen and say, I'm going to hide the ball here.

Morris: No. No. No. I don't believe that. I firmly do not believe that.

Judge Sullivan: Then why would that—no one can disagree that information is favorable. No reasonable person could disagree, right?

Morris: That's correct.

Judge Sullivan: All right. So someone made a conscious effort to shade that information and keep defense counsel from learning of it, and I just reject the answer that that was done because that person believed that the favorable information had already been disclosed to the defendant.

Morris: No. No. Judge, please, I don't—I'm not— I can't explain away something that—

Judge Sullivan: Well, is there someone on your team who can explain it?

Morris: Judge, I don't believe that there should be, Judge. All I can tell you is that it wasn't material.

Judge Sullivan: How does—

Morris: It was just a mistake. It was bad judgment.

* * * * *

At that point, Judge Sullivan cut to the heart of it. He asked, "How does the Court have any confidence that the Public Integrity Section has integrity?"

Brenda Morris, to my surprise, agreed, saying, "You're right."

But Judge Sullivan had more to say: ". . . How do I have that confidence? . . . It's about integrity. It's about officers of the Court looking at information and saying, you know what, I've got a duty to disclose favorable information to the defendant."

Again, Morris interrupted, "And that's what we did."

Judge Sullivan continued, "As opposed to, in the still of the night, getting a black felt tip pen and crossing out favorable information and then saying, well, one reason it was probably done, Judge, was because they already had it. That's. . ."

Trying her best to sound aggrieved, the prosecutor boldly cut in: "Judge, there was no nefarious intent in there. There was no nefarious intent in there."

Judge Sullivan: Then why did it happen?

Morris: But, Judge, it's unfair to say 'in the still of the night' or however you just phrased it, Judge. It was just a matter of—it was a matter of us trying to provide information, and it was hastily done. That's the best explanation I can give. It was hastily done.

Judge Sullivan: That's not good enough, counsel.

* * * * *

Judge Sullivan was giving the prosecution a public dressing down, but it was one they richly deserved. Still, Brenda Morris, who should have known better than anyone in the courtroom that what the judge was saying was absolutely accurate, kept trying to deflect the criticism.

"But, Judge, please understand that, again, it was not a material omission. It was not something—it may have been bad judgment. I think you're right, and that's why we thought, let's turn it over. But at the same time, Your Honor, they had that information and more in the sense that Allen has already said that he wanted to pay for everything, and I think that the materiality issue is something that should not be just wished away. I understand, Your Honor, that this is a very serious—and the Court takes it very seriously, we take it very seriously."

Judge Sullivan said, sternly, "I don't know if the government is taking it seriously."

"No, Your Honor, we are. No, Your Honor, we are," Morris shot back. "This is not something we take lightly at all. And this is not something that's not done lightly or without stress. This is causing us undue stress. We are really worried about this because. . ."

Judge Sullivan: The government *should* be worried about it.

Morris: That's right. . .This is our word, Your Honor. We are career prosecutors here, and I—you know, we don't want our integrity— and I think any trial attorney that I've been up against in all my years from state court through federal will tell you that my word is my bond. Mr. Sullivan can tell you that.

[This was interesting. I knew Brendan had never had a case against her.]

Mr. Sullivan I don't think will deny that. He may not agree with it right now in this forum, but I think he knows that.

Judge Sullivan: The Court's not attacking anyone personally. I'm just very disturbed that—

Morris: I understand.

Judge Sullivan: —that this happened.

Morris: And we're not taking it lightly, Your Honor, not at all. Not at all. But I do want to be make sure that the Court does understand that there is a weighing here in the sense of what was material and that this doesn't in any, in any way, come close to material. We're not saying that it shouldn't have been turned over. I think that was just—it should have been turned over. I can't—I can't say anything about that other than we should have done it, but it was a mistake that was realized, and we're going back.

Judge Sullivan: But at some point, you can't explain it that way, though. You've got a federal judge telling you on more than one occasion, you're aware of your obligations. Everyone knows what the *Brady* doctrine stands for. I cited Circuit opinions, District Court opinions. I did it more than once. I take this very seriously. I said, you're aware, you're aware, you're aware.

Morris: I understand. Uh-huh.

Judge Sullivan: Everyone knew what they had to do.

Morris: Right.

Judge Sullivan: But, nevertheless, the government didn't do it.

Morris: We made a mistake.

Judge Sullivan: The public has to have some confidence in these proceedings. The defendant is entitled to his fair day in court.

Morris: That's absolutely right, and he—we have—that's absolutely right. And, Your Honor, I know that you don't know me. I know you don't know the rest of the members on this team. I do. I've worked with them for years now, and I can tell it was a mistake. I can just tell you it was a mistake. Nobody had any, any conscious decision or any militant intention to come forward with this Court to try to deliberately deprive this defendant of any, any information or this Court of any order that it issued.

We understand the stakes are high. Whether or not this man was a sitting senator or whether or not he was someone who just walked in off the street and nobody knew, we take our responsibility very, very seriously. And we've got people—the Justice Department is watching us. The Justice Department is asking what's going on. We not only take our duty and our responsibility as officers for the Court, but we like our jobs. We do this not for the money, Judge, we do it because we love our jobs, and we do believe in justice, and that's what we're trying to get done here. And I don't believe that the defendant should be able to take a mistake, a mistake, because they are not harmed, they are not prejudiced in any way, but they keep on wanting to drill it home because they know they see a weakness, they see an Achilles heel for us right now, and they're trying to drive a wedge into us.

Judge Sullivan's response to Brenda Morris's self-serving speech was exactly what I would have said: "Why shouldn't they?"

Morris: I don't blame them. I said that this morning. I don't blame them, it's their job.

Judge Sullivan: But they have to rely upon the integrity of the government in order to get this information.

Morris: That's absolutely right. That's absolutely right.

Judge Sullivan: And it's only the government who knows that this favorable information exists. That's why the stakes are so high here.

Morris: And that's why we turned it over. That's why we turned it over. That is why there is absolutely no way that we tried to rationalize it or tried to say, oh, well, if it went to an appellate kind of issue—because you can rationalize that there was no harm, no foul; but, no, it was making sure, yeah, we had to come in here and let the Court know. We had to come in here and let the Court know and let the defense know. And, again, it wasn't because of late last night the thing went out that we waited around, it's because we were going through everything to try and make sure—I was hoping that we could go through and do a complete 302 review, but we couldn't get it accomplished in the time frame. We understood that this was severe. We understood the ramifications of it, and we had to step up and take our medicine, and that's what we've done. That's what we've done. And, Judge, it's not easy. I don't know what—how this is going to be portrayed, but I know people who know me. I know people who know all of us prosecutors here and know good and well we did not do this intentionally."

* * * * *

Judge Sullivan turned to me and asked, "Anything else?"

I responded, "Yes, Your Honor. On September 9th, it was purported that full *Brady* information was provided to the defense. We now know that it was not full *Brady* information. September 17th, they provided 302s. They were affirmatively redacted of *Brady* information. September 22nd, they sent Rocky Williams home to Alaska—and he had *Brady* information that was never disclosed to us. We only got it because we were lucky. We got *Brady* information last night because they were going to put on Special Agent Pluta . . . and they needed to provide her *Jencks* material. We got lucky again.

"But—I speak for the entire defense team—we don't have confidence that we've gotten all the *Brady* information. We don't have confidence in these proceedings. There's a pattern of critical *Brady* failures, and we submit that the appropriate sanction here is dismissal or mistrial in the alternative."

* * * * *

Judge Sullivan faced the problem that there was not a lot of precedent for a case like this to be dismissed at this stage. In fact, we could not find a perfectly analogous precedent.

And, only 16 months earlier, Judge Sullivan had had one of his decisions reversed by an appellate court when he granted a new trial after *Brady* information was withheld from the defense. The appellate court had decided—just as the government was arguing here—that the new information would not have made a difference. In other words, "no harm no foul".

That was exactly the argument that the government was making now, except that the government was also saying, now you have the information. Go knock yourself out with it. (This ignored the fact that we actually prepare for trial in advance and it is difficult to change strategy on a dime when for the first time in the middle of trial the government discloses information that should have been disclosed before the trial started).

* * * * *

Judge Sullivan decided not to dismiss the case or grant a mistrial. However, he did order that all interview memoranda be produced. And he gave us a continuance—a long weekend during which to study them.

Craig Singer whispered in my ear that I should also ask for the grand jury transcripts of the witnesses. I did so. Judge Sullivan asked for the government's position. Morris said she was not in a position to withhold them. The judge ordered the grand jury transcripts released as well.

Now we would have lots of information to work with, and a bit of extra time.

But all the while, the devastating "covering his ass" testimony would be poisoning the jurors' minds.

Chapter
10

False Evidence

Judge Sullivan had ordered the prosecutors to provide *all* interview memos and grand jury testimony. Twice over the weekend of October 3rd the government told us that they had produced everything, and twice our team discovered they had not. For example, we found in one of the grand jury transcripts that the lead FBI agent said she had testified earlier before the grand jury. When we looked for her earlier testimony in what the government had provided to us, we could not find it. But as the grand jury testimony and interview memos rolled in, our team divided them up and read them as fast as we could.

As anticipated, they contained a wealth of additional information favorable to the defense. For starters, we learned that Bill Allen's nephew, Dave Anderson, was not even in the state of Alaska when VECO time records introduced by the government through Cheryl Boomershine showed that he was supposedly working more than 500 hours on the cabin. Anderson testified to the grand jury that he was in Oregon at the time.

This was stunning. What made this all the more so was the fact that the government had tried to keep us away from Dave Anderson. We knew that the government had paid for some of his living expenses and that they intended to call him as a witness. But we could not locate him, so I made a simple request to Brenda Morris for his address so that the defense could subpoena him. Morris refused.

Only when Judge Sullivan scolded the government for taking Rocky

Williams from us did the prosecutors relent and make Dave Anderson available for service of a subpoena. It turned out they had flown Anderson into Washington, D.C. to prepare his testimony, just as they had flown Williams to Washington, D.C. Reading his grand jury testimony that he was in Oregon when the government claimed he was working on the cabin, I now understood why they were so determined to keep him away from us.

We found other examples of favorable evidence in the previously undisclosed transcripts and memos. We learned that an electrician who had seen Catherine Stevens remembered her asking him about the cost of the fixtures, which obviously showed that she intended to pay for them and was not trying to get something for nothing. We learned that John Hess had said, "[Bob] Persons' job was to make Stevens happy since Stevens did not have a lot of time to be bothered with the details of the remodel." We also learned that a neighbor of Senator Stevens had told the government Senator Stevens was always adamant that he pay all bills. But the big *Brady* news was Dave Anderson's presence in Oregon when he was supposedly spending 500 plus hours working on the cabin in Alaska.

* * * * *

Time was the one thing we could hardly spare, but, having discovered these additional examples of the government's concealing favorable information, we took the new pieces of the puzzle and put together a chronological picture of what had happened. (I find that organizing facts into chronological order often makes otherwise incomprehensible facts make sense.) Here is what we found:

As reflected by the interview memos provided during the middle of Allen's testimony, Allen had told prosecutors *two years before trial* that he believed Senator Stevens would have paid any bills that had been sent.

We first asked for *Brady* information at the arraignment on July 31, 2008, and in a letter the next day.

Because we did not feel as though the government was taking our

Brady requests seriously, on September 2, 2008, we filed a motion asking the court to order the disclosure of favorable information.

The Court was to have a hearing on our motion on September 10, 2008. However, on the day before, September 9, 2008, the government re-interviewed Allen by telephone and extracted from him a contrary statement that Senator Stevens would *not* have paid a VECO bill because it would have been too high.

At 8:37 p.m. that same evening, the government sent us a letter revealing only Allen's new harmful statement that Stevens would not have paid a bill, while not disclosing his earlier statement that Stevens would have paid. In other words, the government was hiding favorable information from the defense and generating harmful information in its place.

The next day, on September 10, 2008, prosecutors represented to Judge Sullivan that there was no need to have any further arguments, because they had already given us all the information to which we were entitled.

We continued to press for actual interview memos, not just the government's summary of what was in them, and on September 16, over the government's vehement objections, Judge Sullivan ordered the government to disclose all favorable information in interview memos by the next day. The government blacked out anything they did not want to disclose.

Also on September 16, the lead FBI agent assigned to this case prepared a new memorandum reporting on the Allen re-interview of September 9. Apparently she did so because the government had just been ordered to produce it.

On September 17, 2008, one day later, in apparent compliance with the Court's order, the government produced interview memoranda purporting to contain all favorable information for the defense. On the subject of whether Senator Stevens would have paid the bills, the government produced only Bill Allen's newest incriminating statement that Senator Stevens *would not have paid* a bill in its brand new September 16 memorandum and not the two earlier statements favorable to the defense that Senator Stevens *would have paid* any bill presented to him. In fact, the government affirmatively blacked out the favorable information in one of the 302s (the one relating to paying John Hess).

* * * * *

From this chronological set of facts—which took quite a bit of time and resources to put together during the middle of trial—we could only conclude that the government intentionally chose to conceal the critical favorable information that Bill Allen believed Senator Stevens would have paid any and all bills sent. And rather than disclose that information favorable to the defense, the government chose to extract a new and harmful statement in its place from a witness who was working to reduce his jail time, eliminate his family's potential jail time, and earn the seventy million holdback.

When Judge Sullivan questioned Brenda Morris, the lead prosecutor, the previous week about whether Allen was re-interviewed on September 9th, she said no, but it was now clear to us that the prosecutors had re-interviewed him on that very day. The prosecutors were jerking us around. And, they were also jerking around Judge Sullivan, which was even more dangerous.

* * * * *

I am often asked to speak to bar associations about government misconduct. When I speak about how to deal with government misconduct, I counsel defense lawyers to be very cautious about alleging intentional misconduct. It can undermine your credibility. Judges are reluctant to find that prosecutors and law enforcement officials have acted in bad faith. It oftern hurts your cause.

But I also tell people to call it like they see it. The time had come for us to call it like we saw it. We prepared a new motion to dismiss over the weekend that began like this:

> Until today, defense counsel have refrained from alleging intentional misconduct by the government. We can no longer do so in good conscience. Defense counsel have now conducted

113

an initial review of material produced for the first time on the evening of Thursday, October 1. Defense counsel have also now had the opportunity to review in greater detail the material produced late Wednesday night. The evidence is compelling that the government's misconduct was intentional.

* * * * *

The government's response accused us of "pure and unsupported conjecture," repeating the common refrain I so often hear in litigation over *Brady* issues: the government did not need to turn over this information because it was not "material." In other words, they again tried to argue, "no harm, no foul." The government argued that the Senator was getting a fair trial.

* * * * *

Judge Sullivan held another hearing, at which I emphasized the chronology, pointing out how they extracted a new story from Bill Allen the night before they made their *Brady* disclosures, and then concealed his earlier inconsistent version. I emphasized that the billing records were false and that the government had to have known it. Nicholas Marsh, who introduced evidence in court of more than 500 hours of work by Dave Anderson, was the same attorney who heard Anderson tell the grand jury that he was in another state at the time.

I called the records false evidence, saying:

> This was false evidence and Ms. Boomershine may not have known it, but the government did. And to this day, there's been no apology, no contrition, no attempt by the government to do what they're supposed to do . . . if the government . . . knowingly puts on false testimony, they're supposed to bring it to the court's attention.
>
> . . . They still don't understand their obligations, and when I was before the court last Thursday, I made a reference to the playing field not being level in this case. And as I thought about that, I regret that analogy because this is about much more

114

than a game, Your Honor. This is a criminal case with a career on the line. The Court has responsibilities, the defense has responsibilities, and the government has responsibilities.

And time and time and time again the government has not lived up to them. . . . Enough is enough, Your Honor . . . this case ought to be dismissed.

* * * * *

Judge Sullivan pointed out that somebody knew that the billing records were false.

Marsh, responding for the government, argued yet again that it didn't matter because all they needed to prove was an undisclosed gift over $265. He said the billing records were nothing more than a "placeholder."

Judge Sullivan was upset anew. "We're talking about the United States using documents that the government knows are false, not true." And he expressed an understanding of what it must be like to be in our shoes: "They can't attack Boomershine because she doesn't know anything about it. Anderson didn't testify. Williams was sent away in the still of the night on a plane by the government."

The judge continued, "Someone on that team had an obligation to say something smells here, and we have an obligation to ensure this man gets a fair trial. It doesn't have to be the luck of the draw. It doesn't have to be his lucky day. People shouldn't have to rely upon luck to get justice."

He went on: "What I have doubts about, though, is whether the government is concerned, indeed, with its obligation—its obligation to be the gatekeeper for information and material that's favorable to a defendant. That's a prosecutor's job, as well, that the prosecutor has to take just as seriously as preparing his or her case in chief. It's an obligation, because, otherwise, no one knows about that information. The government has exclusive control over that information."

Marsh responded, saying, "We believe there's absolutely no harm that's befallen. These proceedings have not been undermined. The credibility of these proceedings has not been undermined. The defendant has got everything now, and we have worked very hard to comply with the Court's order and get them everything . . .”

More "no harm, no foul" argument. And later, we'd discover these were lies. But at the time I responded, "We don't feel like we've gotten a fair trial when we get ambushed and dumped on in the middle of trial with things that we should have gotten before trial as we prepare. . .”

Judge Sullivan asked if we wanted a continuance. I said no. With witnesses from Alaska waiting to testify and an election coming up, we were not in a position to wait any longer.

Marsh argued again, "I think we do respectfully disagree with the Court because it's not material. It's not material in the context of all the other stuff going on, and that's the way we looked at it, Your Honor." More "no harm, no foul."

I was beside myself. I had to point out that what they were doing appeared intentional to us. "I don't believe we heard anything from the government," I said, "about the September 9th Bill Allen interview and that *Brady* violation. I don't know what other inference to draw from the fact that the day before coming to court [on September 10], at 8:37 that night [September 9], we got faxed a letter that is 180 degrees opposite from the *Brady* material that's in their files. They interviewed him the day they've got to come to court and answer for their *Brady* violations. I take no joy in reaching that inference [of intentional misconduct], but I can't come to any other conclusion, and we've never gotten an explanation from the government about it."

Judge Sullivan pointed out that he never got an answer from the government on what prompted its re-interview of Bill Allen on September 9. "What prompted it?" he asked.

Morris replied, "What prompted it was, basically because there were some variances with regard to Mr. Allen. As you were able to see during his testimony, Mr. Allen at times has said that what he gave the defendant wasn't a gift. He says that he wished it could have been a gift that he would have given it to him.

"What it mainly comes down to is that Mr. Allen liked the defendant and did do a lot of things for him that was either unsolicited or unknown to the defendant at the time he did it. And what happened is on September 9th, there was a reach to Mr. Allen before we actually drafted the letter to get it concrete, to get it . . . .

"And so, anyway, we called him and whether or not it should have been documented in a 302, we thought that was a better choice to do that so there was some documentation, but it was not an effort to create a new memory for Mr. Allen. . . ."

When the judge didn't say anything, Morris bore on, probably hoping he wouldn't interrupt with another question that would require another verbal dance. Remember that Morris had told Judge Sullivan a few days earlier that the government had not re-interviewed Bill Allen on September 9. Prosecutor Morris continued:

"So the confusion in the courtroom came when you were asking me, and I think you had the 302 in your hand and was asking about the September 9th 302. I thought about the September 9th 302—I saw you with something in your hand and was thinking about the September 9th letter. So I kept saying no, no, no about a 302 and kept referring to this 2006 302 that had been provided to the defendant and where I read into the record about Allen recalled that Ted Stevens wanted to pay for everything. . . ."

Perhaps reading Judge Sullivan's mind, the prosecutor hurried on: "So there was no effort to try and pull a fast one. . . It was more of us trying to be encompassing and giving as accurate a sum up because we were summing up in the letter of what Mr. Allen's statements had been."

Huh? They re-interviewed him to get him to say the opposite of what was in their files. That was the only conclusion one could draw. They concealed favorable evidence from us and created new evidence they liked better in its place.

Judge Sullivan took a break. When he came back to the bench, he issued his ruling: "It's very troubling that the government would utilize records that the government knows were false. And there's just no excuse for that whatsoever, and therefore, the sanction for the utilization of those records for Williams and the other gentleman, Anderson, is that they'll be stricken from the evidentiary record and also the jurors will be instructed tomorrow that the government presented evidence to those jurors that the government knew was not true and, therefore, the court has stricken the records, the business records for those two gentlemen, and the Court will instruct the jury not to consider that evidence at all."

Despite my firm belief that the case should have been dismissed, I was heartened that Judge Sullivan would be telling the jury that "the government presented evidence . . . that the government knew was not true." That would be a very powerful statement to the jury. The tide was turning again, but this time, it was turning our way.

* * * * *

When court reconvened on Tuesday, October 6th following the four day break, the government closed Bill Allen's testimony by playing three recordings of telephone conversations Allen secretly taped without Senator Stevens' knowledge. Many times in the tapes, Allen is quiet, presumably because he knows he's being taped, and in many ways comes across as much older than the Senator, who was at least ten years Allen's senior. The two men seem very far away from each other, with Allen in remote Alaska and Stevens thousands of miles away in Washington, D.C.

The first tape was dated August 31, 2006, the day after VECO's offices were raided; on that tape they discussed the fact that search warrants were executed the previous day.

In the second, dated September 12, 2006, they discussed whether there would be an investigation of political fundraising in campaigns for federal office in Alaska. The government did look into that, but nothing was found amiss—certainly nothing that involved Ted Stevens.

The third call took place on October 10, 2006. The Senator first gives Allen a pep talk about taking care of his health, telling Allen that he has to get some exercise and lead a normal life in the community. Senator Stevens then tells Allen that he was recently discussing his investigation with his lawyers—at that point, two years prior to the trial, he believed he was being investigated under campaign finance laws—and that we had said the most important thing was not to interfere with the investigation. The call concludes bizarrely with Allen telling the Senator (while secretly taping him), "I love you, Ted."

* * * * *

Brendan's cross-examination of Bill Allen went pretty well, I thought. Allen admitted that he never tried to bribe Ted Stevens, because he knew Ted Stevens could not be bribed. Allen acknowledged that Dave Anderson and Rocky Williams were alcoholics and that they did not properly supervise the renovation. He admitted that VECO workers spent more time at the chalet than they should have. Allen conceded that he did not consider what he did to be a gift to Ted Stevens. And Allen testified, in response to Brendan's questions, that Ted Stevens always insisted on paying his share:

Q: And isn't it true that on every occasion you had a meal with him, he insisted on paying his share?

A: Yes, he did.

Q: And isn't it true that on occasions when he flew with you on some private jet that he would pay his share of the cost as required by the government, namely, first class fare rates?

A: Yes.

Q: And isn't it also true that you were in a couple of investments with him where a bunch of guys threw some money in to purchase a horse or two or three?

A: Yes.

Q: And isn't it true that with respect to those little ventures that you had that Ted Stevens always insisted on paying all of the money that was properly his share?

119

A: Yes.

But the 800 pound gorilla in the courtroom was still the "covering his ass" testimony. Brendan had to confront Allen about it, and he did:

Q: Well, you came in here the other day on your direct examination, and you said, well, despite the fact that I saw this letter, I heard from Mr. Persons that I shouldn't send a bill because this was just Ted covering his ass. Do you remember that testimony?

A: That's exactly right.

Q: When did you first tell the government that Persons told you Ted was covering his ass and these notes were meaningless? It was just recently, wasn't it?

A: No. No.

* * * * *

We still thought Bill Allen was telling a lie, but we couldn't prove it. The late John Henry Wigmore, author of the leading American text on evidence and one of history's most famous law professors said that "cross-examination is the greatest legal engine ever invented for the discovery of truth." The Supreme Court has repeated this adage, often referring to cross-examination as a "crucible" from which the truth is likely to emerge. But the crucible of cross-examination does not work without evidence to confront the witness. It is very difficult to prove a lie without evidence of the truth—even for Brendan Sullivan.

* * * * *

After Brendan's cross-examination of Allen, the government put on three more witnesses: an FBI Agent who read emails into the record; another worker who repaired a boiler; and three recordings of calls between Bob Persons and Bill Allen in which Allen gets mad at Bob Persons for faxing some documents to Ted Stevens, indicating that Stevens had only paid for materials—and not labor—on a boiler repair. What did the Senator do when he read the documents and realized the invoice for labor was missing? He asked for a bill.

120

* * * * *

At that point, the government said it was done and rested its case. We filed another motion to dismiss, which is traditionally filed once the government rests. But moments after we filed our motion, the prosecutors changed their minds and announced that they were going to call Dave Anderson to the witness stand the next morning.

This was a clear violation of our agreement with the government that we would give each other 24 hours' notice before calling any new witnesses. But these prosecutors didn't feel bound by their word. Apparently they wanted to present Anderson in front of the jury to say that he wasn't there when the time records said he was so that they would get some credit for letting the jury know the records were false.

They would pretend that they were doing it out of the goodness of their hearts, that they were being honest with the jury. The jury would never know that it was only because of our hard work, the judge's hard work, and some luck that this information had come to light.

* * * * *

Unfortunately, Judge Sullivan not only let Anderson testify but he also did not give the instruction that he'd said he was going to give—the instruction about the government knowingly presenting false testimony. (There is no requirement that judges explain the reason why they do what they do.) It was a tough break for us, and a good one for the prosecutors. By this point, everyone on the defense team was in agreement that the government was playing fast and loose with the rules. Our great hope was that it would catch up with the government before the case went to the jury.

* * * * *

The next day, Dave Anderson, the nephew of Bill Allen, took the stand. Anderson was burly, and he wore his longish hair slicked back from his forehead. The process server who located Anderson

121

had reported that he obviously had been drinking on the day he was served with our subpoena.

On the stand, Anderson had the odd habit of laughing at inappropriate times while testifying. Perhaps he was worried that we were going to bring up his strained relationship with his uncle. Although a generation apart in age, he and Allen had once fought over the affections of the same woman. Anderson got the girl, but Bill Allen got revenge: he had Anderson's mobile home razed with a bulldozer.

According to Tony Hopfinger, writing for the *Alaska Dispatch*, Anderson in 2004 "took up with Allen's former girlfriend. . . The uncle was so angered he fired his nephew, destroyed his Anchorage mobile home [by bulldozing it] and threatened to kill him, according to Anderson and a series of letters he provided that document the feud."

Anderson's testimony was as strange as his manner. He said that he did a lot of work at the chalet—including presiding over what he called "a compactor rodeo" and cutting down a tree. As his testimony continued, Anderson increasingly gave the impression of being a sad sack who clearly wanted to be anyplace but where he was.

We knew we could show he was wrong about the tree. And when the government asked him, at the end of his testimony, if he had ever submitted a false affidavit, he said, "Yes," he had submitted a false affidavit stating that the government had conferred immunity on his family. (The prosecutors had obviously decided it would sound better if they brought out that information rather than have us reveal it on cross-examination.)

We made a strategic call not to cross-examine Anderson. He had admitted that he was not in Alaska when he was supposedly working on the chalet, his manner was peculiar and he had admitted to lying. So we decided to let him go back to Alaska without any further questions. His testimony was not worth the ammunition it would take to shoot it down. This time the government really did rest its case.

Chapter
11

"The Kind of Guy You Take on a Long Patrol"

Trial lawyers have the power to issue subpoenas, which are essentially court orders to witnesses requiring them to appear in court and testify. In theory, a trial lawyer controls the order of witnesses. He or she issues subpoenas, thus compelling all the witnesses to show up, and then calls them to the stand in the order he or she chooses. In *reality*, however, a trial lawyer must work with the witnesses' schedules.

One of the last things any trial lawyer wants is for a witness to be upset because other commitments are not being honored. For that reason, lawyers tend to accommodate witness's schedules, which means that the order in which witnesses are called is often less than ideal. Not having complete control over the order of witnesses, and the fact that each witness may only have a small piece of information means that the presentation may well seem disjointed.

Lawyers sometimes tell juries that their cases are like jigsaw puzzles. Each piece may look insignificant, but once assembled they create a picture. Our defense was like that.

We had special difficulties in our case for the simple reason that our witnesses were primarily from Alaska. In order to juggle the complicated schedules of witnesses who had to make an all-day plane trip to D.C., we ended up spending hundreds of thousands of dollars at a local Marriott to put them up. A few of our other witnesses were busy public officials from Washington, D.C., all of whom had other responsibilities that we had to juggle. The witnesses we originally lined up to start our case had to be rescheduled, because just when we thought we were going to open the case for the defense, the government reopened its case in order to have Dave Anderson testify.

* * * * *

An important piece of the puzzle in the Stevens case was what we call character witnesses. At trial, we were allowed to call five character witnesses to testify about Senator Ted Stevens' good character.

Former Secretary of State Colin Powell had known Senator Stevens for decades, starting with the Secretary's days on the National Security Council and as Chairman of the Joint Chiefs of Staff. Secretary Powell and Senator Stevens had worked closely together on national defense issues. Secretary Powell, one of the most admired people in America, testified strongly about his admiration for Senator Stevens. Using a reference from his days in the Infantry in the U.S. Army, he said, "Senator Stevens was the kind of guy you take on a long patrol," and he added that Senator Stevens had a "sterling" reputation for honesty.

Powell called Senator Stevens: "a trusted individual . . . someone whose word you could rely on. I never heard in all of those years a single dissenting voice with respect to his integrity, with respect to his forthrightness, and with respect to the simple fact that when you shake hands with Ted Stevens, or you made a deal with Ted Stevens, it was going to be a deal that benefited the nation in the long run, one he would stick with. And there was [never] any suggestion that he would be doing anything that would be improper or that would suggest any, any, possible lack of integrity."

Republican Senator Orin Hatch, of Utah, also testified. He described Ted Stevens as "One of the true lions of the Senate, along with my friend Ted Kennedy. . . . If he gives you his word, he will keep it. He's totally honest, totally straightforward." Senator Hatch called Senator Stevens "a wonderful man who has been one of the strongest, toughest, best, most decent, honorable people I've known in the whole time I've been in the Senate."

Senator Hatch's reference to Senator Kennedy made sense, because the three men, Senator Stevens, Senator Hatch, and Senator Kennedy, had been friends for decades. Their friendship transcended politics. In fact, it was Senator Stevens who had recommended the doctor at Duke University Medical Center who operated on Senator Kennedy's brain tumor. Senator Kennedy also had volunteered to be a character witness at trial for Senator Stevens, but his deteriorating health would not allow it.

Donna de Verona, an Olympic swimmer in the 1960s, American's first female sportscaster and a champion of and for women's sports, testified that she had known Senator Stevens for 33 years through their joint interest in the Olympics and in advancing opportunities for women in sports, in particular Title IX. She testified that Senator Stevens was the "go to" person on Olympic sports, and that he had a reputation for "consistency, loyalty, responsiveness [and] courage."

And Gwendolyn Sykes, then Chief Financial Officer at Yale University and later Chief Financial Officer and Vice President for Business and Finance at Morehouse College, testified that she worked for Ted Stevens for ten years and that the Senator was "a trusting character and a trusting soul." She testified that he was "definitely honest. He was always one of the guys who would go to the mat for you, and whatever he told you, you can take his word. . . . [He] was always trustworthy."

The late Senator Daniel Inouye—the senior Senator from Hawaii, Ted Stevens' best friend in the Senate, and a Democrat—testified that he and Stevens shared common values: in World War II, both had served in combat units that suffered high casualty rates. Senator Inouye, who had lost an arm fighting for the Allied Forces in Italy, had become a lawyer and a public servant because his intended profession—surgeon—was no longer a possibility.

Senator Inouye testified that the United States Senate had absolute faith in Ted Stevens, and that he could not imagine his friend Ted ever telling a lie:

Q: Would you trust him with your life?

A: Yes, sir.

Q: Would you trust his work on matters of national security?

A: Absolutely.

Q: Is there any secret in the whole United States of America that you and he don't share?

A: He and I are one of the few Members of the Congress who are privy to certain classified information.

Q: And his representation for truthfulness and integrity are what, sir?

A: Absolute.

* * * * *

Our next important piece of the puzzle was the fair market value of the renovation work. What was it worth? The question was a key part of our defense. If the Senator had paid less than the work was worth—less than its fair market value—and knowingly failed to disclose that fact, he would have been guilty as charged. But he and Mrs. Stevens had paid more than the fair market value. How could it be a "gift" at all?

And if Senator Stevens was told that the renovations were worth less than $160,000, but he had paid more than $160,000, how could anybody say he had intentionally accepted—and deliberately refused to disclose—a "gift"? When you pay a higher price for something than it is worth that certainly is not a "gift." As they say: Do the math.

And so we set out to prove the fair market value of the renovations, and what Senator Stevens knew about the value of the renovations, because that went directly to the heart of guilt or innocence. The first of our witnesses on this issue was a neighbor named Keith Tryck, who testified that a few years before the Stevens' renovations he was planning to renovate his own Girdwood cabin, which was just down the road from the Senator's cabin. Tryck looked into

126

what this should cost, and figured that $40,000 would do it. He told the Senator this, and even prepared a written analysis, which we introduced into evidence. Of course, what Tryck contemplated was not exactly what Ted and Catherine Stevens did, but it was in the ballpark. Tryck's testimony showed what Senator Stevens believed.

This was a neighbor with a similar house just a few blocks away estimating the fair market value of the renovations. Surely that was better evidence of the value of the renovation than the (false) business records introduced into evidence by Nicholas Marsh.

* * * * *

The next piece of evidence on this matter was the building permit, which Bob Persons, the Stevenses' friend and neighbor, obtained for them because they were in D.C. The building permit required an estimate of the cost of the work, and Bob Persons estimated that the renovations would cost $87,000.

In order to pay for the bulk of the renovations, Senator and Mrs. Stevens took out a $100,000 line of credit from the National Bank of Alaska, with the cabin serving as collateral.

When property is being used as collateral for a loan, the bank issuing the loan usually hires an appraiser to determine its value. The National Bank of Alaska hired Gary Randall of Anchorage, who had 33 years of experience appraising Alaska real estate.

According to Randall, who testified his estimate was based on his survey of local builders, the cost of renovating the chalet should have been $80 per square foot for the living space and $34 per square foot for the garage

There would be 1204 square feet of finished space plus 558 feet of garage space. He estimated the cost of the deck to be $8,500. Added up, the total cost of the renovation should have been $123,792.

Finished Space	$80 × 1204 sq ft	$ 96,320
Garage:	$34 × 558 sq ft	$ 18,972
Deck:		$ 8,500
Total	=	**$123,792**

* * * * *

Finally, we had assessors for the City of Anchorage testify. (Although Girdwood was over 40 miles from downtown Anchorage, it was part of Anchorage's tax district.) The assessors testified that it was their job to determine the value of the property in order to assess local real estate taxes. Our associate Beth Stewart presented their testimony. The assessors testified that they appraised the value of the cabin (not including land) at $87,500 before the renovations and $192,300 after renovations. The difference, $104,800, was the value of the renovations.

* * * * *

Keith Tryck thought the fair market value of the renovations was about $40,000. Bob Persons estimated they would cost $87,000. Gary Randall, the veteran appraiser, thought they should have cost $123,792. The official tax assessors thought they were worth $104,800. All three of these estimates were far cries from the $188,000 of the VECO time records.

The Senator and Catherine Stevens paid over $160,000. This was more than anyone's estimate of the value, except, of course, the government, which relied on records it knew were false and grossly inflated.

* * * * *

Before the renovations could begin, the Stevens' property needed to be re-graded, along with a small bit of excavation. In Alaska, it is difficult to dig down into the permafrost, so, once the foundation of the first floor is excavated, there isn't much more to do. Bob Persons arranged to have the excavation work for the renovations done by the H.R. Redmond Company, a family-owned business down the road from the cabin. The H.R. Redmond Company had done the snow removal work for the Stevens family for many years.

H. R. Redmond having died, the company was owned by his widow, Jean, and their son Bob. They ran the business out of the family home, a modest contemporary 1970s style house, about a mile down the road from the Senator's cabin.

Before the start of the trial, Simon Latcovich and I had gone to Girdwood to meet with as many potential witnesses as possible. After interviewing Mrs. Redmond and her son, we gave them a subpoena to testify in Washington at the trial.

When we called them to the witness stand at trial, Bob and Jean Redmond testified that they used their equipment to move dirt and re-grade the property for the renovation. The work was routine. The Senator was never at the chalet when they were there, and Catherine Stevens was only there twice. They testified that Catherine paid the bills in full: $1,200 and $2,256, for a total of $3,456. These payments were consistent with the habits of the Stevens family over the years, they told the jury.

Williams & Connolly partner Alex Romain, whom we added to the trial team after indictment because of the good work Brendan and I had seen from him in other cases, asked Jean Redmond:

Q: Have you ever submitted a bill to Senator Stevens that was not paid?

A: No, sir. It has always been paid.

Q: Every penny?

A: Always. Everything.

* * * * *

One of the proposed renovations to the cabin was to lift the house onto stilts so that new rooms could be built underneath. Bob Persons arranged to have an Alaskan named Tony Hannah lift the house onto stilts, which was Hannah's specialty.

Due to Mr. Hannah's work and hunting schedule, we had difficulty tracking him down. In fact, when he arrived in court to testify he came directly from an elk hunting trip in Wyoming.

Hannah testified that Bob Persons was leading the job and was his primary contact during the work. In fact, he testified that the Senator and Catherine were not present at all during the five weeks he did his work. He also testified that he was paid in full for the work done in three checks as they were billed: $1,875, $1,845 and $1,188. As with the Redmond Company, the bills were submitted to Bob Persons, who passed them on the Catherine Stevens, who paid them all in full "upon receipt."

* * * * *

In the course of the investigation, we found records that mentioned a check for $400 Catherine had written to a man named Tom Swanson. It was to pay him for removing a large tree on the property that was interfering with the renovation—the same tree that Dave Anderson had claimed to have removed using VECO equipment. This inconsistency bothered us, so we decided to track Swanson down. We knew Anderson was wrong and wanted to prove it.

We had a cell phone number for Swanson, but little else. We heard he lived "in the mountains"—pretty much all of Alaska is mountainous—but fortunately we were lucky enough to reach him by cell phone. Swanson asked us to meet him at the Girdwood Town Hall. We did, and he told us he needed to "move a bear box." We East Coast lawyers wondered what on earth a bear box was.

We pulled into the parking lot of the Girdwood Town Hall—a small community center with a post office and space for locals to hold meetings—to wait for Swanson. Soon enough, a rugged-looking fellow in an old pickup truck pulled in to a spot near us and introduced himself.

With our help, this mountain man unloaded a very heavy metal box from the bed of his truck. Neither Simon nor I had any doubt that if we had not been there, even though the big box must have weighed several hundred pounds, he would have unloaded it all by himself.

It was, he explained, a bear box, and it was used to protect trash cans from rummaging bears.

Swanson told us that he had cut down the tree at the Senator's chalet himself. He gave the bill for $400 to Bob Persons, who passed it onto Catherine and she promptly paid it. Dave Anderson was flat-out wrong about cutting down the tree. Cases can turn on small points.

We explained to Tom that his recall of the facts was important, and that at trial we'd need him to testify in court. He accepted the subpoena we handed him, and drove off in his pickup—minus the heavy bear box that had been in the back when he arrived.

Tom Swanson was typical of the number of good Alaskans our team met while we were investigating the government's allegations. We received smoked salmon and moose meat jerky from Alaskans while we were serving them with subpoenas. And while our job was made more difficult by the fact that it was hunting season—we had no idea how many people in Alaska go on extended hunting trips—to a person, the witnesses who agreed to meet with us were good, friendly, honest people.

Swanson came to Court to testify that he, not Dave Andersen, had cut down the tree. He arrived at court timely, but almost didn't make it onto the stand because he arrived at court with a hunting knife. Simon Latchovich was in charge of getting him to the courtroom. When Simon arrived at the entrance to the courthouse, Swanson was explaining that he had been allowed to bring his knife to court in Alaska. "This isn't Alaska," the security officer responded. Fortunately, Simon was able to mediate a resolution that allowed Swanson to take the stand in time. He testified consistently with what he had told us in Alaska.

* * * * *

Augie Paone, who had left Italy with his parents as a boy, grew up in Brooklyn, New York. He served in the U.S. Army during the time of the Vietnam War, and at one point was stationed at a base in Alaska. He loved Alaska, so after his discharge he returned. Because he was a union carpenter, he easily found work. Eventually, he bought out a local general contracting business, Christensen Builders, and became a small business owner in Anchorage.

I first met Augie on an earlier investigative trip to Anchorage with Brendan Sullivan. Augie turned out to be a fit man in his mid-fifties with black hair and a black beard. He struck us as a real straight shooter, an honest and hard-working man. He told us he had been working on a renovation of VECO's office space when he met Bill Allen. When it became obvious to Allen that Bob Persons did not have the expertise to supervise the Stevens' renovation by himself, Allen started talking to Augie about taking over the job. Soon enough, he was hired.

In court, he testified that the arrangement between the Stevenses and Allen is common in Alaska:

"Mr. Allen was good friends with the Senator, and . . . since the Senator was hardly in town . . . he probably would watch the project for the Senator, and this was not unusual for what goes on in Alaska. There are a lot of people that flee the state for the winter, and I've done quite a few projects where a friend or a family member watches out for a remodel."

Paone testified that he never talked to the Senator or Catherine, though he did correspond with Catherine by fax machine. He testified that Catherine promptly paid every bill presented without question. He testified further that Rocky Williams and Dave Anderson were at the cabin, but that they added little value. He said Anderson in particular was not helpful. Augie testified, "I think Dave had a problem with drinking, and I noticed quite a few times that you could smell alcohol, and. . . I'm not a drinker so I wasn't sure if it was just from the drinking that he had done [on the job] or [from] the night before."

We pointed out that the bills from Christensen Builders included general entries for labor and overhead, and attached backup invoices for electrical and plumbing supplies. Rocky Williams often made the purchases of supplies on behalf of the builder, so his name appeared often on the invoices. Since the labor costs were not itemized, it was logical to conclude that Williams' time was included in the charges for labor and overhead. All told, the bills from Christensen Builders were over $130,000, paid in five installments. Any reader of these bills would think the plumbing and electrical work was included.

Paone admitted that there were some workers that Bill Allen sent to the job whose labor costs he, Paone, did not pass on to the Stevenses, notably, those of Rocky Williams, Dave Anderson, an electrician and a plumber. Paone testified that Anderson and Williams were totally inefficient, that they stood around and got very little work done. But, he said, this was not reported to the Stevenses; instead, the decision was made to charge them only for the electrical and plumbing materials and not for time spent standing around.

* * * * *

In addition to building and construction costs, Catherine Stevens wrote four checks to Sears for appliances, a check for over $6,000 to a flooring company and one for over $700 for hardware. She wrote a check for $10,656 for various building supplies—and she paid Rocky Williams a $2,000 bonus in appreciation for the attention he paid to the project.

In total, the money she spent was:

H.R. Redmond (excavation)	1,200.00
H.R. Redmond	2,256.02
Hannah (lifting house)	1,875.00
Hannah	1,845.00
Hannah	1,188.00
Tom Swanson (tree removal)	400.00
Christensen Builders (general contractor)	15,374.60
Christensen Builders	16,633.01
Sears (appliances)	199.88
Sears	838.81
Sears	499.99
Christensen Builders	31,483.75
Christensen Builders	37,898.28
Restoration Hardware (hardware)	776.52
Christensen Builders	30,616.17
Classic Floors (flooring materials)	6,225.43
Rocky Williams (tip/bonus)	2,000.00
Penco (various building supplies)	10,656.98
Total	162,863.08

* * * * *

At the end of the day, Ted and Catherine Stevens had spent more than the value of the renovations. The money had gone for a range of goods and services, including bills for a general contractor that included large labor charges. In the face of this evidence, how could the government say, as Prosecutor Brenda Morris had in her opening statement, that "The cost is always right when the price is free"?

* * * * *

Another player with a good-sized part in the drama of *United States v. Stevens* was Bob Persons. Born and raised in Mobile, Alabama, both Persons and his wife, Deanna, were from Louisiana (she was a Cajun). He'd headed to Alaska after dropping out of college, and stayed a few years. But he had always wanted to return, so, after a decade of corporate life in the Lower 48, he and Deanna did.

They started a hamburger joint in Girdwood which quickly became a success. In 1979, when the Double Musky Inn, a nicer restaurant, went out of business for the sixth time, Bob Persons, totally unfazed by the fact he had no training as a chef other than on-the-job training at the hamburger restaurant, bought it for a song.

And then a big break came. One day while Persons was looking through magazines for recipes, he saw an article about Paul Prudhomme, a rising Cajun chef from New Orleans. On a whim, Persons called him. He told Prudhomme that he and his Cajun wife had just bought a new restaurant in Alaska, and that he, Bob Persons, didn't know what to do.

Figuring that Persons' restaurant in the far reaches of Alaska wasn't going to compete with his own restaurant in the French Quarter of New Orleans, the celebrity chef generously invited Persons to come see how a real chef did it.

"He invited me down," Persons testified, "and gave me a month's training. And then he sent a chef named Buddy Fitzpatrick up to Alaska with me for a year, and we just got lucky. People . . . liked Cajun food."

Twenty-nine years later, the Double Musky Inn—known for generous portions of Cajun-spiced steaks and jambalaya featuring Alaska seafood—had become one of the most popular restaurants in Alaska.

The Double Musky was a couple of miles from the Senator's cabin—

just off the main road from Anchorage. Senator Stevens got in the habit of stopping in for dinner on his way to the cabin if it was meal time (especially if Catherine was not with him). He and Persons became dear friends. As they did, or tried to do, with many witnesses who had something good to say about Ted Stevens, the government tried to keep Bob Persons from testifying. They said that he needed to be advised of his Fifth Amendment rights before being allowed to testify. The government claimed that they were concerned about him, because—they contended—he lied to them in an interview and they didn't want him to expose himself to criminal charges for lying in court. In fact, they were just trying to scare him out of testifying. They insisted that he be advised of his Fifth Amendment rights in open court. So we had to get Bob's lawyer in Alaska, a former judge named Eric Sanders, on the phone. Sanders told Judge Sullivan and the parties that he had advised Bob Persons of his Fifth Amendment rights and that Persons wanted to testify anyway.

Persons, a genuinely nice guy who didn't deserve to be jerked around, was not intimidated by the government's tactic.

As Persons told it, one day he and Senator Stevens started talking about renovations to the cabin: "Well," Persons told the jurors, "Ted and I were talking one day and he has—his house then, I hear people refer to it as a chalet now, but a chalet is actually just a little mountain hut. So Ted always called it a chalet, and we were sitting there one day. He says . . . [his daughter] is going off to college and she'll be coming home with friends and there is no place for them to sleep. He says, you know what I would like to do is lift that home up and put a big room underneath and put bunks around the walls and . . . maybe put a bathroom down there, and that was how it started."

Persons testified that he volunteered to keep an eye on the renovations. He arranged to have Hannah Construction raise the house and the Redmonds do the excavating, and he was the one who asked Tom Swanson to cut down the tree. Persons also testified that Catherine Stevens paid the bills promptly, even though Persons thought one of the bills from Hannah was too high.

Several years earlier, Bob Persons was told by his doctors that because of a heart condition he needed to get more exercise, so he started walking five miles a day through Girdwood. The neighbors quickly nicknamed him "Walking Bob."

As the renovation work took place, Walking Bob would pass the site nearly every day, keeping an eye on things. He testified that Bill Allen did not stop by that often, that Augie was in charge, and that when Dave Anderson was on site, Anderson mostly sat in his truck doing nothing.

Walking Bob testified that from time to time he would give reports to the Senator and that at one point Persons expressed concern about how much the project was costing, but the Senator's response was, "Don't worry about the cost. We're taking out a mortgage to pay the freight."

* * * * *

After methodically going through some of the details of the renovation, we got to the heart of Bob Person's testimony. I asked him:

Q: Did you say to Bill Allen, "Bill, don't worry about getting a bill, Ted is just covering his ass?" Did you say that to Bill Allen?

A: No. Crazy.

* * * * *

We also considered it important to point out that the government had never asked Persons about Allen's alleged statement, even though they had interviewed Persons multiple times.

Q: How many times have you been interviewed by the FBI?

A: Three.

Q: On any of those three occasions, were you asked about the comment that you supposedly made to Bill Allen, "Ted is just covering his ass?"

A: Absolutely not. Nobody's ever asked me that question before.

137

* * * * *

How could the FBI do its job without trying to corroborate the bombshell testimony? Why didn't the prosecutor ask the FBI to confirm this statement? Wouldn't any responsible lawyer check with Persons? Wasn't that the prosecutors' job? Wouldn't even a rookie cop have done so?

I could think of only one reason why the prosecution never asked Bob Persons to corroborate Allen's statement. The statement had only been fabricated by Allen recently—about a month before trial, at that September 9th FBI interview—and if they asked Persons about it and he denied it, they would be required under the *Brady* decision to tell the defense about it—and that would ruin their surprise.

The failure to ask Persons if he made the "cover his ass" statement to Allen was proof positive that the government was well aware that it was a recent fabrication. Bottom line: the prosecutors knew that Allen's "covering his ass" testimony was a lie, and they also knew that Persons would deny saying it. So why ask?

* * * * *

I asked Persons if the Ted Stevens he knew always paid his own bill.

Q: Does Senator Stevens eat at your restaurant, sir?

A: Yes, sir.

Q: How often?

A: When he's in town, quite a bit.

Q: Is there a . . . habit he has with respect to bills for dinner at your restaurant?

A: He always pays his own bill.

* * * * *

Persons had also testified about the way Persons was treated by the FBI, which had interviewed him three times. He described one of the FBI agents as "the most hateful human being" he had ever met. In describing the tactics used, Persons said it "was like being mentally water-boarded." Referring to one agent, he testified— "That guy made me understand why there's a lot of innocent people in prison."

* * * * *

Back in the late 1970s, there was a pop country hit (by the Bellamy Brothers) called "Tumbleweed and Rosalee," a ballad about a cowboy named Tumbleweed and the love of his life, a woman named Rosalee. Catherine came into the Senator's life after he lost his first wife Ann in a tragic plane accident in 1978. The Senator liked the song, and he loved Catherine, so he nicknamed her Rosalee.

Catherine had a nickname for the Senator, too. When they went on their first date, the widower Senator was sharing an apartment with another friend. They called themselves, Felix 1 and Felix 2, based on Felix Unger, the character from the movie and television show "The Odd Couple." As most people recall, Felix was a fastidious bachelor, and his roommate, Oscar Madison, was the opposite. Actually he was so laid back as to be considered sloppy. Catherine told the Senator, "You're no Felix, you're an Oscar," and the nickname stuck.

A native of Anchorage, Catherine attended the Georgetown University School of Foreign Service, after which she went to law school and then became an Assistant U.S. Attorney in San Diego, eventually returning home to Alaska to become an Assistant State Attorney General. Her jurisdiction was the Fourth Judicial District, which covered the Northern-most part of Alaska. By coincidence, it was roughly the same geographic region that Ted Stevens had covered as a U.S. Attorney a couple of decades earlier. Catherine next went into private practice in Fairbanks, working for private land owners and the International Pipefitters' Union in cases against the major oil companies.

When she and the Senator married, she became stepmother to his five grown children, 19 to 23. Catherine and the Senator had a daughter, Lily, the year after they were married. For the next eight years, Catherine devoted herself to raising Lily and doing volunteer work. In 1989, she returned to work outside the home, and held a number of jobs related to law and the arts.

The newlyweds had a home on Capitol Hill in Washington, D.C., and a condominium in Anchorage. In 1983, they traded the condominium for the cabin in Girdwood. The six children eventually produced eleven grandchildren, and at that point Ted and Catherine talked about expanding the cabin. The Senator wanted something simple—a garage and one large room with bunk beds all around the sides.

I asked Catherine at trial, "What was your reaction to that idea?" She responded, "I was not happy with that concept. . . You have to have some kind of bedrooms. I mean, a play area, but you didn't want to have everybody in the same room."

Catherine and the Senator decided to begin the renovations in 2000. As Catherine was between jobs, the timing worked well. She testified that she "wanted to take some time off, and since I had the time and the interest I was the one that was going to be in charge of the renovation. Ted was too busy."

She elaborated on his work habits: "He works all the time. He's the classic workaholic. He gets up early, and on his typical day in Washington, will go down for . . . a breakfast meeting, a conference before the Senate starts. He'll have a Senate day that goes from, say, nine o'clock in the morning, [until] six, seven, eight o'clock [at night]. He does other meetings, receptions in the evening. And since Alaska is four hours earlier, there are a lot of conference calls that go on with the state, so your day goes on forever with that."

As for the renovation, Catherine testified that their friend Bob Persons would help them get started and would make sure they found the right people to help with the construction. She testified that Persons found the workers to do the excavation work, the lifting of the chalet and the removal of a big tree.

She testified that Bill Allen "was a friend who volunteered to find some people that might be available to work to renovate the chalet and find a contractor for us." Bill Allen found Christensen Builders, owned by Augie Paone, to be the general contractor, and he also found Rocky Williams, whom Catherine believed "was a laborer who had time off from his job. He had, as I understood it, worked for VECO, the company that Mr. Allen founded, and he had some personal issues, that he had time available to work." She testified that she believed that he was being paid by Christensen Builders for his time. She testified that she met Dave Anderson and his son on two occasions. She testified that she believed Anderson and his son were also being paid by Christensen Builders.

I took Catherine through every bill. She testified she had paid every one promptly. We walked through one of the bills that showed that she was paying for substantial labor and materials, including lumber, sheetrock, and electrical and plumbing supplies. Rocky Williams signed on behalf of Christenson Builders for many of the supply purchases. From her perspective, everything seemed to be in order as expected for a renovation being conducted thousands of miles from Washington, D.C., where she was living and working.

Catherine testified that she and the Senator borrowed money and paid over $160,000 for the renovations. She testified that she received the appraisal showing the renovation to be worth much less than that. How could the government be saying that the renovations themselves were worth more than $250,000?

Brenda Morris' cross-examination of Catherine was rude. Morris mocked Catherine repeatedly for believing that Rocky Williams' labor costs were paid by Christensen Builders. She tried to paint Catherine as a member of an elite, privileged, wealthy political class. It reminded me of a political campaign. I hoped that her rude demeanor would hurt the government more than it would help it.

Ted Stevens (left) volunteered for service in the Army Air Corps during World War II. Here he is shown with Leroy Parramore with whom he flew cargo planes in support of the Flying Tigers. Stevens flew 228 combat missions and received two Distinguished Flying Crosses. (Anchorage Daily News/McClatchy-Tribune/Getty Images)

Senator Stevens was diminutive in stature, but earned the nickname "the Incredible Hulk" because of the tenacity with which he advocated for legislation that was important to him. (Scott J. Ferrell/CQ-Roll Call Group/Getty Images)

This modest cabin 40 miles from Anchorage was the Senator's official residence and the focus of the criminal case against him. The Senator and his wife Catherine paid over $160,000 for renovations that independent real-estate experts estimated were worth less than $105,000 and should have cost $124,000. (Williams & Connolly LLP Photograph)

The Acting Assistant Attorney General held a nationally televised press conference to announce the indictment of Republican Senator Ted Stevens one day after the Department of Justice had been criticized by its Inspector General for pro-Republican hiring practices. (Susan Walsh/Associated Press)

The three prosecutors who examined witnesses at the trial of Senator Stevens were, front-to-back, Brenda Morris, Nicholas Marsh and Joseph Bottini. (Jose Luis Magana/Associated Press)

Judge Emmet G. Sullivan presided over *United States v. Stevens*. Democratic and Republican Presidents appointed Judge Sullivan to the bench. (© Beverly Resnick: used with permission)

Bill Allen was the star witness against Senator Stevens. In exchange for his "cooperation," he was able to reduce his own prison term for bribing state legislators, sell his company for hundreds of millions of dollars and achieve immunity from prosecution for his children. (Lauren Victoria Burke/Associated Press)

Bill Allen's son, Mark Allen, received immunity from prosecution as a a result of his father's "cooperation." He owned "Mine that Bird," winner of the 2009 Kentucky Derby. (Ed Reinke/Associated Press)

In this handwritten note from Senator Stevens to Bill Allen, Stevens wrote: "You owe me a bill—remember Toricelli, my friend. Friendship is one thing—compliance with these ethics rules entirely different. I asked Bob P[ersons] to talk to you about this so don't get P.O'd at him—it just has to be done right." We argued that this note was the heart of the defense and a snapshot into the mind of an innocent man intent on doing things the right way. (Trial Exhibit)

Bill Allen testified that Senator Stevens' friend Bob Persons told Allen that the "it has to be done right" note was merely an effort by Stevens to "cover his ass." This surprise testimony instantly transformed the "it has to be done right" note from evidence of innocence into evidence of a cover up. We believed this testimony to be a recent fabrication, but on cross-examination, Allen denied that he had only recently told the government about this alleged conversation. (William J. Hennessy, Jr./CourtroomArt.com)

Bob Persons denied that he had told Bill Allen that Senator Stevens was merely "covering his ass" when he requested a bill. "Crazy!" he said. (William J. Hennessy, Jr./CourtroomArt.com)

Former Secretary of State Colin Powell testified that Senator Stevens had a "sterling reputation for honesty." Borrowing an expression from his days as an Army infantry officer, Secretary Powell described Ted Stevens as "the kind of guy you take on a long patrol." (Susan Walsh/Associated Press)

Emphasizing the Government's theme, Prosecutor Joseph Bottini argued that Senator Stevens was merely "covering his ass" by sending the "it has to be done right note." Bottini repeated the word "cover" 14 times during his closing argument. (William J. Hennessy, Jr./CourtroomArt.com)

"The U.S Department of Justice is proud of our team, not just for the trial but for the investigation leading up to it," Acting Assistant Attorney General Mark Friedrich announced from the courthouse steps after the guilty verdict, as lead prosecutor Brenda Morris looked on. (Bill Clarke/CQ-Roll Call Group/Getty Images)

Senator Stevens returned to Alaska two days after the verdict and six days before the general election. He told a campaign rally upon his return, "The verdict was driven by prosecutors who were willing to do anything to win. If I had had a fair trial in Alaska, I would have been acquitted." (Al Grillo/Associated Press)

Attorney General Eric Holder decided to dismiss the case when he learned that prosecutor notes of an Allen interview contradicted Allen's "covering his ass" testimony. On the day that the Department of Justice announced the Attorney General's decision, Brendan Sullivan and I held a rare press conference. This photograph captured our mood. Brendan emphasized that this was a "sad story" because "anyone can be found guilty if the prosecution ignores the Constitution of the United States." (Haraz N. Ghanbari/Associated Press)

On the day Judge Sullivan granted the Government's Motion to Dismiss, Senator Stevens told the packed courtroom, "It is my hope that when the dust settles I may be able to encourage the enactment of legislation to reform the laws relating to the responsibilities and duties of those entrusted with the solemn task of enforcing criminal laws." (William J. Hennessy Jr./CourtroomArt.com)

Senator Stevens leaves the courthouse for the last time after Judge Sullivan dismissed the case. With him, from left to right, are his daughters Beth Stevens, Lily Stevens Becker, and Susan Stevens Covich. The Senator kept this photograph on his desk for the rest of his life. (Susan Walsh/Associated Press)

Eulogizing his friend Ted Stevens, Senator Daniel Inouye drew an ovation from 3000 funeral-goers when he said, "I knew it and we all knew it. He was not guilty. He was vindicated, cleared of all charges." (Rick Bowmer/Associated Press)

Senator Stevens is laid to rest at Arlington National Cementary by the U.S. Air Force as two of his grandchildren look on. (Win McNamee/Getty Images News)

Independent Prosecutor Henry Schuelke and his partner Bill Shields concluded that the "investigation and prosecution of U.S. Senator Ted Stevens were permeated by the systemic concealment of significant exculpatory evidence which would have independently coorborated Senator Stevens and his testimony, and seriously damaged the credibility of the government's key witness." (Haraz N.Ghanbari/Associated Press)

Alaskan Senator Lisa Murkowski won re-election as a write-in candidate after being defeated by a tea-party candidate in the Republican primary. Senator Murkowski has carried on the legacy of Ted Stevens, including the introduction of proposed legislation designed to insure fairness in criminal prosecutions. So far, Congress has not enacted any of her proposed legislation. (Brendan Smialowski/Getty Images)

Chapter 12

The Alaska Project

The prosecution alleged that Senator Stevens had received other gifts that were not disclosed on his Senate ethics forms—but they would not specify what all the gifts were. The government having refused to answer our questions as to what they were, we had to make educated guesses based on the exhibits they had marked and the documents they had requested from the Senator. For the most part, we were able to figure it out, but here, as so often happened in this case, *Alice in Wonderland* came to mind.

The *United States v. Stevens* prosecutors argued that these additional (alleged) gifts went to the question of the Senator's guilt—in not disclosing the value of the renovations to the chalet—because they demonstrated a devious, scheming mind, intent on concealing them from the American public.

* * * * *

One alleged gift not related to the chalet was actually specified in the indictment: a car swap with Bill Allen. In 1999, Ted Stevens decided he needed a bigger, safer car. Bill Allen had a Land Rover he was trying to sell, and the Senator made him an offer: he'd give Allen his beloved vintage 1964 Mustang convertible, plus $5000 and the cost of shipping the Mustang, in exchange for the Land Rover.

Prosecutors alleged that the trade was not fair—that Bill Allen's car was worth more than Ted Stevens'. Everyone involved thought it was a fair transaction at the time. But the ever-cynical government alleged that Stevens got the better end of the deal and that any difference in value should have been reported on the disclosure forms. The truth was that the trade was perfectly fair. Judge Sullivan effectively dismissed that allegation in any event, because prosecutors concealed records regarding the transaction from us.

* * * * *

Prosecutors also claimed that the Senator should have disclosed receiving a piece of stained glass that hung in front of a window in the cabin. The facts should not have been controversial. Jeanne Penny—a friend of Catherine's long before Catherine, or Jeanne, even knew Ted Stevens—had given Catherine the stained glass. Jeanne knew that Catherine appreciated art, and Jeanne wanted to assist the struggling Alaskan artist who'd made stained glass. The artist's studio was a little cabin in the parking lot of the Double Musky next to the trash dumpsters where Bob Persons allowed the artist to stay rent-free. Jeanne, Catherine and the artist worked together on the design of the piece given to Catherine.

For his part, Ted Stevens could not have cared less about the stained glass-art piece. When Bob Persons was walking by the chalet and reported to the Senator that they were hanging the stained glass, the Senator wrote back: "I don't think I want to ask about the stained glass!" What he meant was that this was Catherine's area, not his. He had no interest in stained glass.

The Stevens prosecutors suggested that this statement of disinterest was part of the "covering his ass" campaign. The prosecutors wanted the jury to believe the Senator cared so deeply about the stained glass piece that he created a false document stating that he was not interested in it. In the government's jaded view, we were living in *Wonderland* where everything meant the opposite of what it said: Yes meant no, up meant down—and evidence of innocence was really evidence of guilt.

According to the disclosure form, "Gifts to your spouse or dependent child totally independent of his or her relationship to you" do not need to be reported. This is fair and applies to the gift bans as well. Otherwise, Senate spouses could never accept gifts over a certain value, even from friends (like Jeanne Penny) whose relationship with the spouse predates the marriage to a Senator.

That did not keep Stevens' prosecutor Bottini from arguing the opposite to the jury: "And it doesn't matter if they say, well, this was just intended for Catherine Stevens, it wasn't intended for the both of them, because he's got to report gifts not only to himself, and you see on the form, 'Did you, your spouse, or dependent child receive any gift in excess of this dollar amount?' " However, Bottini conveniently ignored the language on the form that said that gifts to a spouse independent of his or her relationship did not need to be reported. The truth was that the Senator paid no attention to his wife's stained glass. It was Catherine's stained glass and it never occurred to him that it needed to be reported.

* * * * *

Other alleged gifts involved furniture that belonged to Bill Allen. Allen used the chalet more than the Senator did. Indeed, he acted as though he owned the place; it seemed he was always there. Acquaintances of Allen reported that he liked to invite people over to watch football games. On occasion, the Senator's grown children would stop by to spend the night only to leave without entering upon discovering that Allen was already there. In fact, Allen felt so at home in the Girdwood chalet that he took the Senator's furniture out and replaced it with his own. This was quite upsetting to the Senator because some of the furniture that was removed had belonged to Ted's deceased first wife.

It was also upsetting to Catherine Stevens because the old furniture was smaller and more feminine, while Allen's furniture was massive and marked by cigarette burns. The Stevens family wanted their furniture back, and they asked and asked for it, but to no avail. (When the prosecutors indicted him, the Senator asked me to find his old furniture, as it had meant a lot to him. I tried, hard. I even issued subpoenas for it. But it appeared that nobody had it, and to this day, we have no idea where it went.)

When the Senator testified that he asked for Allen to remove the furniture Allen had brought in and to return the Senator's furniture, the government mocked him and said that he should have gotten a restraining order.

* * * * *

Another alleged "gift" of furniture was a massage chair that got attention in the press. Bob Persons thought that the Senator would like a chair that plugged in and could give you a massage when you sat in it, and so he bought one for the Senator's Washington home and had it delivered. There was no discussion with the Senator. No notice. When the Senator learned of this, he said he could not accept it, because it would violate Senate Ethics rules to accept it as a gift.

The Senator and Persons decided the chair needed to be shipped back to Alaska where Persons would pick it up. This was a considerable project, given that the chair weighed over 700 pounds. The Senator and Mrs. Stevens had plans to move some furniture to Alaska at around the same time and intended to ship the chair to Persons with that shipment. The shipment never happened, because the investigation started, and the Senator could not move, or remove, anything for fear of an obstruction of justice charge.

* * * * *

In another strained attempt to portray Ted Stevens as a greedy lawmaker trying to profit illegally, the government put on evidence regarding a statue of several fish, another alleged gift not specified—or even mentioned—in the indictment. The statue was purchased at a charity auction by a group of Alaskans for a nonprofit foundation known as the North to the Future Foundation, which wanted to build a library to house the official papers of Senator Stevens for historical purposes (similar to the Presidential libraries where documents are preserved and scholarly research can take place).

The Senator did not serve on the board of the North to Alaska Foundation and by law he did not own any of its assets, which amounted to the seed money to build the library.

These well-intentioned Alaskans thought this particular sculpture would go well in the library, so they bought it, and one day, it just showed up, in a packing crate on the chalet's porch. Ted Stevens, who did not know how it arrived, and did not want it, kept it in its original box on the porch. He felt he did not own it—and he had no good place to put it. But once the investigation started, it too, like the chair, could not be moved.

The government prosecutors claimed to have caught the Senator once again: clearly the North to the Future Foundation was just a ruse to "cover the Senator's ass" so that he could accept a fish statute. Today, the North to the Future Foundation has the fish sculpture on display in a hotel lobby while they raise the funds to complete the library. It belonged to the Foundation the whole time, not to the Senator.

* * * * *

Bill Allen would hold fundraisers at the chalet. There was talk that Bill Allen had entertained women there. True or not, he certainly spent a lot of time there. Lots of people did—the Stevens family was rarely there, and they wanted it to be used. Mrs. Stevens testified that at one point 21 different people had keys to the cabin.

One day the Stevens family found that Allen had installed a Viking outdoor gas grill on the deck. The Senator and Mrs. Stevens were furious. They were worried about kids using it, and told Allen that they did not want it. They specifically told him that they could not accept it. What's more, they never used it, not even once. However, as with so many other things, they had to keep it in place as required during the investigation. But they did put a lock on it so that their grandchildren did not accidently blow up the place.

* * * * *

The craziest "gift" allegation of all involved a sled dog that had been purchased—for $1,000—by a group at a charity auction and then given back to the charity. In a perfectly legal transaction, the charity then gave the dog to Senator Stevens. (Charities are allowed to make reasonable gifts to legislators subject to requirements that were fulfilled in this case.) The Senator himself bought the dog's sister for $250. Unaware that the group had paid four times that amount for the dog, he listed the gift—even though Senate rules would have allowed him to keep it (because it was a gift from a charity)—and declared a value of $250, based on the Senator himself having paid that same amount for the dog's sister. The government claimed that the value should have been $1000—the inflated value that the group paid in order to make a charitable donation.

We had to bring in several witnesses to testify about this sled dog, and they turned out to be colorful characters. One was Jim Vargos, Alaska's most famous recording artist who goes by the nickname "Hobo Jim." One of his biggest hits in Alaska is "The Iditarod Trail," named after the famous dog sled race held every winter in Alaska.

Hobo Jim testified that he found a runt dog whose owner donated it to be auctioned off at the charity auction. Jim also testified that items at the auction often went for much more than they were worth, because people knew the proceeds were going to charity. He told the jury he intentionally sought a runt, a dog that was not particularly valuable, because he didn't want the donor to give up a good dog.

Hobo Jim testified that he had gotten the dog from a breeder named Dean Osmar, a dog racer, which in Alaska is known as a "musher." Dean had raced in the Iditarod twice, winning it once. Osmar himself testified and described the dog as a "little, blue-eyed white puppy," a runt of the litter. He testified that blue-eyed white sled dogs are not very valuable. Under questioning from Joe Terry, he estimated it to be worth $50 to $100.

169

Brenda Morris cross-examined Osmar, who, in a rare occurrence, turned the tables on her. When Morris seemed incredulous at hearing the dog was worth so little, Osmar asked *her* questions.

Osmar: Do you know anything about the problem with blue-eyed, white color dogs?

Morris: I know nothing about animals, period.

Osmar: Have you heard of wheezers?

Morris: No. I'm afraid of everything.

Osmar: [A] lot of Alaskan natives won't own blue-eyed, light colored dogs because a certain percentage are wheezers. That means they have breathing problems. I think it's a recessive gene. I have had some very good blue-eyed dogs, but I don't have very many in my lot.

Sensing she was barking up the wrong tree, Morris quickly finished her questioning of Dean Osmar.

The final witness was Dave Monson, a well-known musher who also had won the Iditarod. Monson was the widower of Susan Butcher, Alaska's most famous musher. Butcher, a friend of the Stevens family, was the second woman to win the Iditarod, and the first person of either gender to win four out of five years. A true Alaskan hero, Susan Butcher died two years before the trial of leukemia.

Monson testified that when it became clear that the dogs were ill-suited to the Senator's busy life and long hours working in steamy Washington, D.C., he and his wife offered to take the dogs themselves. The Stevens family agreed, but insisted on paying Monson and Butcher to take the dogs. Monson testified that neither of the dogs were well-suited to be sled dogs and had little value, and that he eventually gave both of them away.

* * * * *

Because the government did not identify these specific, individual gift allegations in the indictment, there was no way to tell whether the jury found any of them to be undisclosed gifts. Each of these "gifts" is easily explained if one is inclined to believe that the Senator was acting in good faith. But if one has a jaded, cynical view of the world fueled by the notion that the Senator was simply "covering his ass," the world looks quite different. Everything in the case was becoming tainted by the theme of "covering his ass."

Edward Bennett Williams used to call looking at the world with an overly cynical attitude "looking at the world through dirty windows." Looking at the world with an unbiased view he called "looking at the world though clean windows."

I believed Ted Stevens to be utterly honest, and so did everyone else who actually knew him. But when one is facing an indictment that does not even list the charges and when the government presents fabricated testimony that falsely alleges that an innocent man was "covering his ass," and then plays up jurors' distrust of members of Congress, and hostility to Republicans, what you have is a Washington witch hunt.

* * * * *

Another one of the misguided arrows the government shot at Ted Stevens was to suggest that he took official action that benefitted VECO. This was an unfair attempt to suggest that there was a quid pro quo when there wasn't. The government was allowed to put on what it claimed was evidence that the Senator took action that benefitted VECO, even though the government conceded that there was no conceivable argument of bribery.

While this presented a challenge for the defense, it also presented an opportunity. If prosecutors could put on evidence that Stevens took action that benefitted VECO, we could put on evidence that the Senator would take any legitimate action that benefitted Alaskans (and was consistent with the national interest), that being what Ted Stevens was all about.

While the rest of our team got ready for trial on issues relating to the renovations, we dispatched Williams & Connolly partner Joe Terry to Alaska to collect witnesses who would testify to the many beneficial things Senator Stevens did for Alaskans. Joe didn't have much time, but fortunately it wasn't hard to find Alaskans whose

171

lives had been touched by the Senator. Bill Phillips gave him a list of people to track down. Joe Terry had another advantage: his father was a fisheries economist, and Joe had spent the first years of his life in Fairbanks. We called Joe's work "the Alaska Project."

One of our pro-Stevens Alaska witnesses was a man named Orie Williams. After Alaska became a state, Ted Stevens sponsored the legislation that created the Alaskan Native Corporations, which empowered indigenous peoples rather than simply locating them on a reservation. Orie Williams was a Native Alaskan who served as the Chief Executive Officer and board member of an Alaskan Native Corporation called Doyon Limited. Williams had also been involved in a number of small non-profit entities over the years.

Doyon was in the business of providing services to the oil industry, just as VECO was. In fact, Doyon and VECO often competed for the same work. Williams told the jury the notion that VECO had special access to Senator Stevens was wrong. All had access to their Senator. Williams said, "It's been an honor and a privilege to know the Senator for many years. And access was a key issue. I consider the Senator a mentor; I consider him a great leader. He has always given access. Whether it was a small corporation or a small non-profit or a large company, his access has always been unlimited."

It simply wasn't true, as the government was implying, that VECO had special access because of renovations to the chalet.

* * * * *

Heldi Sandvik was a similar witness. She worked for NANA, a Native Corporation based in far Northwest Alaska, hundreds of miles from Anchorage. The shareholders of NANA were 12,000 Inuit Eskimos and their descendants who originated from Northwest Alaska. In addition to her position with NANA, Ms. Sandvik was on the Executive Committee of the Alaskan State Chamber of Commerce and had previously worked for the State of Alaska.

Joe Terry asked her to "describe the nature of the access, if any, that you have had to Senator Stevens and his staff?" Ms. Sandvik answered, "Well, if we needed to work with the Senator's office, we would simply contact the office and make an appointment and meet with either the Senator directly or with his aides. I've never had a situation where we desired to meet with the Senator where we haven't been able to do so."

In her cross-examination, Brenda Morris tried to show that Heidi Sandvik was biased. "Ma'am," Morris asked, "would you agree that your organization is in large part indebted to Senator Stevens for the work he's provided to your group?"

Ms. Sandvik answered, "I wouldn't consider us indebted to Senator Stevens. Senator Stevens has certainly worked hard to understand how we benefit our shareholders by taking advantage of programs that are designed to specifically allow for our type of involvement. He's there to represent the interests of Alaskans, and he has listened to the Alaskan native community as well as the other groups, such as the Indian tribes and native Hawaiian organizations, to understand how important this program is to allow us to deliver economic benefit to our owners, and as a result he has advocated on our behalf."

Morris followed-up: "So in short, you are grateful to Senator Stevens?" Sandvik answered, "Oh, certainly we're grateful to him."

There's a difference between "grateful" and "indebted," and Ms. Sandvik had drawn the line well.

* * * * *

We also called Julie Kitka, president of the Alaska Federation of Natives (AFN). As described by Ms. Kitka, the Federation of Natives was like the NAACP. It represented the 22 percent of the population of Alaska who were Indians, Eskimos and Aleut people. It was formed in 1966, and Ms. Kitka had been the president for 17 years.

She described the 13 regional native corporations and the 200 village native corporations that were established by legislation sponsored by Ted Stevens in 1971. The Native Corporations were

173

established to empower Alaska's natives, and it had worked. Native corporations were set up in the oilfield services, oil development, tourism, timber, government contracting and a whole range of business activities. She testified that these native corporations competed with VECO, and that her organization wanted 20 percent of all professional, management, technical and clerical workers on any natural gas pipeline set aside for Natives Alaskans so that Native Alaskans who were there first would share in the economic benefits of a gas pipeline. VECO did not agree with that, so AFN asked Senator Stevens for his support, and he gave it to them.

Kitka attempted to state that before Senator Stevens set up the Native Corporations, the poverty rate in Alaska was over 60 percent, but that within the last 30 years working with Senator Stevens and Senator Inouye and others. . .

"Objection," prosecutor Bottini interrupted.

Heaven forbid the jurors hear that Senator Stevens had greatly reduced poverty in Alaska. That would be inconsistent with the government's theory that he was scheming to enrich himself at the public's expense.

* * * * *

The first of the final witnesses we put on to counter the allegation that Senator Stevens sought favors in return for helping Bill Allen and VECO was Louise Johnson, a wonderful woman who worked for Senator Stevens for 30 years. Born in Louisiana, she had traveled to Alaska in the early 1960s, stayed in Fairbanks and got a job with Senator Stevens in 1971. She worked as a secretary, a receptionist and then did constituent service casework for the Senator. She explained that every Congressional office has constituent service caseworkers on the staff, and that "constituent casework is when the constituent is having problems with the federal government or with the various agencies, and requests assistance from Senator Stevens because they don't know where to go or who to go to, and so they contacted our office, and we try to help them resolve it."

She testified that she worked on hundreds of cases for constituents: civil service retirement, social security and visas, just to name a few. She said that Senator Stevens would "always just give me a case, I would do it, and get back to him with a status report; but I just did it all on my own."

She testified that she once helped a friend of Bill Allen's get a visa. Joe Terry asked her, "And in comparison to the other constituent requests that you received, how did you treat that request?"

"I treated all my case requests the same," Louise Johnson replied.

That one visa request—among hundreds—was one of the things, the government said, that gave Ted Stevens a motive to lie.

* * * * *

Pro-Stevens witness Mano Frey was the vice president and Northwest Regional Manager for the Laborers International Union of North America. He had lived in Alaska for 33 years and had previously been President of the Alaska AFL-CIO, which he described as "the Chamber of Commerce for unions." Mr. Frey testified that Senator Stevens would always meet with him, that his unions supported oil and gas exploration in the Arctic National Wildlife Refuge, that he, Frey, asked for language to make sure that labor union contractors could do that work, and that Stevens always agreed. The oil industry was not in favor of this.

The government objected, and convinced the judge to agree. So Mano Frey did not testify in full. He would have testified—and in colorful language—that Senator Stevens rejected the views of the oil companies because he thought requiring that some of the work be done by union labor was best for Alaskans.

The government suggested strongly that Senator Stevens was a captive of the oil industry, and especially that of VECO. We knew that simply wasn't true, so it was our job to prove it wasn't. But at every turn, the government used every tactic in the book to try to block us.

* * * * *

The government suggested that the Senator's support of the natural gas pipeline was a result of his relationship with VECO. Hogwash. Jim Sampson, also a president of the AFL-CIO, testified that the AFL-CIO, which represented construction employees, was very much in favor of a natural gas pipeline. The AFL-CIO wanted a project labor agreement, making that work available to union members. Sampson testified that VECO was opposed to this and was on the opposite side of almost every issue from that of the unions. Senator Stevens, he said, often sided with the unions.

* * * * *

The government put on evidence that Ted Stevens had helped to establish a job training program on Sakhalin Island that benefited VECO. According to his prosecutors, this gave Ted Stevens motive to falsify his disclosures. The problem was it wasn't true.

Sakhalin Island, which is in between Japan and Russia, belongs to Russia. Closer to Alaska than anyplace else in the United States, it is a cold harsh place, but a cold harsh place with oil.

Joe called Russell Howell of the Russian American Center at the University of Alaska. The Russian American Center promoted commercial and cultural ties between Russia and the United States. The Russian American Center ran the training program, which was a good opportunity to train Russians and provide work opportunities for Alaskans on Sakhalin Island.

Howell testified that Senator Stevens supported the job training program because he viewed it as a good employment opportunity for Alaskans. And he testified further that the companies that took advantage of the program were Federal Express and an Alaskan Native corporation called NANTA. VECO did not take advantage of the program. Of course, Ted Stevens supported it because he thought it benefited Alaskans. VECO was not even a beneficiary. End of story. So much for that so-called motivation to lie.

By the time we had finished with this line of witnesses, we felt we had effectively defused the government's ill-founded charge that Ted Stevens had only helped Alaskans when he benefitted personally. But we had one more witness to put on the stand because what she had to say was special.

* * * * *

That Alaska Project witness was Dr. Dani Bowman, a pediatric intensive care physician at the Alaska Native Medical Center, which had been founded to take care of Eskimo, Inuit and American Indians. Dr. Bowman had spent her professional life taking care of critically ill Native Alaskan children. Joe Terry asked her, "In connection with your job have you ever called on Senator Stevens for assistance with a matter?"

Dr. Bowman answered, "Yes, I have. And that's why I'm here today because he helped me save a baby that needed to be transported, a baby who was dying."

"Dr. Bowman," Joe asked, "could you tell me what you requested of Senator Stevens?"

"I requested his help in getting the United States Air Force to help us transport a baby who would surely die just because the baby happened to be in Alaska. It was dying of severe pneumonia, and we had come to the end of the medical care we could offer that child. I asked him to help us, and he said, yes. He didn't ask me the rest of the question. He didn't listen to the rest of the question. He didn't need to know the rest of it. He said, yes, I'll help you. We needed to have a mobile transport, air medevac. . . capable of. . . transferring the baby on something called 'extracorporeal membrane oxygenation.' It's very much like a form of cardiac bypass that's used in the operating room to stop the heart and [then] beat for the patient and push blood around. In order to benefit from that technology, you have to be living in an academic place reachable in the Lower 48 and have an academic medical center, and we don't have that."

Nothing upset Senator Stevens more than somebody from Alaska having a disadvantage merely because they lived in Alaska.

"After you made this request of Senator Stevens what happened next?"

"Within a few minutes, he contacted me back and said he had been able to have the child designated a dependent for medical purposes, a dependent of the Department of Defense. Twenty medical personnel came and saved the baby's life."

Tears were streaming down Dr. Bowman's cheeks as she left the stand. The government objected. Apparently it was too touching. Judge Sullivan struck it from evidence. It was too far removed from what the case was supposed to be about.

A common tactic on television shows is for a lawyer to ask a clearly improper question, for the answer to come out, for the judge to tell the jury to disregard the answer, and for the offending lawyer to say "Question withdrawn," figuring that the jury has already heard the answer.

That was *not* what happened here. The government was implying that Senator Stevens' office was for sale. They were saying that he was corrupt. We were desperate to show this jury what kind of person Senator Stevens was, desperate to show them how much Senator Stevens cared about all Alaskans, how much he cared about Native Alaskans especially. That is why the Alaska Project was so important.

The idea that the government can use almost any evidence to try to establish guilt, while the defense is more limited is a disturbing trend in the law. The government introduced an unrelated real estate transaction into evidence to support its theory. But our evidence that Senator Stevens saved the life of a Native baby was inadmissible.

Chapter 13

"My Bottom Wasn't Bare"

Traditionally in the United States, a criminal defendant testifies last. And he has the absolute right, under the Fifth Amendment of the Constitution, not to testify. If he chooses not to do so, the judge instructs the jury that when deciding to vote guilty or not guilty it *cannot* take into account the fact that the defendant did not testify. Of course, all trial lawyers wonder if jurors really abide by that instruction. But that is the law.

By the time *United States v. Stevens* was reaching its conclusion, the press had reported that the government's case had many problems. According to some arm-chair quarterbacks, why should the defense subject the Senator to a potentially harmful cross-examination when things were going so well for him?

The problem was that the government's bad moments were occurring outside the presence of the jury. They did not hear Judge Sullivan say that the government had knowingly presented false evidence to them; they did not hear Judge Sullivan say that he was the only reason that the Senator was getting a fair trial; and they did not hear Judge Sullivan question whether the Public Integrity Section had any integrity. What they did hear was Bill Allen's "covering his ass" testimony—which had undoubtedly stayed in their minds through the many breaks while we fought for a fair trial.

We thought the Senator had to respond. What's more, he had promised the people of Alaska he would testify in his own defense. So he was determined to testify, and I did not blame him.

* * * * *

Ted Stevens' testimony began with a clear and unequivocal denial of the charges. Brendan began the questioning:

Q: Senator, when you signed those Senate disclosure financial forms, and you've seen them in this case, did you believe they were accurate and truthful?

A: Yes, sir.

Q: Did you ever intend to file a false statement with the United States Senate where you've served for 40 years?

A: No, I did not.

Q: Did you engage in any scheme with any person to conceal anything from the Senate?

A: No, sir.

* * * * *

The Senator then gave the jury some personal background—growing up during the Depression, his military service during World War II, and how he came to live in Alaska. He testified about his marriage to his first wife, Ann, her tragic death, and his marriage to Catherine. He then spoke about his duties in the U.S. Senate and his work habits. He told the jury that he spent most of his time in Washington, D.C., with an average of only twenty nights a year in Girdwood.

* * * * *

The Senator next testified about the renovations to the "chalet"; about the $40,000 estimate from his neighbor Keith Tryck; about liquidating a trust and borrowing money to pay for the renovation; and about Bob Persons and Bill Allen volunteering to help find workers and to keep an eye on the renovation while the Senator was in Washington, D.C. He testified about Catherine having time between jobs to deal with the renovation and manage the checking account. He got choked up as he talked about how hard she had worked in her previous job and how she deserved some down time. He testified about his original idea to put in a big bunk room, and how that was—correctly—overruled by Catherine. He testified about the appraisal and the assessments. And he testified that he believed that appropriate bills were sent and paid in full.

* * * * *

And the Senator testified about the heart of the defense, the "it has to be done right" note.

Q: Now, sir, let's turn to Government Exhibit 495. . . . Read it slowly, and I'll ask you some questions. This is dated what, sir?

A: This is October 6th of '02.

Q: And to whom is it addressed?

A: To Bill Allen.

Q: Please read.

A: It says, Dear Bill, when I think of the ways in which you make my life easier and more enjoyable I lose count. Thanks for all the work on the chalet. You owe me a bill. Remember Torricelli, my friend.

Q: Hold on right there. What did you mean when you said remember Torricelli after you said you owe me a bill?

A: Well, this is an election year. I'm up for election. Torricelli was up for election. I had heard . . . that he had withdrawn from his race and quit because of some problem with regard to his taking money or something from someone in connection with his campaign.

Q: Based upon what you knew, did Torricelli's issues have anything to do with home renovations, as Mr. Allen testified to?

A: No, not that I know of. . . . But it was a serious problem because he had not—he had taken something from someone in connection with a friendship deal, as far as I knew.

Q: What was the purpose of you saying to your friend, Bill Allen, remember Torricelli?

A: What I'm telling him, he's not going to give me anything. I want a record of what he's done on the chalet and I want to pay for it.

Q: Continue with the letter. Next sentence?

A: Friendship is one thing, compliance with the ethics—entirely different. I've asked Bob to talk to you about this, so don't get p.o.'d at him. It just has to be done right. Hope to see you soon. My best, Ted

Q: Now, when you wrote this letter did you mean it?

A: Absolutely.

Q: When you said, quote, I asked Bob P. to talk to you about this, so don't get p.o.'d at him, end of quote, what did you mean?

A: You know, this is a period after [a motorcycle] accident in which Allen seriously was injured and he was getting sort of short-tempered. It wasn't easy to tell him anything and I didn't want him to get upset about it, but I wanted to make sure he understood that I wanted the bills for this work that was going on at the chalet, so I asked Bob Persons to talk to him . . . I was telling Bill Allen not to get p.o.'d at Bob because I was the guy that told him to talk to him about it and get me a bill.

Q: Did you ever tell Mr. Persons anything which could lead to the conclusion that you were trying to cover your ass by this letter?

A: No.

* * * * *

Brenda Morris' cross-examination of the Senator was mocking and sarcastic. I thought this was dangerous. The jury might resent Morris's lack of respect for a war hero, who was also one of the oldest and longest-serving members of the U.S. Senate. But she had charged him with being a criminal, and so she let it all hang out.

And she was consistent with the government's theme that the Senator was scheming to "cover his ass."

After asking about some emails indicating that he knew nothing about any free work, she pushed, "And, Sir, aren't these emails really what you're doing, covering your bottom?"

The Senator responded, "No, my bottom wasn't bare."

Later, Morris drew the Senator into an argument and elicited again the testimony that his "bottom was bare."

Q: You don't ask Bill Allen for any of these gifts, correct?

A: I don't know of a gift you're talking about.

Q: Okay.

A: If it was a gift, why did I ask for a bill?

Q: To cover your butt.

A: My butt wasn't bare, ma'am.

182

* * * * *

Morris had made the Senator mad. I always tell clients that they need to remain cool, calm, and collected when being attacked on cross-examination, as getting into an argument with a prosecutor rarely helps. One of the jurors later confirmed that the Senator's feisty demeanor had been harmful to him.

But imagine yourself innocent. Imagine yourself having given most of your life to public service only to find yourself accused of being a criminal in your 85th year. Imagine listening to lies about your own actions. We knew that the government "just covering his ass" theory was predicated on false testimony. But we did not have the conclusive evidence to prove it. At least not yet. We were left with getting mad. The Senator should not have gotten in an argument with Morris, but I did not blame him. Every one of us was angry.

Chapter
14

"Just Covering His Ass"

The Senator's testimony, which began on Thursday, October 16, and concluded on Monday, October 20, was the last testimony in the case. On the intervening Saturday, the 18th of October, Judge Sullivan held a hearing on what the jury instructions would be.

This hearing was the conclusion of a long process. Jury instructions, the last thing that the judge tells the jury before they begin their deliberations, are a very big deal. In federal court, the marshals usually lock the doors to the courtroom during the reading of the instructions so that there are no distractions. (The reading of instructions is open to the public, but once it starts, judges do not want jurors distracted by observers coming and going through the doors of the courtroom.)

The judge tells the jury that only they are supposed to decide what the facts are. Only the jury can decide whether to believe witnesses and how much credit to give documents and other evidence. But the judge does tell the jury what legal rules apply to determining whether somebody is guilty or innocent. He or she lays down the rules and tells the jury that it is the jury's duty to accept the law as handed down by the judge. The judge tells the jurors that they may not ignore the instructions on the law.

In some types of common cases, such as bank robbery cases, the instructions are routine and unlikely to be controversial. The instructions have been used many times before and can be found in books of standard instructions. But in many white collar criminal cases, the instructions are anything but routine. As our case was sailing through relatively uncharted waters, there was a lot of argument and discussion about what the jury instructions should be.

When a specific jury instruction has been challenged after a trial but then approved by an appellate court, it is considered a good instruction. This means that many instructions get repeated over and over again, whether they are easy to understand or not. Just like the long contracts we often have to sign as consumers that have been used over and over again, our legal system tends to use the same jury instructions over and over again—whether or not they are written in plain English or not. For that reason and because instructions on the law are less scintillating than testimony or argument, lawyers sometimes wonder whether the jury pays attention to them. But they are important, and lawyers can quote from them in their arguments.

* * * * *

In our case, Craig Singer and associate Neelum Wadhwani handled most of these arguments. They worked very hard conducting extensive research, submitting draft after draft of the jury instructions to the other side and to the Court, and putting together objections to the government's proposed instructions. On a number of occasions, in order to meet the deadlines of our demanding case, Neelum worked through the night

* * * * *

Some of the arguments over jury instructions in our case were interesting. We asked for a jury instruction used in a number of cases on how to determine the value of the alleged gifts, i.e., that the value of an object is its fair market value. It had never been used in a Senate Financial Disclosure case, but our case was unprecedented. We had put on evidence of the fair market value of the renovations through an appraiser and assessors. It seemed to us that the jury should be instructed that their opinion mattered. It did not seem objectionable. The government fought us tooth and nail on this, and Judge Sullivan did not give our requested instruction.

All lawyers agree that appellate courts pay careful attention to jury instructions. If the instructions are wrong and the defendant is convicted, a new trial is likely. We believed that the failure to give a fair market value instruction would likely lead to a new trial if needed.

We also thought that the entire prosecution was a violation of the Separation of Powers provision of the Constitution. Only Congress has the power to discipline one of its own for alleged violations of Senate Rules. This was too weighty an issue in the amount of time we had, but it would have made an excellent appellate argument.

* * * * *

There are only two times in a case when the lawyers are allowed to speak directly to the jury: during opening statements, and during closing arguments. And the closing argument is the only time the lawyers are allowed to argue—meaning arguing what the evidence proves (as opposed to just describing what the evidence is) to the jury. Another way of thinking about it is that opening and closing are when the lawyers get to show how the pieces of the puzzle fit together.

In closing arguments, the government goes first and last. The government argues first. Then the defense argues, and then the prosecution responds. That gives the government a tremendous advantage. Studies have shown that the first and last things people hear make the greatest impression. The government argues twice—at the times that matters most.

Why? The government is given the advantage of going twice because it bears the burden of proving the charges beyond a reasonable doubt. Because this is considered an advantage for the defense, the government goes twice to make up for it. At least that's the theory.

186

* * * * *

Prosecutor Joseph Bottini gave the government's first closing. He began by arguing, "Ted Stevens knew that his friend Bill Allen was wealthy. Bill Allen was generous. And he knew that his good friend, Bill Allen, would help him and give him hundreds of thousands of dollars' worth of free benefits."

Bottini argued that Senator Stevens received the renovation work for free, all but ignoring the $160,000 the Stevens had paid (for $120,000 worth of work). And, he argued that the "it just has to be done right" note was simply a part of a scheme to cover it up. As Bottini told the jury, "He's just—pardon my French—covering his ass."

Even though Bottini spent much of his argument talking about the sled dog, he admitted, "[T]he case isn't about the dog. It's never been about the dog." Nonetheless, he then accused the Senator of lying about the dog, saying "If he's willing to mislead and cover-up about a small-ticket item like that dog, what does that tell you what he'd be willing to do when he talks about things like the remodel of his home?"

He made a similar point with the massage chair, arguing that his refusal to accept it as a gift was a cover-up, arguing that the fact the Senator had not moved the chair was proof he was lying about it. (Of course Bottini ignored the fact that had the Senator moved the chair he would have been accused of obstruction of justice.)

The government's theme was clear: Senator Stevens was covering his ass. Bottini used the word "cover" 14 times during his closing argument. True to government form, he referred to Senator Stevens as the "defendant" over 80 times, apparently to lump him in with all of the other criminals in America.

After listening to Bottini's argument, I concluded that the government's case was based on fabricated testimony and cynicism. If only we could prove that the testimony was fabricated, we could negate the cynicism.

187

* * * * *

Unlike Bottini, who had paraphrased what had been said by the witnesses, in closing arguments Brendan likes to quote from transcripts. He likes to read the actual testimony. The government had apparently read our arguments from prior trials, because they filed a motion for an order that Brendan could not read from transcripts during closing argument. They argued that reading from the actual transcripts would confuse the jury and make closing arguments longer.

Are you kidding me? I thought.

Judge Sullivan, of course, denied that motion.

Brendan began:

> You've heard a very twisted interpretation of the evidence. . . . Not only were you given a twisted interpretation of the evidence, but you've been given a twisted interpretation of real life, the way the Stevenses lived it at the time not, seven, six, eight years later.

> To believe the government's version of the evidence you've got to think [Senator Stevens is some kind of] mastermind of a conspiracy [who] goes through life, doesn't mean what he says in the documents, writes something so it will protect him seven or eight years later out there somewhere. . . You see, the problem is, if you look at life through a filthy dirty glass, we've all seen those places, just dirty glass that doesn't get washed for five years or ten years in some hard-to-get-to-place, then the whole world looks dirty. . . . To believe the government you have to ignore the written record. . . The government doesn't want you to understand the evidence here.

Brendan then turned to the Torricelli note—that "it just has to be done right" note:

> This is a letter written on October 6th, 2002, by Ted Stevens to Bill Allen. The government wants to make you think this is a cover-up, just a letter written by a man thinking someday he's

188

got to account for something. You read that letter to yourself
. . . [and] it will take you straight into the mind of Ted Stevens
on that day. That shows his intent, that shows why he's not
guilty, that shows why he didn't do anything willfully or knowingly to violate the law. . . . The government of the United
States tries to take that and erase it out, put it off with the
false testimony of a witness they brought in this courtroom
who got on that stand and said to you Mr. Persons told me don't
pay any attention to that letter, that's just Ted covering his
ass. An explosion in the courtroom wipes out a letter that was
written by a man on October 6th, 2002. I'm going to prove to
you that's an absolute lie that brought this lie into the court.

Brendan told the jury that the government never asked Bob
Persons about it, and Bob Persons denied ever saying that the Senator was just covering his ass. "No. Crazy," he said. Brendan pointed
out that Allen was protecting his children and protecting his $70
million holdback and trying to minimize his jail time.

Brendan pointed out that, according to most of the witnesses, the
Senator was hardly ever at the cabin.

He took the jury through emails and documents at the time showing that as they lived it, the Stevenses were willing to pay, and did
pay, more than $160,000. He took them through the bills that were
paid—every bill presented to the Stevens family, totaling over
$160,000. He pointed out that Dave Anderson was wrong when he
testified that he took down the big tree.

In addition, Brendan pointed out that the bills the Stevenses saw
only contained general lines for labor, and Rocky Williams signed
for supplies seventeen times. From where Ted and Catherine
Stevens sat, it looked like they paid for everything they got—as
they lived it, looking at the world through clean glass.

He paraphrased for the jury the testimony of the appraiser and the
assessors, who had valued the renovation at much less. And he took
them through the character testimony.

After the lunch break, Brendan spoke for another hour taking the jury through the flaws in the government's case. His final lines were:

> The government comes here late in the night of a good man's life, and they try to brand him a criminal. The evidence won't permit it. The law won't permit it. And your gut won't permit it. Because you have here a man that has lived 84 years honorably, truthfully, abiding by the law and serving people. . . [T]hey ask you to brand him a criminal, to tarnish everything he has done for 84 years, despite the fact that the evidence is unrefuted that he is an honorable, truthful man.

* * * * *

"What!" screamed Brenda Morris, who went next for the government. "Were we at the same trial? Because the evidence I saw was totally different than that imaginative display we just sat through. Because the trial I sat through told me that no one is above the law: not a teacher; not a social worker; not a lawyer; and, certainly, most certainly, not a sitting United States Senator from the State of Alaska who thinks he is entitled to break the law whenever he thinks it's to his benefit."

"He believes he was above the law," she argued, asserting that he thinks "the law simply didn't apply to him."

Thus far, she hadn't talked about any actual evidence. Instead, she had simply appealed to what she had assumed from the beginning was a natural bias against Members of Congress.

When she did turn to the evidence, she spoke in generalities, not giving specifics other than to say that nobody really seemed to know who was in charge or who worked for whom. She then accused us of throwing Catherine Stevens under the bus. She said that our witnesses were trying to "cover the defendant's butt."

She even made fun of Ted Stevens for stuttering, which he did from time to time: ". . . he was perfectly eloquent when it came to discussing all matters about himself. The words just flowed. As soon as you started asking him about those renovations and how

190

they got paid—*umba, rumba, butta, uh, umba, rumba*—he started stuttering and sputtering. . . ." This prosecutor knew no limits.

She accused him of "trying to paper the trail." The "it just has to be done right" note was covering his ass. If he could write that note, he could write a check, she argued. The note was just "cover." He was trying to "paper the trail."

She compared the 84 year-old U.S. Senator to a six-year old who was cheating while playing hide and seek. ". . . I was talking to a friend, and he was telling me this reminds him of his little six year-old-son [who] likes to play hide-and-go-seek, but what he likes to do is he likes to cover his eyes and then when you say hey, hey, I see you, he goes, no, no, no, I don't see you. I'm not looking. You know, you tell him he's cheating and then he starts laughing. But," she said, "the defendant is not a six-year-old, and his actions aren't cute."

Then, just moments after comparing the Senator to a child, she made fun of his advanced age. ". . . you weren't born yesterday," she said, "referring to the jurors," ". . . and certainly [he] wasn't— the defendant wasn't either."

She said that a friend told her, "Brenda, maybe since the defendant lives so close to the North Pole maybe Santa and his elves came down and did this work and completed it . . . he had been very, very good."

She also mocked Catherine Stevens for believing that Rocky Williams' and Dave Anderson's time was paid through Augie Paone's bills.

She closed by, once again, invoking prejudice against politicians. Interestingly, not once during her final argument to the jury had the prosecutor referred to my client as "Senator Stevens" or even "Mr. Stevens." It was always "the defendant," as if being a defendant was tantamount to being guilty (which, in the minds of many people it is, unfortunately). But she certainly let the jurors know what he did for a living, at least the way she preferred to phrase it.

191

"When you are dealing with politicians, that's a whole different ball game because politicians are used to the constant scrutiny of their lives. They carry themselves differently. They talk differently. They're much more guarded, and they talk in a way so as not to expose their vulnerability. . . The defendant is a powerful politician," she told the jury. "He makes a living off his sharp, sharp mind and off his influence."

Then she asked the jurors to "do something that very few people have done, it's to stand up to him because at the end of the day behind that growling and that snappy comeback and all that righteous indignation, he's just a man. . . Make him responsible, ladies and gentlemen, just like any other defendant would be."

I wanted to scream right back at her. How dare you call this good man a liar? How dare you call this World War II veteran a criminal?

But the rules do not permit talking to the jury at all at that point, much less screaming back at the prosecutor. As I said, the government gets the last word, and at that point all a defense lawyer can do is hope and pray that reason and open-mindedness will prevail over bias and testimony that (I believed to the core of my being) was fabricated.

Wouldn't they see that Ted Stevens was not covering his ass? Wouldn't they see that Allen had just made up the covering his ass testimony? Surely the government's tactics wouldn't work.

Chapter 15

"Proud of Our Team"

I have a routine while waiting for a jury to return to a verdict. I make sure that I am in the courtroom every time the jury enters or leaves so that they know how much I care about what they are doing. But in between these appearances, there is often lots of downtime. I try to use that downtime to work on other cases for other clients. I find a quiet place to work near the courthouse with my cell phone on so that I can be there in a few minutes if called by the court. But my mind always wanders to the jury: What are they talking about? Are they looking at the exhibits? Are they close to a decision? This usually makes it impossible to concentrate on other work for other clients. When that happens, I usually read a book or watch a movie on video. *My Cousin Vinnie* is a favorite.

In this case, we did something different. Hoping for the best, but planning for the worst, we used our downtime to put together a letter to the Attorney General complaining about the prosecutors' misconduct during the trial. If this jury returned the wrong verdict, the Attorney General should do something about it, we believed, but we needed to lay it out for him in some detail. Craig Singer and Simon Latcovich took the lead, but we all pitched in.

* * * * *

The jury got the case just before noon on Wednesday, October 22. Judge Sullivan excused the alternates, instructing them not to talk to anybody about the case in the event that they needed to return if

193

one of the deliberating jurors needed to be excused. Judge Sullivan told them that their lunch would be provided and that he would keep them until 4:45.

At 3:55 p.m., the jury sent out a note that read: "Can we leave a little early today? Would that be a problem, Your Honor? Kinda stressful right now. We need a moment of clarity for all."

Judge Sullivan, of course, accommodated their request. That ended the first day of jury deliberations.

* * * * *

At 11:30 the next day, the jury sent out another note: "Please clarify (liability costs) as it is not reading clear in Senate regulations."

At noon, they sent another note: "We need page 20 from the indictment. It is not in our possession."

They were clearly reading the indictment very carefully. Why they needed the indictment, I've never understood. It is written by prosecutors. But most federal courts allow it to go into the jury room with the evidence.

Twenty-three minutes later, the jury sent out the third note of the day:

"We the jury request that Juror #9 be removed from the jury. She is being rude, disrespectful, and unreasonable. She has had violent outbursts with other jurors and is not helping anyone. She is not following the law and rules that were stipulated to us in the instructions."

We spent the afternoon at the courthouse, mostly in our courthouse warroom, discussing what we thought Judge Sullivan should say in response to the jury notes and then waiting for the next inevitable note from the jury. As for the note about Juror No. 9, Judge Sullivan gave the jury a "pep talk" (at our request) about civility and mutual respect. While there was some down time and I was deep in thought, I looked up to see John Holton, our young paralegal who was about to start law school, sitting at a table playing no-stakes poker with Simon Latcovich and Senator Stevens while we waited for the jury to return a verdict.

At 4:05 that day, the jury sent a fourth and final note of the day:

> We have given the evidence consideration and have exhausted ourselves for this day. We are unanimous in requesting we break and continue deliberations [tomorrow].

That ended the second day of deliberations.

* * * * *

That evening, everybody was thrown a curveball. Judge Sullivan covened an emergency hearing to inform us that Juror No. 4 had told one of the U. S. Marshals that her father had died and that she needed to leave immediately for the funeral. She departed and left no forwarding information. What to do now?

The next day, the Court brought in the first alternate. Judge Sullivan asked some standard questions. Then he asked, "Is there anything that would prevent you from deliberating impartially?" The alternate juror paused, and then said, "No."

Judge Sullivan replied, "I'll have to ask you, you kind of paused or hesitated, and I just have to ask you why you paused or hesitated." Answer: "I was just—I paused because I was trying to think if I had already formed an opinion and I just wanted to make sure I hadn't."

* * * * *

Over the weekend, we waited for Juror No. 4 to reappear. She did not. On that Sunday evening, the judge replaced Juror No. 4 with the first alternate, Juror No. 11.

* * * * *

Believe it or not, the law provides that when a juror is replaced, the deliberations have to start over. In theory, it is as if they never started to consider the case. The jury theoretically began deliberations anew on Monday morning, October 28. At 3:15 that afternoon, the jury sent a note saying they had reached a unanimous verdict.

The jury entered the room, the courtroom deputy read the verdict form while I stood next to Senator Stevens. Guilty on all counts. The Senator's eyes filled with tears. Mine did too.

* * * * *

It was pandemonium as we left the courthouse. The marshals, professional as always, cleared a path for the Senator to our waiting van. Leaving the building, Brendan took the Senator by the arm, thereby breaking Senator Hutchison's rule. Brendan was determined to stand by the Senator at his worst moment. A photograph of Brendan and the Senator exiting the courthouse was on the front page of the *Washington Post* the next day.

While we left the courthouse in our van, the Acting Attorney General for the Criminal Division, Matthew Friedrich, rushed to the scene to hold a press conference on the courthouse steps. He said, "The U.S. Department of Justice is proud of our team, not just for the trial but for the investigation leading to it."

I'm not suggesting that Acting Assistant Attorney General Friedrich was involved in the misconduct, but for him to claim that the U.S. Department of Justice was "proud" of its prosecution team was offensive. The judge had repeatedly found the prosecution team to have engaged in misconduct. Sure, the jury had found the Senator guilty after the government was caught cheating repeatedly. And they had managed to keep the case from getting dismissed. So far. And I understood the instinct of a leader to praise one's troops. But the Department of Justice's performance at trial was nothing of which to be "proud."

To express pride in unethical prosecutors after a fiasco of a trial was over the top and unbecoming of the United States Department of Justice. The Acting Attorney General had completely ignored Judge Sullivan's criticism of the case.

We were contemplating whether to send the letter we had written. Could writing to the Attorney General backfire? The press conference made our decision easy. The notion that the Department was proud of its team was something that could not stand. We decided to sleep on it, and if we still thought it was the right thing to do, send it the next morning. I went home to try to sleep, but could not.

Our team met the next day with the Senator and Bill Phillips. We were unanimous in our decision to send the letter. We did not discuss who would sign the letter. After we disbanded, Brendan called and told me that he would sign the letter by himself. "This one is going to be hot," he said. "Whoever signs this letter may ruin their career. I can take the risk. My career has been long. You should not."

I called every member of the team and told them what Brendan had said. Every person on the team reported to me that they understood the risks and wanted to sign the letter. Some were still burdened with massive loans they had taken out to pay for law school. My eyes filled with tears as I told Brendan that every member of the team wanted to sign the letter. Brendan, who has a strong will, would not hear of it. He signed it alone. We hand-delivered his letter to the Attorney General's office that morning.

There was a clamor on Capitol Hill to have Senator Stevens removed from the Senate. To help the Senator beat that back, we gave a copy of our letter to him to give to a few Senators so that they would understand how bad the government's conduct had been. We redacted some grand jury testimony that the government might object to people seeing (even though we did not think there was anything wrong with making it public). Within the day, it was available to the public on the internet.

It began:

> We represent Senator Ted Stevens. We write to request that the Department of Justice commence a formal investigation into the repeated misconduct by federal prosecutors in connection with this case. We also request that the Department take immediate steps to preserve all information related to its investigation and prosecution of Senator Stevens.

We had four complaints: the prosecution's knowing presentation of false billing records to the jury; the prosecution's intentional concealment of *Brady* information; the prosecution's use of the "cover his ass" testimony, which prosecutors must have known was false; and the government's granting of excessive and unprecedented benefits to Bill Allen to coerce false testimony.

* * * * *

The letter was addressed to Attorney General Michael Mukasey. It was detailed—over 16 pages long. We offered to meet with him and his staff. We never heard back from him or any member of his staff.

Chapter 16

"F*#@ The Feds, Vote for Ted"

Ted Stevens spent the day after the verdict discussing legal strategy and getting organized to go to Alaska to campaign for an election that was now only six days away. The story of the government's misconduct was being widely reported in Alaska. He left the next day.

* * * * *

Back in my office, I watched the news coverage of the Senator's return to Alaska. Hundreds of Alaskans were waiting for the Senator when he arrived at Ted Stevens International Airport. They gave the Senator a hero's welcome. Signs read, "Welcome Senator Ted" and "Give 'em hell Ted." Many in the crowd wore tee-shirts that said, "I love you Uncle Ted." Others wore tee shirts that read, "F*#@ the Feds, Vote for Ted."

Prominent Alaskans such as U.S. Senator Lisa Murkowski and former Governor Bill Sheffield showed up to support their senior Senator. A popular Alaska radio host told the crowd: "I don't particularly like it when outsiders tell me what to do." He told the crowd that those in Washington who had attacked Senator Stevens could "kiss his Alaska moose-hunting behind."

The Senator told the crowd that he "naively trusted someone I thought was an honest friend, when he was neither honest nor a friend."

"He's a scoundrel!" a voice shouted back from the crowd. The Senator told the crowd that he had kept his promise to testify in his own defense, that he believed his disclosure forms were accurate when he filed them, and that he would never compromise the honor of Alaska or the Senate.

The Senator said that he wanted to continue to "represent Alaska in the Senate while my lawyers pursue the appeal to clear my name."

The people in the crowd shouted out, "We trust you Ted!" over and over.

He told them, "The verdict was driven by prosecutors who were willing to do anything to win. If I had had a fair trial in Alaska, I would have been acquitted." The crowd roared.

Back in Washington, D.C., I thought to myself that if he had had a fair trial *anywhere*, he would have been acquitted.

* * * * *

The Democratic Senatorial Campaign Committee ran very negative ads. One showed a painting of the founding fathers and reported that there had been 1897 Senators in American history, but only ten had been indicted. Ted Stevens became the eleventh.

One of the nastiest ads showed actors pretending to be FBI agents sitting in a van wearing headphones. They were supposed to be listening to wiretaps. One of the pretend FBI agents says, "He doesn't miss a perk. He even got a Viking Grill. Top of the line." Another pretend agent says, "I'm going to call the U.S. Attorney. He thinks he's above the law." A female pretend agent turns around and says, "And I voted for him," with disgust in her voice. It was powerful stuff.

200

* * * * *

But in the days just before the election, the Senator's campaign ran some powerful ads as well. A number of ads showed Alaskans from all walks of life talking about their respect for Ted Stevens. One had Alaskan after Alaskan repeat the mantra, "I'm sticking with Ted." Another emphasized how much Ted Stevens had meant to the state.

Danny Seybert of King Salmon said, "People talk about change. Ted Stevens has already been changing Alaska for over 40 years."

Gene Strong of Klukwan said, "He is down to earth and honest and forthright."

Buckwheat Donahue of Skagway says, "I trust his judgment. That's why I voted for him."

Roger Schnabel of Haines: "He loves Alaska."

Rob Babiak of Naknek: "We cannot afford to be without his presence in the Senate. We simply can't."

Steve Hynes of Skagway: "I wouldn't change out my Senator right now for a bet on anything."

And finally, Mary Ann Jones, of Naknek: "Without Ted, we're toast."

* * * * *

My favorite ad showed a lumberjack wielding an ax while he delivered this monologue:

You know, Ted Stevens has been there for Alaska.

Year after year.

Again and again.

Nobody's perfect, but them fellas in D.C., they worked Ted over pretty good.

Prosecutors withheld evidence that could have cleared him.

They offered other evidence that wasn't even true.

Those folks in Washington, they already cast their ballots. Soon

Alaskans will get to cast ours. Ted's always been there for us. Come Tuesday, I'm going to be there for Ted.

Ted Stevens had fought for respect for Alaska in Washington, D.C. Many Alaskans thought that throwing out Ted Stevens was throwing away the respect the state had earned in Washington.

The lumberjack ad said it all: "Prosecutors withheld evidence that could have cleared him. They offered other evidence that wasn't even true."

Juror No. 4 did not reappear before the verdict or for several days afterwards. We were troubled by that. Before leaving, she said her father had died. Steve Cady, a wonderfully conscientious associate, researched whether her father had in fact died. He researched newspapers, funeral homes, and death announcements in the juror's home town in North Carolina. He even visited the family burial plot and took a photograph of the site where the father was supposed to be buried. He concluded that the juror's father was very much still alive. But we didn't know quite what to do with that. She had lied to the court and was unfit for jury service.

Judge Sullivan issued an order for her to appear in court and explain why she had failed to respond to Judge Sullivan's "numerous and continuing attempts to communicate." The hearing was held on November 3, the day before the election. Judge Sullivan appointed a lawyer for Juror No. 4, who showed up in court that day. Juror No. 4's lawyer spoke:

> Your Honor, Juror No. 4 is present. And, Your Honor, Juror No. 4 has authorized me to make a brief statement on her behalf, which is, that she appreciates the Court's concern over her well-being, and she is fine. She also asked me to say that she apologizes to the court, that in fact her father did not die, that she was in a state of mind where she had to go to California as opposed to being able to continue to deliberate here, and the story about her father was just one that popped into her mind . . . as an excuse. So she apologizes for that as well.

The juror herself explained that she had left to attend a horse race in California called the Breeder's Cup. Judge Sullivan invited the parties to file papers if they would like. It was upsetting; a juror had lied to the judge and gotten away with it. That's not right. But there wasn't anything to do.

As Juror No. 4 walked to the subway, she was followed by a bevy of reporters. When asked what she thought about the Stevens case, she said, "He didn't do anything any other congressman or senator or governor or president has not done. He was guilty but these other ones are just as guilty if not more guilty." Not exactly a clear statement. Or a very reassuring one.

* * * * *

The Senator himself addressed the State of Alaska in a two minute ad that ran across the state. It began with a powerful statement from his daughter Lily. "Sometimes it takes knowing someone for a long time to know when they're speaking the truth," Lily said.

Senator Stevens himself then addressed the camera:

I love Alaska. Just like most of you, I raised my family and built my future here. These past few months have been difficult for all Alaskans including my family. I deeply regret that. From the bottom of my heart, I know that I am innocent. Everyone has a right to a fair trial and an appeal because sometimes innocent men are found guilty. This is one of those times. As my defense team clears my name, I assure you that I will continue to serve in the Senate while I earn your vote. Overzealous prosecutors violated the Constitution by knowingly withholding evidence confirming my innocence. Even the Court said the prosecution lied to the jury. . . My future is in God's hands. Alaska's future is in yours. . . I ask for and need your vote tomorrow because this election is all about Alaska.

* * * * *

On Tuesday, November 4, 2008, the United States elected Barak Obama as its first African-American President. I watched his victory speech from Chicago with great emotion. Regardless of how one felt about then-Senator Obama's proposed policies, it was an historic and important moment for our country.

But I was also trying to keep an eye on the election in Alaska. Bill Phillips was in Alaska and was sending text messages that the early returns were looking good. At 3:15 a.m., I received the following text message from Bill: "We're up by 4,100, Lead is holding. The bush is yet to report. The bush should be for Ted. A little early to call anything but we're in pretty good shape at this point. 60,000 ballots will be left to count over the next 2 weeks. We think we gain from the 60,000. Ted says hello and thanks again for all your help."

I went to bed not knowing the outcome. The next day, I learned that the Senator had won the *election day* voting by a margin of about 3,257 votes.

But Alaska has early voting and absentee voting. And there were still some questioned votes to count. Alaskans had cast about 224,000 votes on Election Day, but there were over 60,000 early and absentee votes to be counted. They would be counted beginning on the eighth day after the election. Bill Phillips told me conventional wisdom was that early and absentee votes tend to favor Republicans because wealthy and military families are more likely to vote early or absentee. Things looked good for the Senator's re-election chances.

But conventional wisdom did not hold true. The counting began on Wednesday, November 12. By the afternoon, it was reported that the Senator's lead had dropped to 971 votes. By later that day, Senator Stevens' opponent, Mark Begich, had a three vote lead. By the end of the day, the Senator was down 814 votes. By Friday, November 14, the Senator was down by 1,022 votes.

By Tuesday, November 18, 2008, the Senator was down 3,724 votes. Tuesday, November 18, 2008, was also the Senator's 85th birthday. His friends and staff had a birthday celebration at a Capitol Hill townhouse. Everybody who attended paid $20 at the door to make sure that there were no ethics issues. Craig Singer, Beth Stewart, Simon Latcovich and I attended. Senator Inouye expressed his love for Senator Stevens no matter what. There was a birthday cake and a lot of awkward small talk. Everyone knew the election was lost. We slipped out into the cold night and went back to the office.

Friends urged the Senator to ask for a recount. He declined to do so. Senator Stevens conceded the election that night after his eighty-fifth birthday celebration was over. "Given the number of ballots that remain to be counted, it is apparent the election has been decided and Mayor Begich has been elected. I wish Mayor Begich and his family well. My staff and I stand willing to help him prepare for his new position."

* * * * *

Two days later, the Senator gave his last speech on the floor of the United States Senate:

> I feel the same way now that I did in 1968. I really must pinch myself to fully understand that I am privileged to speak on the floor of the U.S. Senate. Coming from the boyhood I had, I could never even have dreamed of being here today. And home is where the heart is, Mr. President. If that is so, I have two homes—one is right here in this Chamber, and the other is my beloved State of Alaska. I must leave one to return to the other.
>
> My mission in life is not complete. I believe God will give me more opportunities to be of service to Alaska and to our Nation. And I look forward with glad heart and with confidence in his justice and mercy.
>
> I told members of the press yesterday that I don't have any rearview mirror. I look only forward, and I still see the day when I can remove the cloud that currently surrounds me.

The Senators on the floor and weeping staffers in the gallery gave him a standing ovation.

* * * * *

When Ted Stevens was defeated because of an illegal verdict, the balance of power in the Senate shifted—the loss of his seat gave the

Democrats a one-vote margin—a 60 vote majority that could pass any piece of legislation without it being blocked by a Republican filibuster. Having achieved a filibuster-proof majority, the Democratic Senate passed the Obama health care reform legislation on a straight party-line vote.

The illegal prosecution of Senator Stevens enabled passage of the most controversial legislation of the Obama administration. I take no stand on whether the Patient Protection and Affordable Care Act (a.k.a. ObamaCare) was good legislation or bad legislation. I do know that the legislation was controversial and that many Americans have strong feelings about it. And I know that a piece of legislation so controversial should not have been affected by an indictment that never should have been brought, much less a trial in which prosecutors cheated over and over again.

* * * * *

At 4:47 a.m. on November 15th, more than a week after election day and more than two weeks after the verdict, our firm received an extraordinary fax, a letter to Judge Sullivan—with copies to the prosecutor and to the Stevens defense team. It began, "My name is David Allen Anderson and I was the final prosecution witness in Senator Ted Stevens trial. I am writing this letter to you to clarify my testimony during the trial. I testified to the fact that there was never immunity for me or my family and friends. That is simply not true."

Anderson reported to Judge Sullivan that he was "instructed" by the government how to "sugar coat" the agreement that he and his family would not be prosecuted and how to get that agreement "swept under the rug during the trial as [the prosecution team] had told the court just the opposite." Anderson also said that a letter written by prosecutors in which they stated he had lied about the immunity status of himself and his family was "not true" and "completely false."

Anderson's allegations had the ring of truth to them. Defense lawyers often suspect that the government makes secret immunity deals with witnesses. This can be done with a wink and a nod or in coded language. We did not know whether Anderson's allegations were true or not, but one thing was certain: somebody was lying—either government witness David Anderson or the federal prosecutors.

Anderson made another allegation that rang true. He said, "[T]he prosecution had always known where I spent my time and how," and that he "was told by the Department of Justice they did not have to provide the defense with my testimony from the grand jury until 24 hours before I took the stand."

This, of course, proved our point that the government knowingly put on false testimony when they introduced business records indicating that Anderson had worked on the cabin for many hours when in fact he was in another state. This confirmed our belief that they weren't going to call him as a witness because they didn't want to produce his grand jury testimony (which would prove that the time records were false).

* * * * *

Reacting to this new information, Brendan sent another letter to the Attorney General asking for "an immediate and thorough investigation," and requesting "that those responsible for this wrongdoing be appropriately dealt with. . . . In addition, should the impartial investigation confirm the facts delineated in detail in my letters, I request that the government take action to dismiss this case, on its own motion. We are prepared to make available to an impartial investigator voluminous materials that support the facts set out in my correspondence. The trial of Senator Stevens was irretrievably tainted, and the Department of Justice has the obligation to redress this manifest injustice."

Once again, we never received a response.

* * * * *

We also made a motion to Judge Sullivan to hold a hearing to get to the bottom of Anderson's allegations. But, just when I thought I couldn't be any more surprised by the unfairness of these prosecutors, they submitted a *secret* response to Judge Sullivan. The government notified us that they had submitted a response but the contents of the response were not disclosed to the defense or the public.

The government was essentially saying: *Do not worry about it; we are convinced that Dave Andersen is now lying. You cannot see it, but we have given proof to Judge Sullivan.*

We complained harshly about this tactic, citing legal precedent that, "particularly in criminal cases," such secret filings "are contrary to the most basic concepts of American justice and should not be permitted except possibly in the most extraordinary cases involving national security."

Judge Sullivan did not consider the secret filing, and the government withdrew it when we called their bluff.

I learned one important lesson from the Dave Anderson episode. Open trials and media coverage of those trials can give citizens the courage to speak up. Citizens are often scared to death of the government: the I-don't-want-to-get-involved syndrome. But when an independent judge like Emmet Sullivan stands up to prosecutors and demonstrates that they are not infallible, or it somehow becomes known that something very unfair is going on, oftentimes citizens are emboldened to speak out. That was about to happen again—but this time from a credible source deeply embedded in the prosecution team.

* * * * *

Filing a motion for a new trial is standard procedure for a defendant who has lost a criminal trial. Our motion for a new trial was due by the close of business on Friday, December 5. Motions for new trial are almost never successful with the trial judge, but it is usually necessary to raise the issues with the trial judge before taking them up on appeal with appellate judges.

We had several issues that we wanted to raise and some we wanted to highlight, including, among others, the lack of a jury instruction on the value of the renovations and separation of powers. Our team had been hard at work preparing the motion. Although we knew that such motions are rarely successful, given the government's misconduct in our case and David Anderson's recent allegations we thought it likely that ours would be and we would get a new trial. Judge Sullivan had not even scheduled a sentencing date in our case, he was so concerend by what he had seen.

Filing dates scare defense lawyers to death: if they miss a filing date, they may be deemed to have waived their arguments, both before the trial court and before the court of appeals. This was uppermost in our minds as we were putting the finishing touches on our new trial motion, readying it for a filing before 5:00 p.m. when the following email message popped into my email in-box:

> The government writes the Court to inform it that we expect to make a filing under seal next week. This filing relates to information received on Tuesday that may raise privacy and confidentiality issues that we are still sorting out. While we believe the information will have no impact on the verdict, we anticipate a filing nonetheless as a cautionary measure.

What? Judge Sullivan convened a conference call at 4:00 p.m. to find out what was going on. Prosecutors declined to say much more than what was in their email. They repeated that they just had to sort out some privacy issues. Judge Sullivan judiciously offered us more time to file the motion now due in less than an hour. Worried that an appellate Court might someday find that we had waived our arguments, we politely declined the offer and filed anyway. The government again assured the Court and us that whatever information it had was no big deal, and said they would file something on Wednesday.

The following Wednesday, we received another email. This one informed us that they were not yet ready to file. The next day, the government did make a filing. It was filed under seal—meaning it was hidden from the public. Here is how it began:

> The United States of America, by and through its undersigned

209

attorneys, hereby respectfully files this Memorandum and a redacted copy of a self-styled whistleblower complaint, authored by [FBI] Special Agent Chad Joy with the court. A copy of the redacted complaint and this accompanying memorandum have been provided to defense counsel.

As explained herein, the government does not believe that any of the allegations contained in the Joy complaint affect the integrity of the trial proceedings or the verdicts in this case. One of the case agents in the Stevens prosecution has filed a self-styled whistleblower complaint against another case agent. Neither case agent testified as a witness in the Stevens trial. Given the fact that neither one of these individuals testified as witnesses in the Stevens trial, as well as other reasons mentioned herein, the Joy complaint—even if all allegations set forth therein are assumed to be true—does not affect the integrity of the trial proceedings or the verdicts. Nevertheless, out of an abundance of caution, a redacted copy of the Joy complaint is being shared with the court and defense counsel.

One thing I had already learned in this case and others was that when prosecutors say that they are making a disclosure out of an "abundance of caution," chances are good that the disclosure is going to be a bombshell. And that's exactly what this was. I skipped past the government's downplay and got to the Joy complaint itself, which had been filed by Chad Joy, an FBI agent.

Joy wrote: "As a co-case agent on Polar Pen for the past five years, I have witnessed or learned of serious violations of policy, rules, and procedures as well as possible criminal violations."

He was talking about possible criminal violations *by the prosecution team*, not the citizens they were investigating. Was this a joke? How could the government team say that the integrity of the trial was not affected? Were they going to call their own agent a liar?

The complaint was hard to read because the government redaction team had been at work again. More than half of the document was redacted so that we could not read it. But even though more than half of the document was redacted, it contained some douseys.

First, Joy believed that members of his prosecution team had "intentionally redacted *Brady/Jencks* material that defense counsel was entitled to receive." So much for "good faith mistakes."

Second, Joy said that prosecutor Nick Marsh "inappropriately created a scheme to relocate [Rocky Williams who] was also subpoenaed by the defense." According to Joy, "After the final preparatory session [with Williams], prosecutors decided Williams was not a witness the prosecutors wanted to use." It wasn't done for Rocky's health after all.

Third, Joy said that prosecutor Marsh had argued that a 302 written by Special Ageny Pluta should not be turned over, even though it contained exculpatory information under *Brady* and had to be turned over under *Jencks* since Pluta was going to be a witnesss. According to Joy, Marsh was "absolutely against" turning it over. This confirmed my belief as to why we had gotten 302s during Bill Allen's testimony.

Fourth, Joy reported that Kepner had inappropriate relationships with the media, suggesting that she had inappropriately leaked confidential information to the media. The irony that the government was trying to keep the allegations against it from being made public was not lost on me.

Fifth, Joy complained that Special Agent Kepner had inappropriate dealings with Bill Allen. She met with him alone in her hotel room and she wore a skirt as a surprise present for Allen during his testimony. (He pointed out that she does not usually wear skirts.) Joy said that he knew that Kepner repeatedly shared confidential information with Allen that should not have been shared and stated his belief that she may have communicated with Allen about the underaged sex investigation of him.

Our first job was to get access to the entire complaint. Hadn't the government learned that redacting was a dangerous practice? It was like Groundhog Day. We simply recycled our brief from the

Anderson affair, and submitted it to Judge Sullivan, who quickly agreed that the full complaint should be made available to us. Upon receiving the complete complaint, we learned that Joy had also alleged that the lead FBI agent was accepting improper gifts from somebody she was investigating in Operation Polar Pen. You couldn't make this up.

The next step was to have the Joy Complaint filed publicly. Recent experiences had taught me that almost all criminal proceedings should take place in public, especially when the government's conduct is in question. When I thought back to the government's public relations dirty tricks and the fact that one of Joy's charges was that the government was illegally leaking to the media, I was beside myself. Talk about two sets of rules. They did not want the same rules to apply to them. But more importantly, I knew that public access was the right thing to do.

We filed a brief that began: "This country has always had a strong tradition of access to judicial proceedings. This is especially true in criminal cases, where the Sixth Amendment guarantees the accused a public trial and where First Amendment public access concerns are paramount. The public has an especially strong interest in this criminal case, and Senator Stevens—whom the government publicly vilified—has a compelling interest in the immediate disclosure of exculpatory information.

"Having prosecuted Senator Stevens in the most public manner imaginable, and having lost no opportunity to publicize its allegations against him, the government unfortunately takes a very different position when the prosecution team is the subject of allegations of serious wrongdoing."

The government, for its part, argued that the entire complaint should be hidden from the public. Their "most important" argument was that Joy had requested confidential treatment.

* * * * *

On its marble facade, The Newseum, the news and journalism

212

museum located on Pennsylvania Avenue just blocks from my office, has a 10 story-tall reproduction of the First Amendment, and I drew inspiration driving by it. We were doing the right thing. Public access did matter; it was a fundamental principal of our founders. And the public deserved to know what an FBI agent himself was saying. It's too bad, I thought to myself, that the voters of Alaska did not know about this before the election.

Conscientious as always, Judge Sullivan ruled that the complaint would be disclosed publicly, but he ruled that Agent Joy's identity would remain confidential because the government had repeatedly represented that it had determined him a "whistleblower" which entitled him to confidential treatment.

On December 22, 2008, we filed a motion for a new trial. It began:

> A whistleblower complaint submitted by a Special Agent with the FBI now confirms what the defense has long believed and alleged: the government cheated and lied in order to obtain a verdict against Senator Ted Stevens. The whistleblower reports "many serious problems . . . encountered in the recent trial of U.S. Senator Ted Stevens" and that he or she "witnessed or learned of serious violations of policy, rules, and procedures as well as possible criminal violations" by members of the prosecution team. These serious violations include fostering an improper relationship with the government's star witness (whom the defense contends fabricated the most important testimony in the case), intentionally withholding exculpatory information from the defense, and scheming to keep an important witness away from the defense after the government's attempts to prepare that witness to testify went badly. The new whistleblower complaint shows unmistakably that government representative lied to the Court or stood by silently while other members of the prosecution team represented facts to the Court that simply were not true.

Chapter
17

Contempt

Three days after Christmas, Rocky Williams's mother-in-law called the Stevens family to tell them that Rocky was fading in and out of consciousness, that she thought he only had about a week of life left, and that Williams cared very much for the Stevens family. We took this as an invitation to try to talk to him one last time, so we called his mother-in-law. It was too late. Rocky had died of liver and kidney failure on December 29, the day after his mother-in-law's call to us.

* * * * *

On January 14, 2009, the government informed us they were preparing an opposition to our motion to dismiss—and that they wanted to use the name of the whistleblower in their papers. This was a complete reversal of their previous position.

It was also another mysterious move by the government. I could only conclude that they wanted to use his name so they could attack him by name. But if they did that, then we wanted to refile our motion to dismiss. It wasn't fair that we had to treat him as an anonymous whistleblower using gender neutral pseudonyms, but the government could attack him by name. So we had a hearing before Judge Sullivan on the issue.

Our position was simple: if the government could name the whistleblower, so could we. The government didn't think that was necessary. Judge Sullivan said that he agreed with us, but wanted

214

to take a break before concluding for the day. Judge Sullivan came back after the break with a question for the government which triggered a lengthy dialogue between the judge and the government.

Judge Sullivan said, "Let me just ask you this question, though. When did your office learn that he was denied—that the person was denied whistleblower protection?"

Brenda Morris replied, "It was sometime after our sealed hearing, Judge. Or is that correct? Did we learn—no, I think it was."

"I need to know that," said Judge Sullivan.

At which point, prosecutor Welch chimed in with, "It remained unclear. I think at one point he got a letter but he was afforded the right to re-amend the letter that he had issued."

Judge Sullivan asked, "Was he told that he was denied status before the hearing? That last hearing?"

Morris: "I believe, Judge."

Judge Sullivan: "I don't want to guess about this. I need to know. "

Welch: "Then we need to be clear about it."

Judge Sullivan: "Well, I mean, that's something that the Court should have known because we stayed up almost 24 hours getting that opinion out and doing a lot of other work operating on the assumption that, you know, this man is seeking protection. The Court was extremely sensitive to that, extremely sensitive to that, but I need to know the answer to that. I need to know it now. So if you get someone on the phone, I need to know the answer to that."

Morris: "We can contact [Chad Joy's lawyer]. He would be the best person to know."

Judge Sullivan: "Well, the office of the General Counsel would know. You can contact the Government attorneys. You can call your office."

Morris: "When they alerted Mr. Joy?"

Judge Sullivan: "I need to know when the Public Integrity [Section] knew that he had been refused whistleblower status."

Morris: "Judge, I would have that information on my computer because I was the one that reached out to the Office of Professional Responsibility [known as OPR] to find that information out and they sent me a letter that had been sent to Mr. Joy."

Judge Sullivan: "Does someone—your secretary, someone have access?

215

I just need—well, can't you call the OIG [Office of Inspector General]?"

Morris: "Yeah. Actually I can call OPR [Office of Professional Responsibility], the individual who I spoke with at OPR."

Judge Sullivan kept pressing: "I want a copy of that letter also."

Morris: "I have that. I have an extra copy because it's on my computer. But the copy—and that's what was explained to me from OPR that—because I was keeping OPR apprised of what was going on here, and in apprising OPR—it was after the hearing when we—because after I apprised OPR of what was going on here, that's when I was informed that there was a—that Mr. Joy had been given a letter as early as December 4 telling him he had been denied whistleblower status."

Judge Sullivan: "Why wasn't I told that? I was never told that?"

Morris: "I didn't know that, Judge. I didn't know that."

"Somebody knew that," said Judge Sullivan, whose patience was wearing thin. "That office knew that. We nearly pulled our heads off getting that opinion out, operating under the assumption that his whistleblower status was up in the air. That would have been a dramatic revelation had we known that he'd been denied whistleblower status by the Government."

Morris: "Well,—we didn't know it. The Public Integrity Section did not know."

Judge Sullivan: "They kept it from you?"

Morris: "Yeah. The whole thing was kept from us, Judge. As a matter of fact, the only thing—"

Judge Sullivan: "But you had nine days to investigate this, though. You got the complaint and the Government took nine days before your office told me, right?"

Morris: "Right, and that's true."

Judge Sullivan: "During the nine days, you didn't learn that he'd been denied whistleblower status?"

Morris: "No, sir. Yes, sir. It wasn't that we were investigating—"

Judge Sullivan: "Why don't you come up to the podium."

Morris: "Yes, sir. It wasn't that we were investigating as much as we were trying to make the determination of what we could do. It was a matter of our office working with OPR. In my understanding, and I guess Bill Welch would be better to explain how it came to our attention because it looks like the letter went from FBI Anchorage to

Headquarters, from Headquarters to our Main OPR, to OPR to Main Justice, to Main Justice then to Bill Welch and then to us, the trial team. So it was—"

Judge Sullivan interrupted the lead prosecutor: "I find it incomprehensible that your office didn't know prior to the hearing that this man had been denied whistleblower status. . . ."

After yet another lengthy exchange, it was clear the Judge had heard enough. Clearly he was not getting the answers he needed. In a stern tone he said, "I want a declaration from the Attorney General. I want his signature on this declaration. I want to find out what—how the Government handled this whole matter on whistleblower status, what OIG did when the complaint came in. I want copies of correspondence from OIG to the complainant. I want copies of all correspondence from OIG to OPR and to your office, to Anchorage, to anyone who had any knowledge about this. I want to know what your office knew and when it knew it.

"I find it astounding. If your office knew this man had been denied whistleblower status, it had an obligation to tell me before we had that hearing. You certainly—if you learned about it afterwards, as soon after you learned about it, you had an obligation to let the Court know."

Morris: "Judge, again, I just want to make sure that it's not OIG as much as—"

Judge Sullivan: "I don't care who it is."

Morris: "—OPR."

Judge Sullivan: "I don't care who it is. I want the Attorney General's declaration about what happened, everything that happened with respect to this whistleblower issue, what each arm of the Government knew, when it knew it, what it knew and why I wasn't told relevant information. Today is Wednesday. I want it on my desk by noon on Friday. I'm not going to extend the time."

Welch: "If I may, with all due respect, Your Honor."

Judge Sullivan: "I know he's leaving office, but I want his signature on this declaration before he leaves office."

Welch: "We certainly can't make any promises. We're going to communicate exactly what the Court has said."

Judge Sullivan: "I want it done."

Mr. Welch: "I understand."

Judge Sullivan: "And the fact that he's leaving office next week is not an excuse. This is the most important matter on his desk right now. I want it done by noon on Friday. I want answers to my question, and I want the declaration of the Attorney General before he leaves office, and I'm not going to extend the time."

Lest there be any misunderstanding, Judge Sullivan then added, "*This* Attorney General, not the next one, this one."

* * * * *

Late in the next day, the government filed a motion to reconsider. The basis of the motion was that Joy *was* a whistleblower after all. The government brief read, "The Department has never determined that Agent Joy is not entitled to whistleblower protection, and has never so advised him. We apologize for the error."

I couldn't believe it. The government was flip-flopping again. Surely this move would backfire. I sent the team home. But Brendan said we needed to respond. So I stayed late and wrote a response. Simon Latcovich arrived early the next morning to fill in some details and Craig Singer, always our editor, reviewed it quickly. Here is what we wrote:

> The government never wanted the public to know that one of its own agents, Chad Joy, had submitted a whistleblower complaint asserting that he "witnessed or learned of serious violations of policy, rules, and procedures as well as possible criminal violations" by members of the team that prosecuted Senator Stevens. In its efforts to convince the Court that these allegations should be hidden from the public, the government "strenuously argued that [Agent Joy's] complaint should not be made public based on whistleblower and privacy concerns." The Court disagreed, but redacted Agent Joy's name out of deference to the government's (and Joy's counsel's) representations.

> The defense was forced to prepare its motion to dismiss using generic terms and without using Agent Joy's name. When the time came for the government to respond to the motion to

dismiss, the government did not want to play by the same rules. It apparently wants to attack Agent Joy in public by name. In order to achieve that end, the government told the Court that Agent Joy "does not qualify for whistleblower status" after all and that he "was denied whistleblower protection." Clearly, when it suited its strategic goal to try to keep Agent Joy's complaint confidential and hidden from the public, the government relied on Agent Joy's whistleblower status. But when the government wanted to attack Agent Joy by name in public, the government claimed that Agent Joy was not a whistleblower after all.

Justifiably concerned about this inconsistency, the Court ordered the Attorney General to "sign a declaration under oath. . . and provide copies of all relevant correspondence, detailing precisely (1) who within every office of the Department of Justice knew about the complaint filed by Agent Joy, (2) what those individuals and offices knew, and (3) when those individuals and offices received the relevant information. The Court further ordered that the "declaration must also address all decisions, correspondence, and communication within the Department of Justice related to Agent Joy's status as a whistleblower and the determination that he was not entitled to whistleblower protection."

After the Court issued its Order, the government changed its position once again, telling the Court on January 15, 2009, that Agent Joy is a whistleblower after all and that he was never denied whistleblower protection. Confronted with the falsity of its representations on January 14, 2009, the government now states that "government counsel was mistaken" and "apologizes" for their "error." This is a familiar refrain from this team of Public Integrity prosecutors, calling to mind the Court's inquiry early in these proceedings, "How does the Court have any confidence that the Public Integrity Section has integrity?"

The pattern is unmistakable. Over and over again the government has been caught in false representations and otherwise

219

failing to perform its duties under the Constitution and the Rules. And over and over again, when caught, the government has claimed that it has simply made good faith mistakes. When the government failed to produce Rocky Williams's exculpatory grand jury testimony, the government claimed that this testimony was immaterial. When the government sent Mr. Williams back to Alaska without advising the defense or the Court, the government asserted that it was acting in "good faith." When the government affirmatively redacted exculpatory statements from FBI Form 302s, it claimed that "it was just a mistake." When government counsel told the Court that Allen had not been re-interviewed the day before a hearing on its *Brady* disclosures, this was a "mistaken understanding." When the government failed to turn over exculpatory statements from Dave Anderson, it claimed that they were immaterial.

When the government failed to turn over a critical grand jury transcript containing exculpatory information, it claimed that it was "inadvertent." When the government used "business records" that the government undeniably knew were false, it said that it was unintentional.

The defense (and the Court) was forced to spend hundreds of hours dealing with these "mistakes" in the middle of trial. It strains credulity to believe that these were all good faith mistakes, and the defense submits that an evidentiary hearing will demonstrate that they were not (if the Court is not convinced already). Even after getting caught making one so-called mistaken statement after another, the government as late as Wednesday, January 14, 2009, was still recklessly (at best) making false representations to the Court. The conclusion is clear: neither the defense nor the Court can rely upon the representations of government counsel from the Office of Public Integrity. The defense submits that the Attorney General should be required to comply with the Court's Order of January 14, 2009. The Court and the defense are entitled to know who knew what and when.

* * * * *

One hour later, the judge responded. After quoting our papers at length, he denied the government's motion to reconsider.

* * * * *

The government's next move was to make an emergency appeal. Craig and Simon worked on the appeal while I took a long-planned trip to Florida with my family. Frankly, I was expecting a last minute pardon of Senator Stevens as the Bush Administration ended. It is a modern tradition that presidents wait until the end of their administration to issue most pardons. If ever there was a candidate for a pardon it was Ted Stevens. We had not made a formal request—that is too lengthy a process—but the rumors out of the White House were that things looked good.

When the government told us it was going to file an appeal on the evening of Friday, January 17, Simon was worried that the appeal would ruin dinner plans he had made with friends. Craig knew better. He told Simon that the government would not get their papers filed until well after dinner, which turned out to be true. Simon went to dinner and then stayed up all night preparing a first draft of a response to the government's appeal. Craig took over the next day, edited Simon's draft and got it filed. Simon and Craig wrote a great brief, but on Saturday, January 18, 2009, the U.S. Court of Appeals for the District of Columbia Circuit delayed enforcement of Judge Sullivan's order for the Attorney General to file his declaration, saying it needed more time. This was totally understandable.

* * * * *

Chief Justice John Roberts swore in Barack Obama at noon on January 20, making Mr. Obama the 44th President of the United States of America. I heard the night before and again the next morning that there would be no pardon after all. Pardons had apparently become too controversial. And President George W. Bush must have believed that the system would right the wrong that had

221

been done to the Senator for whom he had recently thrown a White House dinner to celebrate his 40th year in the U.S. Senate. I watched from my hotel room in Florida knowing that no pardon had been issued and that Attorney General Michael Mukasey had left office without doing what Judge Sullivan had ordered him to do. After the President had taken the oath, I sent an email to the team: "At this hour we begin a new chapter in our fight to vindicate Ted Stevens." And then I set a team meeting for the next day.

Our team wasn't alone in worrying about the case over the Inaugural weekend. Judge Sullivan issued an order the next day acknowledging that he could no longer direct the Attorney General in office during the Stevens prosecution to provide a declaration. Instead he ordered the Department to turn over every email and piece of paper in the Department regarding who knew what and when about the whistleblower status of Agent Joy. The materials were ordered to be provided to Judge Sullivan *and the defense* by January 30.

* * * * *

On January 30, 2009, the prosecutors provided the documents to Judge Sullivan but did not provide them to the defense.

We submitted a motion to have the Department of Justice held in contempt.

At a hearing on February 14, Judge Sullivan asked why the documents hadn't been produced to the defense. When a junior government lawyer could not provide a reason, Judge Sullivan held the senior lawyers in contempt.

Obviously displeased, the Judge said, "It's outrageous for the Department of Justice, the largest law firm on the planet, to come before a federal judge and say, yeah Judge, you know, we recognized your order, we realized it and we haven't gotten around to complying with it, and we really don't have a good faith reason or any reason for not having complied with it. That is not acceptable in this court and that's the reason why I'm adjudicating these attorneys in contempt."

* * * * *

I had a growing feeling that maybe "the cloud" surrounding the Senator would be lifted. Our post-trial motions had not yet been heard by Judge Sullivan. And I had to believe that he would give the Senator a new trial, at the least.

Chapter
18

New Prosecutors

Two days after Judge Sullivan held the original prosecutors in contempt, the Department of Justice replaced them with three new prosecutors who did not work in the Public Integrity Section. The new senior prosecutor was Paul O'Brien, head of DOJ's Narcotics and Dangerous Drug Section. Drug wars in Mexico were raging, but apparently the Department thought that it needed somebody fresh with unquestioned integrity to fix things

Assisting O'Brien were David L. Jaffe, the Deputy Chief of the Domestic Security Section and William Stuckwisch, a senior trial attorney in the Fraud Section. All three were stars in the Department of Justice. This was good news. It took Judge Sullivan holding some of the original team of prosecutors in contempt, but at least (and at last) somebody was paying attention at the Department of Justice.

Without delay, the new prosecutors began to disclose documents to us that we had not seen before. In fact, O'Brien and his team provided over a thousand pages of new documents over the course of the next few weeks. I had assumed that the new prosecutors would begin doing what the government usually does, which is to try to protect the verdict. That assumption quickly changed.

I was meeting with some federal law clerks who were considering working for Williams & Connolly when I got a call from our receptionist, Sharon Brown, who said, "Mr. O'Brien is here in the lobby and wants to see you." I could not remember another time in my career when a prosecutor had shown up to see me without an appointment. I excused myself from the law clerks and headed for the lobby.

Mr. O'Brien wasted no time: "I have some more documents to give to you. There's one I wanted to point out to you." After quickly thumbing through the set of documents, he pointed to an email in which four prosecutors were talking about an ongoing interview of Bill Allen. The date was April 15, 2008, four days after we produced the "it has to be done right" note.

"We are looking for a 302 of this interview," he said, "and so far, we haven't found one. But we're still looking." After months of dirty tricks, Paul O'Brien was a breath of fresh air.

* * * * *

I hustled to my office to read the email, which was actually a chain of emails. The first was from Nicholas Marsh. "Am I pushing too hard?" he asked his colleagues while he was still interviewing Allen.

A few minutes later, Joe Bottini responded, "Let's call it for today. . ."

Marsh wrote back, "O.K. Thanks."

Prosecutor Ed Sullivan wrote back, "We may want to talk to [Allen's lawyer, Bob] Bundy immediately afterwards and get him to push BA [Bill Allen] on this issue and get him to focus. BA's position makes no sense and is directly contradicted by his contemporaneous acts. I'd also like to push BA re: why TS [Ted Stevens] is asking for a bill in 10/02 and 11/02. The timing is bothering me. Is it [because] the project is out of control? Only VECO guys are on the site? Neighbors are snooping around? Public is about to find out?"

Marsh wrote back, "Re #2, do you think it's probably that his friend Torricelli withdrew from his reelection campaign a week before the 10/02 note?"

Ed Sullivan replied, "Could be. Could also be that it's a wink and a nod—that he knows BA won't send him an invoice, but he can paper the file. Could be a lot of things. I was hoping BA might be able to shed some light on the timing/context."

＊ ＊ ＊ ＊ ＊

They were clearly talking about the Senator's "it just has to be done right" note to Bill Allen. And clearly they did not like what Allen was telling them about it in April 2008. Until Paul O'Brien delivered this email, we had no clue that there was a government interview of Bill Allen a few days after we provided the note to the government, even though all interviews were supposed to be recorded in 302s and Judge Sullivan had ordered that all 302s be provided to the defense.

The next day, O'Brien delivered handwritten notes of the April 15th interview of Bill Allen. This is what Assistant U.S. Attorney James Goeke had jotted down:

- Note to Bill from [Stevens]

- Refers to Toricelli and [Stevens] needing a bill for the work

- Allen does not recall Bob P[ersons] talking to him about a bill for Ted S.

- If [Stevens] had pressed—would have created an invoice

- Rocky [Williams] and Dave [Anderson] screwed this up b/c always drunk

＊ ＊ ＊ ＊ ＊

My reaction when I saw the notes was simple: case over. They were the reverse of what Allen had said in court. Forget all the gigabytes of irrelevant junk they had given us. Here it was. We now had conclusive proof that the "covering his ass" testimony was fabricated, just as we had said from the minute we'd heard it. Finally we had the proof. When first asked, Allen didn't recall anything about Persons saying that Ted Stevens was just "covering his ass." The covering his ass statement was clearly fabricated. Recently. Just as we had believed from the minute we heard it. Finally, we had the proof. In a white collar case, this was as close as you get to a smoking gun.

* * * * *

The next day, O'Brien's team found some notes of prosecutor Ed Sullivan:

- [Allen] recalls receiving note from [Stevens]. Doesn't recall talking to [Bob Persons] re: giving bill to [Stevens]. . .

- [Allen] not saying it didn't happen, just doesn't recall.

- Doesn't recall having VECO put bill together. . .

- But if they had done the work efficiently, then FMV [Fair Market Value] = $80,000 (estimate)

These notes were also the 100 percent opposite of the most important testimony in the case. There was no way the Department of Justice could defend its ill-gotten verdict any longer.

* * * * *

At 5:30 in the morning of April 1st, 2009, Michael Byrne, a former associate at Williams & Connolly who had moved to my home state of Missouri to become a public defender, switched on his radio to listen to the news on National Public Radio. What he heard caused him to bolt out of bed, pull out his Blackberry and send us an email:

"Congratulations! I just heard that they're dismissing the Stevens case."

I got in the car without checking my Blackberry that morning and was driving down the Rock Creek Parkway on my way to the office at 7:00 a.m. when the phone rang. It was Simon Latcovich. "Have you heard the news?" Simon asked. "What news?" I responded. "NPR is reporting that DOJ is dismissing the Stevens case." I spilled my coffee as I hit the accelerator.

As soon as I got to the building I hustled to Brendan's office. Michael Byrne's email had arrived shortly after 6:30 EST, and soon after that our in-boxes and voicemails were flooded. What was going on? Was it true? Reporters were calling and emailing us like crazy, but we hadn't heard a word ourselves, other than what NPR was reporting.

Paul O'Brien called at 8:30 a.m. Brendan, Simon Latcovich, and I had been scheduled to meet with him and the new team of prosecutors at 10:00 that morning. We had asked for the meeting to urge them to drop the case voluntarily in light of the new evidence. As O'Brien had readily agreed to the meeting, I thought the chances good that after listening to us, he would do just that.

After confirming that the government was in fact dismissing the case, he apologized for the fact that we'd learned about it from the media. "That's not what I had intended," he said. I believed him. To my knowledge, everything Paul O'Brien and the other two new prosecutors had done was honorable.

We called the Senator, who was in Anchorage where it was not yet 5:00 a.m. I told him what was happening, and he gave me his authority to make a statement. He thanked me, and said he was going back to sleep. I thought to myself that it had finally turned out the way he'd always thought it would. Exactly as he had predicted in his farewell address on the Senate Floor months earlier, the cloud had lifted.

A bit later, the government filed a motion which read in part:

> The government recently discovered that a witness interview of Bill Allen took place on April 15, 2008. While no memorandum of interview or agent notes exist for this interview, notes taken by two prosecutors who participated in the April 15 interview reflect that Bill Allen was asked about a note dated October 6, 2002, that was sent from the defendant to Bill Allen. The note was introduced at trial as Government Exhibit 495 and was referred to as the "Torricelli note." The notes of the April 15 interview indicate that Bill Allen said . . . that he (Bill Allen) did not recall talking to Bob Persons regarding giving a bill to the defendant. This statement by Allen during the April 15 interview was inconsistent with Allen's recollection at

trial, where he described a conversation with Persons about the Torricelli Note. In addition, the April 15 interview notes indicate that Allen estimated that if his workers had performed efficiently, the fair market value of the work his corporation performed on defendant's Girdwood chalet would have been $80,000. Defendant Stevens was not informed prior to or during trial of the statements by Bill Allen on April 15, 2008. This information could have been used by the defendant to cross-examine Bill Allen and in arguments to the jury. . . .

Given the facts of this particular case, the Government believes that granting a new trial is in the interest of justice. The Government has further determined that, based on the totality of circumstances and in the interest of justice, it will not seek a new trial. Accordingly . . . the Government moves to set aside the verdict and dismiss the indictment. . . .

* * * * *

Though O'Brien and his team had acted honorably, somebody at the Justice Department had leaked the story. Some people were saying that the Department of Justice simply wasn't going to go after Ted Stevens again because of his age. That wasn't right, and it wasn't fair. So we went to work on a statement of our own. Here is what we wrote:

We are grateful to learn that Attorney General Eric Holder has decided to drop all charges against Senator Ted Stevens. That decision is justified by the extraordinary evidence of government corruption in the prosecution of Senator Stevens.

This jury verdict was obtained unlawfully. The government disregarded the Constitution, the Federal Rules of Criminal Procedure, and well-established case law such as *Brady v. Maryland*, *Giglio v. United States*, and *United States v. Safavian*, which require the government to reveal to the defense all evidence that demonstrates the innocence of the accused.

The misconduct of government prosecutors, and one or more FBI agents, was stunning. Not only did the government fail to

229

disclose evidence of innocence, but instead intentionally hid that evidence and created false evidence that they provided to the defense.

The government also presented false evidence on a key matter when it elicited testimony from its principal witness—Bill Allen—that a crucial hand-written note by Ted Stevens was an effort to "cover his ass." This testimony was false and a recent fabrication. Members of the prosecution team knew that it was false. Nonetheless, it was presented by the prosecution at trial in a manner to give it maximum bombshell effect. Bill Allen had no recollection of the "CYA" statement when first questioned about it on April 15, 2008, in a meeting with four prosecutors and an FBI agent, but was subsequently "pushed" to provide the false "bombshell" testimony favorable to the prosecution.

On February 16, 2009, a new team of prosecutors was assigned after members of the original government trial team were held in contempt of court. The new team of government lawyers provided to the defense clear evidence that the "CYA" testimony was false. In essence, the government tricked the jury into returning a tainted verdict against the Senator based on false evidence.

There are heroes in this story. . .

We went on to praise Judge Sullivan, and to quote some of the most telling observations he made during the course of the trial. We also thanked Attorney General Eric Holder, who had lived up to the responsibilities of his office. Then we made the important point that the majority of prosecutors and FBI agents are honest and ethical and should not be tainted by what happened in the Stevens case.

There are thousands of ethical prosecutors and FBI agents who have our admiration and respect for the work they do. The wrongdoing of a few should not taint the majority. Some ethical government attorneys who came late to this case were lied to by the original trial team. Accordingly, it is crucial that this matter be fully investigated to determine the complete facts and assess responsibility.

We closed with a tribute to our client, and friend, Ted Stevens:

Senator Ted Stevens has served his country with distinction in the United States Senate for more than forty years. He is a World War II veteran and a life-long public servant. He did not deserve this prosecution by rogue prosecutors trying to make reputations for themselves.

Williams & Connolly is proud to have defended Senator Ted Stevens.

Our firm does not have a public relations or a press department. We generally do not talk to the press about pending cases. But this case was different. We were able to cobble together a list of email addresses of reporters and others who had contacted us throughout the case. We sent the press release out by email, and then went to lunch with Bill Phillips.

At lunch, Bill Phillips convinced us that we needed to provide some footage for the evening news. So Brendan and I held a rare press conference to repeat what we said in our press release. Brendan added one more thing. While acknowledging that it was a day of relief, he added that it was a "sad story" because "anyone can be found guilty if the prosecution ignores the Constitution of the United States."

We were not high-fiving each other because of our great victory. We were relieved that the Senator had been exonerated in the eyes of the law, but we were disgusted at what had happened. It was a day of relief more than happiness.

Chapter
19

Dismissal

Judge Sullivan wanted to have a hearing to dismiss the case. Six days later, on April 7, we assembled in his (packed) courtroom. After saying good morning and noting the drama of the day and the weeks that had led up to it, Judge Sullivan got right to the point, and he did not mince words:

> For nearly 25 years I have told defendants appearing before me that in my courtroom they will receive a fair trial and that I will make sure of it. In nearly 25 years on the bench, I've never seen anything approaching the mishandling and misconduct that I've seen in this case.

> Before we hear from the parties this morning, the Court believes it is important to take a few minutes to talk about how we got to this point in this case and to share some thoughts about what we, as a legal community, need to do to safeguard the integrity of our criminal justice system. The United States Government has an obligation to pursue convictions fairly and in accordance with the Constitution, and when the Government does not meet its obligations to turn over evidence, the system falters. Again and again, both during and after the trial in this case, the Government was caught making false representations and not meeting its discovery obligations. And each time those false representations or unmet obligations came to light, the Government claimed that it had simply made a good faith mistake, that there was no ill intent and/or that the Court

had already taken steps to address the problem and therefore there was no need for court action.

When the Government failed to produce Rocky Williams' exculpatory grand jury testimony, the Government claimed that this testimony was immaterial. When the Government sent Mr. Williams back to Alaska without advising the Defense or the Court, notwithstanding the Court's interactions with counsel for the parties that weekend, the Government asserted that it was acting in "good faith."

When the Government affirmatively redacted exculpatory statements from FBI Form 302s, it claimed that "it was just a mistake." "When Government counsel told the Court that Bill Allen had not been re-interviewed the day before a hearing on its *Brady* disclosures, that was a "mistaken understanding."

When the Government failed to turn over exculpatory statements from Dave Anderson, it claimed that they were immaterial. When the Government failed to turn over a critical grand jury transcript containing exculpatory information, it claimed that it was inadvertent. When the Government used business records that the Government undeniably knew were false, it said that it was unintentional. . .

When an FBI agent involved with the investigation and prosecution filed a complaint alleging misconduct on the part of the prosecutors and another FBI agent, not only did the Government seek to keep that complaint a secret, but the Government claimed that the allegations had nothing to do with the verdict and no relevancy to the Defense, that the allegations could be addressed by the Office of Professional Responsibility's investigation and that any misconduct had already been addressed and remedied during the trial.

In fact, as recently as February the 6th, the Government told the Court that there was no need for any post-trial discovery and that the Government was, and I quote, confident that its response to the Defendant's post-trial motions would resolve the need for further inquiry into the allegations as they relate to the trial . . .

And yet, after the Court held three senior attorneys in contempt for blatantly failing to comply with this court's order to produce documents and a new team of prosecutors was assigned to the case, we learned for the first time what may well be the most shocking and serious *Brady* violations of all, that the Government failed to tell the Defense of an interview with Bill Allen in which Allen stated that he did not recall a conversation with Bob Persons about sending the Senator a bill and that Allen estimated the value of the VECO work on the Senator's home at $80,000, far less than the hundreds of thousands of dollars the Government had alleged at trial.

As this Court said during the trial, 'This is not about prosecution by any means necessary,' and as the Court also said, and 'The fair administration of justice does not depend on the luck of the draw or a lucky day or a lucky continuance; indeed, it should not depend on who represents the Defendant, whether an FBI agent blows a whistle, a new administration, a new attorney general or a new trial team. The fair administration of justice depends on the Government meeting its obligations to pursue convictions fairly and in accordance with the Constitution. There was no question whatsoever in this case that the Government knew of its obligations. The Court issued discovery orders and talked about *Brady* from Day One; nevertheless, the Government repeatedly failed to meet those obligations. . . . We must never forget the Supreme Court's directive that a criminal trial is a search for the truth. Yet in several cases recently this court has seen troubling failures to produce exculpatory evidence in violation of the law and this court's orders. Whether you are a public official, a private citizen or a Guantanamo Bay detainee, the prosecution, indeed the United States Government must produce exculpatory evidence so that justice shall be done.

I, therefore, urge my judicial colleagues on every trial court everywhere to be vigilant and to consider entering an exculpatory evidence order at the outset of every criminal case, whether requested to do so or not, and to require that the exculpatory material be turned over in a useable format because, as we've seen in this case, the use of summaries is an opportunity for mischief and mistake, and I encourage the Attorney General, for whom I have the highest regard, to require *Brady* training for new and veteran, experienced prosecutors throughout the country and also encourage an open dialogue between defense attorneys and prosecutors regarding these discovery obligations.

Further, I urge the President and the Attorney General, as they select new United States attorneys, to obtain from those appointees their commitments to fulfilling these important obligations, and indeed, the Senate confirmation process should also address these most important prosecutorial obligations.

Those are a few thoughts about how we got to this point and where we go from here. I'll have more to say in a few minutes, but first I'll hear from the Government.

* * * * *

Paul O'Brien, for the government, spoke next. He confirmed that the Department of Justice was asking that the case be dismissed. And then he apologized on behalf of the United States government.

"I hope the Court appreciates one thing this morning, speaking on behalf of the Department, we deeply, deeply regret that this occurred. We would ask the Court to grant the Government's motion, dismiss the indictment with prejudice, and again, I apologize to the Court and we deeply regret that this occurred. I would ask the Court grant our motion."

I may have missed it, but I did not believe that he apologized to Senator Stevens. Or to the Senator's family. Or to the citizens of the State of Alaska. Or to the United States Senate. Or to the American people. But, I believed then and believe now that he was sincere. Paul O'Brien and his colleagues acted with courage and conviction when others had not.

* * * * *

Then Brendan Sullivan stood to address the packed courtroom:

First off, let me say that I've never agreed more with anything I've heard from the bench than your opening remarks today. I agree with every word of it, including the suggestions that you make about how change might be brought about by high government officials focusing upon the need to educate and instruct and reeducate prosecutors out here who have this tremendous power and tremendous duty and responsibility to make sure our system is fair.

. . . The bottom line of our experience here is that, as the Court said, the most crucial of the *Brady* evidence [of innocence] and material of this whole case was hidden from the defense until just two weeks ago, was finally produced to the defense by this new team of honest and ethical government attorneys, five months after an unlawful verdict was returned, a verdict returned based upon government misconduct. . . .

The extraordinary evidence that we've seen in just three documents that they produced . . . support the multiple motions that were filed by the Defense throughout these proceedings, which sought dismissal and a new trial. More importantly, these documents prove that the Government acted unlawfully to achieve the verdict which the jury returned. . .

Then Brendan turned to an important point that he and I had discussed many times with the Senator, who bristled every time he read that he had been "convicted":

The fact of the matter is, Your Honor, this verdict against Ted Stevens of October 27, which the whole world reports as having convicted Ted Stevens, I know maybe it's legalese, but there's no conviction in this case. There's none. There was a verdict returned, it was unlawful. There never is a conviction

236

against a citizen until a judge reviews post-trial motions, makes rulings and signs a judgment.

So if I had one wish—I know it couldn't, won't be granted—[it is] that I never see again anybody report that Ted Stevens was convicted, because he was not. . .

Brendan then turned to the government's ridiculous press conference at which the top criminal prosecutor in the government of the United States of America expressed the Department of Justice's "pride" in the Stevens prosecution team.

[O]ne of the most remarkable things is that despite this court's many admonitions to the Government throughout this process, some amounting to virtual public censures for their conduct, an Acting Assistant Attorney General of the Criminal Division of the United States Department of Justice goes out to the [courthouse] steps after that verdict is returned, gathers the prosecutors in a family photo, and says to the world, "The Department of Justice is proud of this team."

I'm not suggesting he knew anything about the misconduct, but if he just read the newspapers—how could the leading attorney of the Department of Justice over the criminal division make such a statement? I suggest to you that that says it all. There is the failure of leadership. It's prosecute to win at all costs, and wrongdoing can flourish when that's the attitude of a leader. . . .

You see, what happened . . . here in this courtroom, I think, is easily explained. They indicted a sitting United States senator who is certain to be elected. If there's any certainty in politics, the certainty is that Ted Stevens would have been elected to another term in office after a distinguished 40 years of serving Alaskans. . . .

Ted Stevens believed in his innocence. That's why at age 84 he was willing to submit himself to a court, to the process and to jurors. He believed so much in his innocence that he asked for a speedy trial, and we defense lawyers, who don't generally like speedy trials, agreed. He was indicted a few months before the election, but what neither he nor I nor you contemplated was that the Government would act unlawfully. . . .

The Government cannot do much to make amends, I guess, except to say you're sorry, and that, from Paul O'Brien, is appreciated. He did say that. Sorry we put you through an unlawful proceeding; sorry the Government lied, cheated, violated the law in an effort to convict you; sorry it cost you months of your life at the end of an extraordinary life; sorry prosecutors were dishonest, unethical, caused you to lose an election after you served for 40 years; sorry you were disgraced by a verdict that should never have been that was unlawful. Sorry. Never, never, sufficient.

* * * * *

Senator Stevens spoke next. He walked to the podium while Catherine and three of his daughters looked on from the front row. The witch hunt was over.

Thank you very much, Your Honor, for the privilege of being able to address the Court. I'm deeply grateful for your hard work and all that you've done throughout this case as well as the dedication of your chambers staff and the courthouse staff. I know that you and they have worked many late nights and weekends and holidays during this case; your dedication to public service is an inspiration to me, and without your experience and vigilance, the truth would never have been known. . . And, of course, I'm grateful to this team here [of new prosecutors] that took over this case, and I really was amazed that they reacted so quickly to the evidence that was presented to them and they presented to the Defense team. It really is— really is an indication of a great competence. . .

I'm full of giving thanks this morning, but I do also thank the Alaskans. As I traveled throughout the state, Your Honor, almost every Alaskan said, 'I've said a prayer for you, Ted,' and that was very meaningful to me. I'm blessed to have been able

238

to serve Alaska for 40 years as United States Senator, and I, of course, am grateful to my senate colleagues and former staff and close friends who have supported me. Many of those friends attend these proceedings every day and some of them are here again this morning. Their friendship has been a humbling source of strength to me through this ordeal.

I'm showing that I really don't have the words to express the measure of my gratitude to all concerned, but particularly my wife Catherine who stood by me through this whole process, and my children, my entire family, three of my daughters are here this morning, for their unwavering support in these troubled times, I'm—I'm really fortunate and I love each one of them.

But, Your Honor, I want to be brief, but I say that I've had a long career. I've served the United States for many years. I served as a pilot in World War II in China. I served as a United States Attorney in the Territory of Alaska. I was solicitor of the Department of Interior, and I've been a senator for 40 years. It was my great honor to be a member of the Bicentennial Commission on the Constitution of the United States with Warren Burger, Chief Justice Warren Burger. I've been deeply committed to the rule of law and the Constitution, and I support it to the best of my ability.

Until recently, my faith in the criminal system, particularly the judicial system was unwavering, but what some members of the prosecution team did nearly destroyed that faith. Their conduct has consequences for me that they will never realize and can never be reversed. But today, Your Honor, through your leadership and persistence and commitment to the rule of law, my faith has been restored, and I really can never thank you enough because obviously I watched it every day.

Your actions gave me new hope that others may be spared from similar miscarriages of justice, and it is my hope that when the dust settles I may be able to encourage the enactment of legislation to reform the laws relating to the responsibilities and duties of those entrusted with the solemn task of enforcing criminal laws.

I deeply appreciate your service. Thank you.

* * * * *

I was struck by the words he used: "fortunate," "humbling," and "gratitude." There was no bitterness, though he had every right to be bitter.

* * * * *

Brendan, Senator Stevens and Judge Sullivan all recognized the dedication of chambers staff, especially a hard-working law clerk whom we had all noticed. Judge Sullivan said it best: "I want to recognize someone whom I often introduce as my brilliant lawyer, Addy Schmitt. She is indeed great and she was with me every step of the way, and we're talking about 15–18–hour days and longer and weekends and holidays . . . and I'm deeply indebted to her. I would not have been in a position to discharge my judicial responsibilities . . . without her expert assistance and her brilliance, and I'm deeply appreciative."

Law clerks play an important role in our system of justice, and especially in uncovering injustice. I agreed with the words that Judge Sullivan had chosen: brilliant, great and expert. Of course, the most important attribute for one seeking justice is a willingness to work really hard, and Addy Schmitt worked very hard.

Near the end of the hearing, Judge Sullivan directed a question to Brendan. "On October the 28th, the day after the verdict was returned, you delivered a 16-page letter to then Attorney General Michael Mukasey, detailing at length many of the events recited today and asking the Attorney General to commence a formal investigation into the prosecutorial misconduct in this case. Did you ever receive a response?"

Brendan responded, "Your Honor, I had actually sent three letters to the Attorney General of the United States, Mr. Mukasey. I never received an acknowledgment that they were even received in the office. I received no word back. I made an effort in those three letters to lay out our concerns at the time. To my knowledge, I don't know what he did, if anything."

Having confirmed what he apparently suspected, Judge Sullivan had one more piece of business, which was how to get to the bottom of what happened inside this prosecution team.

The Court has repeatedly been told that the Office of Professional Responsibility at the Department of Justice is conducting an investigation into the investigation and prosecution in this case. The Court first heard about an investigation on October the 2nd during the trial when a member of the prosecution team informed the Court that the prosecution team had, in her words, 'self-reported', . . . to the Office of Professional Responsibility because the Court had found a *Brady* violation.

That was six months ago. The Court next heard about the OPR investigation when the Government assured the Court it need not take any action based on the Joy complaint because OPR was conducting a thorough investigation. That was four months ago. And yet, and to date, the silence has been deafening.

Similarly, the Defense tells us just moments ago they received no response to their numerous letters to former Attorney General Mukasey urging him to commence a formal investigation. Shocking but not surprising.

The Court looks forward to receiving the results of the OPR investigation whenever that investigation concludes. But the events and allegations in this case are too serious and too numerous to be left to an internal investigation that has no outside accountability. This court has an independent obligation to ensure that any misconduct is fully investigated and addressed in an appropriate public forum.

Accordingly, the Court shall commence criminal contempt proceedings against the original prosecution team, including

William Welch, Brenda Morris, Joseph Bottini, Nicholas Marsh, James Goeke and Edward Sullivan pursuant to the Court's authority under Federal Rule of Criminal Procedure 42, based on failures of those prosecutors to comply with the Court's numerous orders and potential obstruction of justice.

Judge Sullivan was almost but not quite finished:

Moreover . . . the Court finds that the interest of justice requires the appointment of a non-Government disinterested attorney to prosecute that matter. Therefore, the Court will appoint attorney Henry F. Schuelke . . . as prosecutor. Mr. Schuelke [who] enjoys an outstanding local and national reputation for fairness, integrity and sound judgment . . . will investigate this matter. . . . Let me stress that I have not, by any means, prejudged these attorneys or their culpability. I do not take this decision lightly and I certainly hope the record will ultimately find no intentional obstruction of justice. Nevertheless, the Court has an obligation to determine what happened here and respond appropriately, and I intend to do so.

Now, at this point, the Court will focus on the Government's motion to set aside the verdict and dismiss the indictment with prejudice. The Court has the highest regard for Attorney General Eric Holder. The Court had the honor of serving on the Superior Court with him briefly and the Court knows that Eric Holder has earned his impeccable reputation as a lawyer firmly committed to fairness, integrity and the rule of law. Accordingly, the Court respects Mr. Holder's decision to seek dismissal of this case in view of the totality of circumstances surrounding this investigation and prosecution, and the Court concurs with the Attorney General that it is in the interest of justice that this verdict be set aside and the indictment be dismissed. . . .

* * * * *

In a case full of surprises, Judge Sullivan's appointment of an independent prosecutor was yet another one. Judge Sullivan was using a rarely invoked provision of the Federal Rules of Criminal Procedure that gave him the power to appoint an independent prosecutor to investigate and prosecute the charge of contempt of court. It is a crime to intentionally disobey a clear and unambiguous court order.

Judge Sullivan concluded the hearing by again thanking the new prosecutors.

> I recognize the circumstances were not those which you relished, but your presence and your efforts have certainly been consistent with all this court ever wanted to do from Day One, which was to afford the Defendant, like any other defendant, and not because of his station in life, like anyone who comes before this court, all this court ever wanted to do was to afford the Defendant his fair day in court, and that day has arrived.

* * * * *

There were many tears in the courtroom that day. It reminded me of the day of the illegal verdict, except that this day the tears were tears of relief.

Our exit was chaotic. The Marshals, as always, did a great job. As we were about to leave the courthouse, I remembered Senator Hutchison's advice and got myself and the other lawyers out of the Senator's way. He walked out of the courthouse with his three daughters. A photograph of the Senator with his daughters—not his lawyers—ran in papers across the country the next day. And sat on his desk for the rest of his life.

* * * * *

There was one piece of unfinished business. Judge Sullivan needed to enter a written order dismissing the case. Craig Singer and I hammered out a draft order with the cooperation of Paul O'Brien. The order made it clear that Senator Stevens was never actually convicted of a crime. It read, "There was never a judgment of conviction in this case. The jury's verdict is being set aside and has no legal effect. The government's Motion is granted. The Verdict is hereby set aside and the indictment is hereby dismissed."

Senator Stevens carried a copy of that order with him every day thereafter so that he could correct people who suggested that he had been convicted. There was *no conviction* in the case.

* * * * *

That night I flew the Alaska state flag—the Big Dipper and the North Star in gold over a midnight blue background—from the front porch of my suburban Washington home. Our entire team and their families came for dinner, including the Stevenses and the Phillipses. Bill and his wife Janet had crab legs flown in from Alaska and we feasted on those while toasting the Senator.

It was a happy event, but not entirely so. As I tried to sleep that night, I asked myself, did the system work? Yes and no. To some extent things had been made right. Judge Sullivan had granted an order exonerating the Senator. But the citizens of Alaska had been robbed of a fair election. And life would never be the same for Ted Stevens.

Other questions raced through my sleepless mind: How could this happen in America? How could people be so cynical? How could our system allow this to happen, even if it was fixed—sort of—eventually? Would the Schuelke investigation get to the bottom of it? Time would tell.

Chapter
20

Tragedy

In August of 2009, every lawyer on our team (except for Brendan Sullivan and Alex Romain who had other commitments) headed up to Alaska to go fishing with Senator Stevens on a trip arranged by Bill Phillips. We were the guests of one of Bill's clients, the GCI Corporation, an Alaskan telecommunications company that was serving those in the most isolated regions of Alaska by expanding access to broadband and wireless internet service. Perhaps the most important service GCI provided was "telemedicine," whereby Native Alaskans in the bush country could have live internet video conversation with a doctor in one of Alaska's larger towns. We stayed at "the Agulawak," a rustic fishing retreat GCI owned in the Bush.

The only way to reach towns within the Alaskan Bush, the remote part of the state, is by airplane. (Technically that applies to the capital, Juneau, as well, but Juneau is not considered the Bush.) The closest town to the Agulawak was Dillingham, which is on the Southwest coast of Alaska, near the top of the Aleutian Islands. To call it remote is an understatement.

GCI's director of corporate strategy was Greg Chapados, a native of Fairbanks, who had succeeded Bill Phillips as the Senator's Chief of Staff. The Chief Executive of GCI was Ron Duncan, also a close friend of Bill's. Ron was married to Dani Bowman, the intensive care pediatrician who had testified about Ted Stevens' saving her young patient's life. On the day that the Justice Department moved to dismiss the case, Senator Stevens had been alone in an Alaskan cabin that had belonged to his mother-in-law. That night, Ron and Dani took Senator Stevens out for dinner. Ron was a wine collector, and they very appropriately (or ironically) shared a bottle of wine called "Justice."

For a total of fourteen hours, the defense team travelled from Washington to Southwest Alaska through a series of connecting flights. As few Americans from the Lower 48 have been to Alaska, most people don't realize how distant the state is, how rugged its terrain, and how breathtakingly beautiful. The route we took went over Whitehorse in the Canadian Yukon and massive glaciers.

From the Anchorage airport, one takes a smaller plane to Dillingham, a town comprised mostly of Quonset huts, supply stores, a medical clinic, and a small airport. We flew the final leg to the Agulawak on a vintage sea plane, a de Havilland "Otter," which has ten folding metal seats, harness-type seat belts and life preservers. There are large pontoons under the wings, and one climbs a ladder to board. The cabin is not pressurized, there are no tray tables, and obviously, no beverage cart. It was nonetheless a beautiful plane, kept in immaculate condition.

Using the Agulawak as our base camp, we flew to several remote locations to fish. We caught lots of fish: salmon, artic char, rainbow trout and Dolly Varden. In fact, we caught (and released) so many arctic char that we lost count. At night, we played cards, drank wine, and had the time of our lives. (The Senator cleaned up in our card games.) But we also spent time wondering how the investigation, which still gnawed at all of us, was going. Would we learn the full truth?

* * * * *

After the fishing, we flew back to Anchorage to visit the Girdwood cabin, the object of so much controversy. We invited Augie Paone and Bob Persons to join us. I viewed them as heroes of the case and told them so; they had told the truth in the face of intense pressure from government prosecutors. Many citizens will not do that. I compared them to other heroes in cases who had stood up to tell the truth in defiance of government pressure. Mrs. Persons and Mrs. Paone, also heroes, were teary-eyed as I spoke. They had spent many days waiting for their husbands' turns to testify. Bill Phillips spoke of what a great team we were. Amen to that. The entire team went to Bob Person's restaurant, the Double Musky, for dinner. Bill Phillips picked up the tab.

* * * * *

In the first week of August, 2010, the Senator and some of his friends planned another Alaskan fishing trip, and, again, it was Bill Phillips who put the trip together. One of their stops would be the Agulawak, where our team had been the year before, and they would fly on the same de Havilland Otter we'd flown the year before. The Otter would take them from Dillingham to the Agulawak, and then to various fishing spots in the area.

On the morning of August 10, I awoke at 5:00 in the morning to catch the 7:00 shuttle to New York for a deposition. I looked at my Blackberry as I headed out the door of my house at 5:30 a.m. An email caught my eye. It was a breaking news alert from the *Anchorage Daily News:* a plane had crashed near Dillingham, Alaska. The paper did not know who was on board.

My next email, from Catherine Stevens, said, "Bad news, please call." Oh God. I called Catherine's cell phone, and reached her at her sister's house in Anchorage, at 1:30 a.m. Alaska time.

Catherine told me the Otter had crashed and that some of the people on board had survived and some had died. The Senator, Bill Phillips, Bill's 13 year-old son Willy, former Stevens staffer Jim Morhard, former Stevens staffer Sean O'Keefe, O'Keefe's 19 year-old son Kevin, GCI employee Dana Tindall and her 16 year-old daughter Corey were on board.

Then she handed the phone to retired Air Force General Joe Ralston, a dear friend of the Stevens family. Ralston had gone to Catherine's side upon hearing the news. He was still trying to figure out exactly what had happened. Some had died and some had survived, he said, but he emphasized that the information was sketchy. He told me that first responders were on the scene, but that the weather was terrible and rescue operations had to be suspended for the night.

Ralston put Catherine back on. I told her we were praying, and I drove to the airport. I had a deposition to cover, and a client counting on me. Remembering Brendan's admonition, I knew that I had to be at my post. But the lack of news from Alaska was torture.

The press was not yet aware that Senator Stevens was on the plane, and I knew it would be a very big story when they figured that out. Though overcome with worry and sadness, I knew what had to be done.

Brendan was on vacation in Maine. I tracked him down, and after telling him the news, prepared a statement from the firm on my Blackberry during the cab ride to my deposition in downtown Manhattan, anticipating what we would say if the Senator had in fact been killed.

At every break in the deposition, I would check my messages. The media eventually reported that the Senator was on board the downed plane, but nobody knew who was dead and who had survived. Finally, I received a voicemail message from Beth Stevens: "We've lost Dad, and we've lost Bill."

I wept briefly, but gathered my composure.

I called Beth Stewart and gave her instructions to issue our statement *after* the family had confirmed his death but not before. Beth and I then reached Brendan on a conference call, and Beth patched in Catherine Stevens. She was still in shock. She said, "Can you believe it?" and then gave us some news: Willy Phillips, Bill's 13-year old son, had survived the crash and was going to live. "Isn't that wonderful?" Catherine said. Yes, we agreed it was.

She told us that Mitch Rose had released a statement on behalf of the family. We told her that we would also be issuing a statement, because there were some things Ted's lawyers needed to say. It read:

We are deeply saddened by the news that Senator Stevens has died.

Senator Stevens was a member of what Tom Brokaw called America's "Greatest Generation." He volunteered for the Army during World War II and flew combat missions with the Flying Tigers. Senator Stevens loved our country, the State of Alaska, the U.S. Senate, and above all else his family. He had many friends on both sides of the aisle. He always did what he thought was in the best interests of the public.

Senator Stevens did not deserve the treatment he received late in his career from some members of the Department of Justice. The presiding judge, Emmet G. Sullivan, stated that "[I]n nearly 25 years on the bench, I've never seen anything approaching the mishandling and misconduct that I've seen in this case." The verdict against him was based on fabricated evidence. The Attorney General asked that Judge Sullivan dismiss the charges when he learned of some of the government's misconduct. In granting the Attorney General's request, Judge Sullivan emphasized that the government's interest in a criminal prosecution "is not that it shall win its case, but that justice shall be done."

Senator Stevens was innocent, and insisted on fighting the charges. Even after the case against him was dismissed, he remained profoundly affected by the government's misconduct and its implications for others. His fervent hope was that meaningful change would be brought to the criminal justice system so that others would not be mistreated as he was by the very officials whose duty it is to represent the United States justly and fairly.

Senator Stevens was an American hero. We were honored to represent him, and we were honored to call him our friend.

We send our condolences to his family and his many friends in Alaska and throughout the world.

249

Our statement was heartfelt, and, we thought, captured his life as we knew it. But on this day it was rightly drowned out by those far more important than lawyers. Among the multitudes who issued statements were President Barack Obama (who had already called Catherine Stevens before we did); former President George H. W. Bush; former President George W. Bush; Secretary of the Interior and former Senator Ken Salazar; Speaker of the House Nancy Pelosi; Senator Orrin Hatch; and former Alaska Governor Sarah Palin.

Senator Lisa Murkowski's statement said it best:

> The thought of losing Ted Stevens, a man who was known to business and community leaders, Native chiefs and everyday Alaskans as "Uncle Ted," is too difficult to fathom. His entire life was dedicated to public service—from his days as a pilot in World War II to his four decades of service in the United States Senate. He truly was the greatest of the "Greatest Generation." The love and respect that Alaskans of all persuasions feel toward Ted Stevens is on par with what the American people felt towards leaders such as John F. Kennedy, Dr. Martin Luther King, Jr. and Ronald Regan. Ted had the vision of a John Kennedy that Alaskans are an exceptional people who would achieve great things in his lifetime; the compassion of Dr. Martin Luther King Jr., in devoting his life to alleviating the Third World conditions that plagued Alaska's Native people; and the unwavering strength of a Ronald Regan whether fighting for the men and women of our military or for Alaska's right to develop . . . and its abundant natural resources. On this sad and tragic day, we pray for all those who have perished, as well as the survivors and their families.

Senator Patrick Leahy also described the Senator exceptionally well:

> He was a tough negotiator and a savvy legislator. But as I told him again last month, he was an old school senator. He always kept his word to me and to other senators. In moments of legislative battle he would come onto the floor wearing his

[Incredible] Hulk tie, and he would growl and act like a bulldog. But then he would spot friends on the floor and give a wink and a grin.

In addition to Willy Phillips, Jim Morhard, and Sean and Kevin O'Keefe survived the crash. The others on board, including the pilot, died.

* * * * *

Kurt Bowden was a legendary U.S. Marshal, who had worked in the federal courthouse in Washington, D.C. for decades before I went to law school. He was often assigned to high profile trials and was assigned to the Stevens trial. He usually chatted with Senator Stevens each day before court and during breaks. One day, he complimented Senator Stevens on the tie he was wearing, which had a print of dozens of rainbow trout on it. The next day, the Senator showed up at our office with a bag from a Washington, D.C. clothing store. He had stopped on the way to pick up the same tie for Marshall Bowden. "Senator, I don't think we should give Mr. Bowden a tie during the middle of trial," I told him. "You're right," the Senator reluctantly agreed.

The day after the Senator died, I received a call from Kurt Bowden, who wanted to express his condolences. Kurt told me how much he liked the Senator. I told Kurt about the tie that the Senator had bought him. Now that the Senator had passed away, surely I could deliver the tie intended for him. I delivered it that afternoon.

* * * * *

Alaska went into mourning, and my wife and I, along with the rest of our team, got on a flight to Anchorage for the funeral. As his funeral procession traveled the streets of Anchorage, Alaskans lined the street with signs that said "Thank you, Ted" and "We love you, Ted."

* * * * *

A remarkable funeral was held in Alaska's largest church. A large

251

overflow crowd watched via video feed in a nearby gym. Alaska television and C-Span covered it live. Brendan and I were honorary pall bearers (along with over 100 others), which I considered, and always will, one of the great honors of my life. A planeload of Republicans and Democratic Senators from Washington, called a "CODEL," Washington-speak for a Congressional delegation, not to mention countless military brass, were there. So were native Alaskans, elected officials and veterans, some wearing their uniforms.

Before she read the Alaskan poet William Ransom's poem "A Legacy of Dreams," Senator Murkowski said, "He taught us about trust and loyalty, he taught us about tenacity and commitment. Never giving up. . . . As important as Ted Stevens is to Alaska's history, he was all about Alaska's future."

The part about not giving up was especially important to Ted Stevens. It certainly applied to the part of his life I had lived with him (though it applied to many other parts of his life as well). Ted Stevens was a fan of Winston Churchill, and his family included some well-known Churchillian expressions in the program. One was especially apt: *"Never give in, never give in, never, never, never, never—in nothing, great or small, large or petty—never give in except to convictions of honor and good sense."*

* * * * *

The first eulogist was Joe Biden, the Vice President of the United States. Turning to the Stevens family, he said, "Your dad, along with some of my colleagues, used to kid me about the fact that I quote a lot of Irish poets. They think I quote them because I'm Irish. I don't do that. . . . I do it because they are the best poets. Your dad had a lot in common with one of the Irish poets that I and many others have quoted for a long time, James Joyce. James Joyce once said: 'When I die, Dublin will be written in my heart.' I have no doubt, not a single doubt in my mind that Alaska is written in Ted's heart. And Ted's heart is big enough that along with Alaska, Cath-

NOT GUILTY: THE UNLAWFUL PROSECUTION OF U.S. SENATOR TED STEVENS

erine and his 6 children, and 11 grandchildren are also written across that big heart.

"You never had to wonder what was in Ted's heart. It was obvious to everyone who knew him, it was obvious to me the day I met him as a 29 year-old kid who had just been elected to the U.S. Senate. . . . Whenever Ted Stevens made a commitment, you could absolutely bet your life on the fact that he would keep the commitment. Everyone in this church also knows, everyone who ever met Ted knows, that Ted's friendship and support was not bounded by ideology. As a matter of fact, it had no bounds. None whatsoever.

"When I came to the Senate in 1973 I was 100 out of 100 in seniority. Just having gone through an accident where I had lost my wife and daughter, many of my colleagues, some of whom are here today, offered help to get me through a pretty tough time in my life, but very few I could count on one hand, and I can name them, offered as warm an embrace as the Republican Senator, who I had never met in my life, who walked across the floor of the Senate to my corner desk, up by that roll top desk, extended his hand and said, 'I want to get to know you. Ann and I want you to come to dinner.'

"Back in those days as some of my colleagues know, we actually hung out together . . . we actually cared a lot about one another and it didn't have anything to do with if we were Democrat or Republican. Ted was part of a close-knit Senate family within a Senate family. There was Ann and Ted and Fritz and Patsy Hollings, Tom and Barbara Eagleton, and Bill and Dolly Saxby. And that family, that inner family, took me in to their family. They were kind of a life preserver in a difficult time. . . .

"To the people of Alaska, I can say with absolute certainty without fear of contradiction what Hamlet said of Horatio, 'We shall not look upon his like again.'"

* * * * *

The sort of bi-partisanship of which the Vice-President spoke was sorely needed in Washington. I was too busy to pay much attention, but the United States underwent the most severe economic crisis since the Great Depression during the Fall of 2008. The U.S. Government and the Senate especially could have used Ted Stevens during that time in the halls of Congress, not a federal courtroom. We could use him now.

* * * * *

Senator Daniel Inouye also eulogized the Senator. He described seeing his best friend just after the Senator lost his first wife: "When I saw him, he said, 'Why Ann, and not me?' He was ready to give up but he realized he had a duty to carry out so he stuck on. Thank God."

After telling several humorous stories, Senator Inouye referred to the trial. "I knew it and we all knew it, that he was not guilty—and he was vindicated, cleared of all charges." The somber funeral crowd broke out into wild applause. My eyes welled up, as did many others'.

Senator Inouye then said, "As the Vice President . . . indicated, his word was good, his word was absolutely good. You could take it to the bank. And he was also tenacious. He called me one day and said, 'I want you to come to Alaska and see the natives,' which we did. As a result of that trip together, we conjured up all kinds of things, not just schools and hospitals, and clinics and roads, but other things. For example at that time, if you lived out in the village, there were no roads. In the winter time you needed a dogsled, you couldn't fly in, but a village usually had a nurse. The only way was to communicate somehow. I want you to know Ted and I began this high-tech business called telemedicine. It was from that trip. Now it's commonplace. . . . He was that type of person.

"We will have no more drafts. Ted said, if a man or woman is willing to put on a uniform and stand in harm's way and risk death to defend me, to protect me, I am going to do everything possible to be of help so that they come home to their loved ones, to their wives, to their sweethearts, to their sons and daughters. And I hope you will join me. That's the kind of fellow he was. The veterans of America, the military family of America lost a good friend but there are so many of us here who will do our damned best to carry on his work.

Farewell friend. We will never forget you."

* * * * *

Reverend Norman Elliot, an Episcopalian priest from Alaska, was one of the last to speak. Like Ted Stevens, he was a World War II veteran. In 1978, he had presided over the funeral of Ann Stevens and the weddings of many of the Stevens children. After emotionally relating the story of the Senator losing Ann, he continued, clearly speaking from the heart: "Alaska and the Nation have lost a mountain. I sincerely hope that somewhere in a mountain range in Alaska, a great unnamed mountain will be found. A mountain which can be seen, not hidden. A mountain which can be seen and named after the Senator. Not named Senator Ted Stevens, not named Senator Ted, but Uncle Ted. Uncle Ted in order that future generations will know a famous man once lived amongst us. A man who not only served Alaska and the nation but loved Alaska and its people."

* * * * *

In Washington, there is always a backlog of veterans waiting to be interred at Arlington National Cemetery, and the Senator's burial had to be delayed for several weeks. So, the Senator was to be buried in Arlington National Cemetery on Tuesday, September 28.

On Monday, September 27, the day before the burial was scheduled to take place, I was in my office discussing firm business with two of my partners when Craig Singer knocked on the door. I asked him if it could wait, but he said it was something I needed to know right away. When I stepped out into the hallway, he told me the media was reporting that prosecutor Nick Marsh had committed suicide.

I didn't know how to react. But I knew that I had to warn the Stevens family, which I did. Beth Stevens, who had loyally attended every day of trial with her father, had just been diagnosed with cancer and was having surgery that day. I knew that the Stevens family needed to hear the news from me, not the press. I managed to get to them first.

* * * * *

Nick Marsh left behind a new wife. I felt horrible for his wife and for the rest of his family. I also felt badly for his friends. But *my friend,* Senator Ted Stevens, upon whom Marsh and his fellow prosecutors had inflicted so much harm, was being buried the next day.

A few reporters called and left messages for me. I felt that out of respect for Marsh's family and the Stevens family it would be inappropriate for me to comment. One of the stories reported that I had not returned a call seeking comment, and a few hours later, when I checked my messages, I found this voicemail: "Mr. Cary, this is a friend of Nicholas Marsh's. You drove him to this. You should say something nice about him. The fact that you haven't commented is despicable."

Shocked as I was by the anonymous caller's words, I stuck with my decision as I still felt it was the respectful thing to do.

* * * * *

On September 28, 2010, the U.S. Air Force buried Senator Stevens in Arlington National Cemetery. Only the sad occasion marred what was otherwise a beautiful day. The Secretary of Defense and more military personnel than I could count were there. Senators from both sides of the aisle arrived by the bus load. As the crowd followed the horse-drawn caisson with the Senator's casket down the rolling hills surrounded by white headstones, the Air Force Band played "The Battle Hymn of the Republic."

The Chaplain of the Senate, Barry Black, a Seventh Day Adventist preacher with whom the Senator had become close, began his remarks by saying "Great men remind us that we can leave more than footprints in the sands of time." After Chaplain Black spoke, the Air Force fired a 21-gun salute. As if on cue, a large red-tailed hawk swooped over the grave site. The circling hawk was such a remarkable sight that I wondered at the time whether it was staged by the Air Force. I later learned that it was not.

Four F-22 fighters approached from the south, flying low over the city. It reminded me that the last time I had seen a fighter flying over the restricted air space of Washington D.C. was on September 11, 2001. As the jets reached the burial site, one peeled off in the missing man formation.

After the jets flew away and their roar subsided, the crowd dispersed in utter silence. The hawk circled the grave again and flew off.

* * * * *

After the burial, The Kennedy Center for the Performing Arts hosted a concert in honor of Senator Stevens. The master of ceremonies was David Rubenstein, who worked for President Jimmy Carter, and who had become a successful business person and philanthropist. He was Chair of the Kennedy Center Board.

We felt we owed an obligation to the Stevens family and to all of his friends to show them how much he meant to us at the Kennedy Center, but also how much he meant to all the people in the country.

The truth is Senator Ted Kennedy was probably the greatest supporter of the Kennedy Center. Of course, it is named after his brother, but Senator Kennedy had one modest deficiency in his support of the Kennedy Center; he wasn't a member of the Appropriations Committee. Senator Kennedy realized pretty quickly that if he was going to do things to help the Kennedy Center, he needed to get someone on the Appropriations Committee to help him. He found another Senator, Ted, and they worked together extremely well for many years. The Kennedy Center is very much in the debt of Ted Stevens for that and we thought today what we'd like to do is, to gather people together here because this is a living memorial.

In honor of the Senator's military service, the U.S. Air Force Brass Quintet played military songs, two cello players from Alaska played Handel, and the Harvard Glee Club sang "Wouldn't It Be Nice" and "God Bless America," a tribute to the Senator's days at Harvard Law School. Five musicians of the Thelonious Monk Institute of Jazz played "Bright Mississippi" and "What a Wonderful World." (The leader of that group thanked Senator Stevens for making that group's trip to Alaska possible several years earlier.) A chamber music group composed of members of the National Symphony Orchestra played the 4th movement of Schubert's "Trout" Quintet for the fish-loving Senator, and mezzo-soprano Denyce Graves, one of America's premier operatic stars, sang "America the Beautiful." The tribute to the Senator was spectacular.

* * * * *

Alaska's Governor, Sean Parnell, and the Alaska legislature declared November 18, 2010, to be Ted Stevens Day in Alaska. It would have been the Senator's 87th birthday. Senator Murkowski, who presided over the ceremonies in Anchorage, told Alaskans that the day he was buried, Congress had named an 8,340 square mile ice field "The Stevens Ice Field." The same act designated the highest unnamed mountain in Alaska "Mount Stevens." Time will tell whether Alaskans will follow Reverend Elliot's suggestion and call Mount Stevens simply "Uncle Ted."

Chapter 21

"We Used to Have a Senator Like That"

The so-called Tea Party movement, which wanted to shrink the size of government drastically, was sweeping much of America in 2010. The Tea Party had special appeal in Alaska where people tend to be suspicious of what happens in the "Lower 48," especially Washington, D.C. A Yale-educated lawyer transplanted from Kansas by the name of Joe Miller decided to ride the Tea Party wave and challenge Lisa Murkowski in the Republican primary. He attacked her for being "too liberal."

The conventional wisdom was that Senator Murkowski would prevail, but her campaign was worried. So, leaving nothing to chance, they asked the Alaskan of the Century to tape an endorsement. By the summer of 2010, Senator Stevens' reputation in Alaska was largely restored, and most Alaskans firmly believed he was innocent and the victim of out-of-control prosecutors. Some Alaskans were trying to draft him to run for governor, or, in 2014 to run again for the Senate seat he had held for 40 years. Few in Alaska doubted that he would win—in a landslide.

On July 30, 2010, less than two weeks before his death, Ted Stevens sat before a video camera and taped a simple statement in support of Senator Murkowski: "I trust Lisa and her commitment to keep fighting for us. She's working for Alaska every single day. We need Lisa and the seniority she's earned now more than ever."

The campaign's idea was to run the ad in the final days of the primary to assure victory. But just a few days before the ad was supposed to run, Senator Stevens was killed in the plane crash.

Consumed by the death of Senator Stevens, and thinking Senator Murkowski would win, many Alaskans weren't paying much attention to the Republican primary.

The funeral was held on August 18, six days before the primary. Out of respect for the Stevens family, Senator Murkowski decided not to run the ad.

On August 24, Joe Miller defeated Lisa Murkowski by 2,000 votes.

The winner of the Democratic primary was Scott McAdams, a commercial fisherman and the mayor of Sitka, Alaska. McAdams issued a statement praising Senator Murkowski: "Lisa Murkowski served Alaska as a state legislator and United States Senator with energy and enthusiasm. We agree on the great majority of Alaskan issues. Lisa Murkowski is a class act who always put Alaska first. By contrast, lawyer Joe Miller ran an unfair nasty campaign that didn't extend to Lisa Murkowski the respect she deserves."

* * * * *

Miller promptly took a trip to Washington, D.C., in anticipation of his election to the United States Senate. While there, he said, on Twitter: "Think I'll do some house hunting while I'm in D.C." And this: "Guess I should pick up some office furniture, as well, while in D.C." And: "Then there's a matter of a name plaque for the door." And finally: "My sincere appreciation for the warm welcome, including from future colleagues in D.C."

Miller claimed that a volunteer with access to his Twitter account had sent the tweets. Whoever did it, Alaskans didn't like it.

* * * * *

Senator Murkowski wasn't willing to surrender the Republican Party to Joe Miller. Not without a fight. So on September 17, 2010, she announced that she would run in the general election as a write-in candidate.

On October 1, 2010, Mayor McAdams launched an ad that some described as one of the best campaign ads in the nation during the 2010 campaign season. In it, Mayor McAdams is seen trying on ties in front of a mirror.

He begins, "I'm Scott McAdams, and my wife Romee told me I'd better start wearing a tie so I can look senatorial."

In front of a mirror, he tries on tie after tie. "Now if it takes a tie to finally get the same oil royalties as Louisiana, then I'll wear one. And if it takes a tie to stop outsourcing our jobs to China or our tax dollars to the Lower 48, then that's a good reason too. I approve this message because for me it's about Alaska getting our fair share again." The ad ends with Mayor McAdams settling on a bolo tie, a style that Senator Stevens favored, especially when he was in Alaska. Most Alaskans knew that this was a salute to the Alaskan of the Century, Ted Stevens.

But in case the bolo tie was too subtle a tribute to Uncle Ted in the ad, McAdams came back with one more message, simply saying, "We used to have a Senator like that." The ad ends with the camera closing in on an Incredible Hulk tie just like Senator Stevens used to wear.

When I saw the ad, my eyes filled with tears. Here was a Democrat saluting the Senator Stevens I had known, in effect saying he was the kind of public official that Democrats and Republicans alike should emulate.

It was a great ad. But the Murkowski campaign had an even better ad to run. They pulled out the Ted Steven's endorsement he had filmed ten days before the plane crash. And what had Senator Stevens worn during that endorsement? A bolo tie like the one Scott McAdams had picked.

The ad begins with one of Senator Stevens' daughters, Susan Stevens Covich, approving the ad and thanking Senator Murkowski for not running it in the days after Senator Stevens had died. "My father, Senator Ted Stevens, endorsed Lisa Murkowski in her run for the United States Senate. What some Alaskans don't know is that my father made a campaign commercial for Lisa that was scheduled to run just days after we lost him. Putting our family before her campaign, Lisa made certain 'out of respect' to my dad and my family, the ad did not air."

Then the ad cut to Ted Stevens saying: "I trust Lisa and her commitment to keep fighting for us. She's working for Alaska every single day. We need Lisa and the seniority she's earned now more than ever."

After the Senator had delivered his posthumous endorsement, Senator Murkowski ended the ad by thanking the Stevens family for their support and for "sharing the Senator with all of Alaska." It was powerful stuff. When I saw it, I cried again.

* * * * *

The election was held on November 2. As in 2008, it took quite a while to count the votes in Alaska, but 15 days later, on November 17, 2010, it became obvious that Lisa Murkowski had won. It was the first successful write-in campaign for the United States Senate anywhere in the country in half a century.

The front page of the next day's *Anchorage Daily News* showed Senator Murkowski and Lily Stevens Becker hugging while announcing the news. That day was November 18, 2010, which would have been Senator Steven's 87th birthday, the day which Governor Sean Parnell and the Alaska Legislature had previously declared Ted Stevens Day in Alaska.

* * * * *

Alaska Natives were especially pleased with the outcome of the election. Myron Naneng, President of the Association of Village Council Presidents, flew in from the bush for Murkowski's victory celebration. "I think everybody [in rural Alaska] really made a commitment after what happened in the primary. [Joe Miller] had no presence other than insulting Native people. We are not 'special interests'. We are people who were here before he ever was."

Lisa Murkowski cared for Alaska's first citizens, just as Ted Stevens had. Her victory had the ring of justice to it.

Chapter
22

"Your Job Is to Do Justice"

One day after the dismissal of the Stevens case, Attorney General Holder attended the swearing in of a new class of Assistant U.S. Attorneys. The new federal prosecutors swore the traditional oath of federal officers to "support and defend the Constitution of the United States." The Attorney General delivered a message to the new Assistant U.S. Attorneys. He spoke to them about the extraordinary role played by a federal prosecutor. He told them, *"Your job as Assistant U.S. Attorneys is not to convict people. Your job is not to win cases. Your job is to do justice. Your job is in every case, every decision that you make, to do the right thing. Anybody who asks you to do something other than that is to be ignored. Any policy that is at tension with that is to be questioned and brought to my attention. And I mean that."*

Brendan and I were so impressed, so moved, by these words—especially after what we had just been through—that we had them memorialized in a Lucite block to keep in sight at all times in our offices. What made the Attorney General's statement even more meaningful to us was that he delivered it in the very courthouse where the Stevens case had been dismissed 24 hours earlier.

Attorney General Holder took another significant step that same day. He made an excellent choice to be the new head of the Office of Professional Responsibility, the office that investigates federal prosecutors accused of violating the ethical rules. The Attorney General named veteran federal prosecutor Mary Patrice Brown, a

264

lawyer of unquestioned professionalism to the post. At a speech during her first month on the job, Brown told a group of prosecutors, "If your gut is telling you you do not want the defense to have this, then that tells you you must turn it over. That's how we were trained. People who don't do that, and hold things too close to the chest, those are the people who run into trouble." I could not have said it better myself.

There were other personnel changes at the Department of Justice. Bill Welch, the Chief of the Public Integrity Section, returned to his home state of Massachusetts to be an Assistant U.S. Attorney. He would later leave the Department of Justice altogether for a private sector job. Welch was replaced by Jack Smith, a well-respected federal prosecutor from New York.

Lead courtroom lawyer Brenda Morris moved to Atlanta, and worked out of the U.S. Attorney's Office there. Later, she turned up in Alabama prosecuting a case of alleged influence peddling involving gambling legislation. In that case, Morris was accused of not turning over evidence to the defense on a timely basis. Like Bill Welch, she has since left the government for a private sector job.

Nicholas Marsh and Edward Sullivan of the Public Integrity Section were transferred to the Department of Justice office that handled extraditions.

Two Assistant U.S. Attorneys from Alaska—Joseph Bottini and James Goeke—remained Assistant U.S. Attorneys. Bottini stayed in Anchorage. Goeke moved to the state of Washington.

FBI agent Mary Beth Kepner remained with the Bureau in its Juneau office. Chad Joy, the FBI whistleblower whose complaint confirmed the government misconduct we had previously alleged, left the FBI. There is said to be an internal FBI investigation of Joy's allegations against Kepner, his one-time partner, but it has yet to be released. The FBI turned down my request to see it.

* * * * *

As for Bill Allen, Ted Stevens' "friend" who had done him so horribly wrong, he finally had to face sentencing. The Department of Justice honored its deal with him, even though I believed that the Department could have withdrawn from the deal on grounds that Allen breached the agreement by lying.

At sentencing, the government emphasized that Allen had "cooperated" and that his sentence should be less than it would have been otherwise. One year and a day after the guilty verdict against Senator Stevens, a federal judge in Alaska sentenced him to three years in prison and fined him $750,000. Though I was tempted to attend Allen's sentencing, I chose not to do so.

While it is true that Bill Allen's sentence was much lighter than it would have been had he not "cooperated" at all, I strongly suspect that if the falsity of his testimony at the Stevens trial had not been revealed Allen wouldn't have spent *a single day* in prison.

I did not spend much time thinking about where Allen was going to serve his prison sentence, when he was supposed to report to prison or what he was up to in the meantime. But an article in the *Anchorage Daily News* when Allen began serving his sentence caught my attention. It turned out that Allen was assigned to "Terminal Island," a low-security federal correctional facility located at the entrance of the Los Angeles Harbor. The *Daily News* quoted a prison spokesman who said, "It's not beachfront property, but it's a beautiful location, as prisons go."

The *Daily News* also reported that Allen had been seen at a Las Vegas auction with his daughter Tammy, who bid on and won a limited edition Mustang. The total price for the Mustang was $352,000.

* * * * *

And then there was the matter of the child sex investigation of Allen. In the final few days of trial, we learned that the sex abuse investigations of Allen had been transferred to the Child Exploitation and Obscenity Section of the Department of Justice in Washington, D.C. We thought that the attorneys at Justice specializing in child exploitations would take the matter seriously. They did. But, on August 22, 2010, the *Anchorage Daily News* dropped a bombshell with the headline that "Federal officials won't prosecute Bill Allen on sex charges." According to the article, "top officials in the U.S. Department of Justice have vetoed the prosecution of imprisoned former VECO Chief Bill Allen on sex charges involving minors, closing an Anchorage Police Department and FBI investigation that began in 2004. . . ." According to the *Daily News,* "the police officer who led the case. . ., Sgt. Kevin Vandegriff, along with Detective Michele Logan, who took over the case when Vandegriff was promoted to patrol sergeant, said they are unhappy with the decision, which was left unexplained to them by federal officials." The article quoted Vandegriff, "I think that we put together a very solid case, we did a lot work on it. It deserved to be indicted and heard before a jury." The article also reported that "the Justice Department trial attorney who had been working with them for nearly two years, along with the supervisor of his section, thought the case was strong enough to seek an indictment from a grand jury. But the two prosecutors, in the Child Exploitation and Obscenity Section in Washington, were overruled by officials atop the criminal division. . . ."

* * * * *

On December 13, 2010, an editoral in the *Anchorage Daily News* addressed the issue. After noting that the Justice Department had not given a meaningful answer to her questions of why DOJ did not "pursue what both federal prosecutors and Anchorage Police invesigators said was a strong case against Bill Allen for sexual expolitation of teens," the editorial went on to say: "The silence of the Justice Department on the matter leads naturally to the suspicion that the sex-abuse case was dropped as part of a plea deal to gain Allen's cooperation in the corruption case. We don't know if that's true. We do know that the protection of Alaska's children is more important than a bribery case. We do know that young women came forward in this case only to be told, in effect, that the justice they sought wouldn't be forthcoming. We do know that this sends exactly the wrong message about the value we place on the safety of our children and justice for victims—particulary those most vulnerable including Native girls from Alaska villages."

* * * * *

Bill Allen was released from a half-way house on November 22, 2011. Standard credits for good behavior and apparently for agreeing to enter into an alcohol abuse program meant that he served less than two years.

* * * * *

There were a lot of ups and downs during the years 2009 through 2011. I was pleased that the Attorney General did the right thing and dismissed the case against Senator Stevens that never should have been brought. I was pleased that the Department of Justice was engaged in reform efforts. I was pleased that so many people were calling for lasting reform. But I was deeply disappointed in the refusal of the Justice Department to agree to any reforms in actual rules. And I was devastated by the death of my friends.

Brendan and the other members of our team shared in the highs and the lows. And while we rode the emotional rollercoaster, we waited and waited for the pair of reports, one ordered by Judge Sullivan and the other to be conducted by the Department of Justice itself.

* * * * *

In my two decades as a lawyer, I'd always been able to work my way out of a funk by practicing total immersion in my current caseload. But the death of Ted Stevens, which came 16 months after his case had been thrown out rattled me to my very foundation.

Thinking back on our relationship, I recalled that in the beginning, before he was indicted, the Senator was a bit difficult, a bit prickly. But from the moment of indictment forward, he was like a grandfather to me, and my affection for him grew exponentially as I saw what he was going through.

Then after the trial, when we both had more time to reflect on things and our respect for one another grew, I would say a true friendship developed.

One thing that helped me get through the saddest days was looking at a photo–taken at my house on the night of our celebratory dinner–and re-reading what he had written along the bottom: "Your commitment to assure final victory gave me a new life. Thanks for your use of your great talent and your friendship."

Chapter
23

"Systemic Concealment"

On March 15, 2012, Judge Sullivan released the long-awaited report of Henry Schuelke, the special investigator he'd appointed in 2009. Schuelke and his law partner William Shields (like Schuelke, a former prosecutor) had labored almost three years interviewing witnesses, reading documents and emails, and writing a report which totaled 525 pages.

Their report was hard-hitting from the outset. Its first sentence almost said it all: "The investigation and prosecution of U.S. Senator Ted Stevens were permeated by the systematic concealment of significant exculpatory evidence which would have independently corroborated Senator Stevens' defense and his testimony, and seriously damaged the testimony and credibility of the government's key witness."

In its dissection of the fiasco known as *United States v. Stevens*, the Schuelke Report revealed that there had been great unhappiness and considerable in-fighting among members of the prosecution team. Even though I had suspected as much, what I read still stunned me.

Schuelke and Shields had learned that top-ranking Justice Department brass asked Brenda Morris to be the lead trial lawyer right before the indictment. Schuelke and Shields read prosecutors' emails, which told the story as the prosecutors lived it. Joe Bottini wrote that Nick Marsh considered the addition of Brenda Morris to be a "slap in his face" and that he was so "pissed" that he was considering leaving the Department of Justice over it.

"There is no joy in Mudville right now," Marsh wrote to a friend on the day of the indictment for which he had worked very hard. And Morris herself told the investigators, "Nick was just livid."

According to the Schuelke Report, all four original prosecutors—Marsh, Ed Sullivan, Bottini and Goeke, were upset. Schuelke and Shields wrote that Morris's "four displaced colleagues resented her appointment, and Ms. Morris, in an attempt to avoid making the situation worse, "[tried] to make herself as little as possible," and "did not supervise the prosecution."

Whoa! Did I read that right? Did the same prosecutor who screamed during her closing and mocked Senator Stevens really try "to make herself as little as possible?" And had she really disclaimed supervising the prosecution?

I read it again. I had read it correctly. The ego, anger and abdication of responsibility I was reading about had turned what should have been a search for the truth into a recipe for disaster.

* * * * *

Reading about the dysfunctional prosecution team, I thought to myself how different it was from how the defense had functioned. One trial observer, Cliff Groh, a former Alaska prosecutor who watched the trial and blogged about it daily, compared our team to "a squad of commandos operating behind enemy lines—tough, ruthless, and decisive." He noted that the number of people he saw working on the case for the government and the defense were roughly the same, but observed that our team was well-organized and decisive while the government's was not.

Groh went so far as to compare our team to Delta Force. When this passage was pointed out to me during the trial I chuckled a bit. Comparing our team to Delta Force was over the top, but we were very organized. And decisive. Moreover, Groh only saw the tip of the iceberg. He did not see the incredibly diligent around-the-clock work of every other member of our team outside of the courtroom. We were not concerned about who was getting the glory. (There was no glory for the defense during the trial in any event.) All we were concerned about was doing the best we could for our client, whom we believed to be innocent.

As I read the Schuelke Report, I thought back to what Groh had written during the trial. It was true; Williams & Connolly functioned as a team. We cared about each other, and we really cared about our client, who always came first.

Ever since the beginning of the trial, I had suspected that the Stevens prosecution was driven more by selfish ambition than by a desire to see justice done. The Schuelke Report proved my suspicion right.

* * * * *

I had been very upset, before trial, when the government turned over 500 gigabytes of electronic documents that were absolutely disorganized, as I suspected that the government was intentionally making it hard for the defense to do its job. This was especially upsetting to me given the short amount of time we had to prepare for trial. Though I complained about the government's disorganization when the electronic document collection arrived, I bit my tongue and decided not to allege intentional misconduct. I didn't have the proof.

The Schuelke Report provided that proof. Schuelke and Shields interviewed a government technology specialist who told them that she had organized the electronic documents into a series of folders so that defense lawyers could find what they needed. But then, she told Schuelke and Shields, she was overruled by Nicholas Marsh, who told her to undo her work. This was especially galling to Alex Romain and Simon Latcovich who had asked Nick Marsh to provide the electronic documents in an organized manner. Marsh told them he didn't understand what they wanted.

According to the Report, he told her to dump all the electronic documents into one directory to make finding them difficult. So my first instinct was correct. The government had intentionally disorganized the electronic documents.

* * * * *

At trial, our team was very interested in learning when Bill Allen had first concocted the "covering his ass" testimony. It was devastating testimony, and we believed—instinctively and immediately—that it was a recent fabrication. The notes produced by Paul O'Brien that had led to the dismissal of the case proved that it was a recent fabrication, but we wanted to know how recent? We were hoping that Schuelke and Shields would find out. They did. Allen first came up with his "recollection" while flying to Washington for the trial and reported his new recollection on September 14, 2008, exactly one week before the trial began.

We learned from the Report that the government was very concerned about the Toricelli note when we provided it to them before indictment. This was not surprising to me. The Toricelli note was, after all, a valuable piece of evidence for Ted Stevens. The Schuelke Report revealed that the prosecution team was concerned about the Toricelli note from the minute they laid eyes on it.

Schuelke and Shields found an email in which FBI Agent Kepner expressed her concern that the note might be "fatal" to their case. Other emails revealed that the prosecutors were so concerned they even pursued a hare-brained theory that the note was a forgery. (They concluded, reluctantly, that it was authentic.)

The court-appointed investigators described the birth of the "covering his ass" testimony: "The Torricelli note worried the prosecutors and Agent Kepner, and captured their attention, in April and May, 2008, but no cure for the problem created by those notes for the government's case was found until the week before the trial began when Mr. Allen's memory suddenly improved, after prodding by Agent Kepner. . . .

"Mr. Allen testified in this investigation that the memory of the

CYA statement came to him during his flight to Washington, D.C., for the trial, after some prodding by Agent Kepner. Shortly before the trip, Agent Kepner told him 'that you better figure out or remember what you done with this Torricelli note from Ted. . . . You got to figure out what you done and when did you talk to Bob Persons.' Mr. Allen and [his lawyer] arrived in Washington on Friday, Sept. 12, 2008, and they met with Mr. Bottini and Agent Kepner on Sept. 13 and 14 for trial preparation.

"During the meeting on Sept. 14, 2008, Mr. Allen told Mr. Bottini and Agent Kepner that he remembered speaking with Mr. Persons after receiving the Torricelli note and that Mr. Persons told him that Senator Stevens was 'covering his ass by asking for a bill.' Mr. Bottini recognized immediately the significance of this conversation and he informed the entire team, except for Mr. Goeke who was still in Alaska."

Shazaam! On September 14, 2008, after being prodded by an FBI Agent, the case turned around dramatically for the government when its richly-rewarded star witness suddenly delivered what the government so desperately wanted to hear—an explanation for the Torricelli note.

In a clear violation of FBI regulations, Agent Kepner did not prepare an interview memo of what had happened, which made it highly unlikely that we would ever have learned the truth but for an amazing series of events: a whistleblower emboldened by the rulings of a courageous judge; original prosecutors getting held in contempt; and their replacement by Paul O'Brien and his team, who found prosecutor notes of an earlier statement by Allen that was entirely inconsistent with Allen's case-breaking testimony. (In yet another violation of FBI regulations, there was no interview memorandum of Allen's earlier inconsistent statement either.)

* * * * *

The government had cheated us. But as bad as that was, there was more. Brendan had asked Allen on cross-examination during trial if he had just come up with the "covering his ass" testimony recently. Allen denied it. Here are Brendan's questions and Allen's answers:

Q: Well, you came in here the other day on your direct examination, and you said, well, despite the fact that I saw this letter, I heard from Mr. Persons I shouldn't send a bill because this was just Ted covering his ass; do you remember that testimony?

A: That's exactly right.

Q: When did you first tell that story? When did you first say those words? Was it in the last—since September 9th? Was it since September 9th?

A: It's been so long that I can't tell you how many days before I talked to him, but I did, and I asked him, hey, I got to get something done. I've got to get some invoices. And he said, hell, don't worry about the invoices. Ted is just covering his ass. That's exactly what he said. . .

Q: When did it come to you, sir?

A: What?

Q: When did you first tell the government that Persons told you Ted was covering his ass and these notes were meaningless? It was just recently, wasn't it?

A: No. No.

Q: On September 9th, you didn't tell them that, did you?

A: Hell, I don't know whatever—

Q: You gave them reasons why you didn't send a bill. You answered you simply wanted to do the work was one of them, and another was part of the reason was that the costs were higher than they needed to be. You didn't tell them then about Persons' conversation with you, did you?

A: You know what, I don't know when I talked to them, but I did talk to him, and it's been quite aback, quite a while back. Whether you like it or you don't.

Q: When did you first come up with this, sir?

A: When did I come up with it?

Q: When did you first tell somebody?

A: Huh?

Q: When did you first tell a government agent?

A: Hell, I don't know I don't know what day it was.

* * * * *

Schuelke and Shields saw this for what it was—undeniably false testimony that should have been corrected by the prosecutor. (If a prosecutor knows that his witness has testified falsely, he is required to bring that to the attention of the Court and defense counsel.) Neither Bottini nor any other prosecutor in the courtroom that day did so.

"Mr. Allen's denial was false," the Schuelke Report stated. "He told Mr. Bottini and Agent Kepner about the CYA statement by Mr. Persons for the first time on Sept. 14, 2008, a week before the trial began, during a trial preparation session for which no 302 was written. Mr. Bottini knew the testimony was false and knew that he had an obligation . . . to correct that testimony there and then, but he did not. . . ."

* * * * *

And, rather than correct the testimony, he capitalized on it during final arguments. Here is what Bottini said in closing:

> [Senator Stevens] says I did ask for a bill for 2002 work. Government [Exhibit] 495 is the note he sent on October 6th, 2002, the Torricelli note, and you remember what Bill Allen said after that? Bob Persons did pay him a visit, came by and he told him, look, he doesn't really want a bill. He's just— pardon my French—covering his ass. . .

* * * * *

How could this have happened in the first place? When Bill Allen said he had no recollection of discussing a bill with Bill Persons—a statement that contradicted Allen's bombshell testimony and contradicted what he had told Joe Bottini and Mary Beth Kepner on September 14—there were four prosecutors and an FBI agent present. Why didn't the prosecutors tell us about the contradictory statement? What was their excuse?

"Memory failure." Each prosecutor who participated in the interview of Allen that day and FBI Agent Kepner claimed memory failure. Every one. Here is what the Schuelke Report said about that:

> The complete, simultaneous and long term memory failure by the entire prosecution team, four prosecutors and the FBI case agent, of the same statement about an important document made at the same meeting by their key witness in a high profile case is extraordinary. Considering the galvanizing effect the Torricelli note had on the prosecutors during the weeks following its receipt, that memory failure becomes astonishing.

* * * * *

Not only is it astonishing, but "memory failure" is also an excuse that most prosecutors would never accept from a citizen whose freedom was in their cross-hairs. And, of course if Agent Kepner had prepared an accurate interview memorandum as she was required to do, and if prosecutors had provided such a memorandum to the defense as they were required to do, there would have been no excuse at all. The contradictory statement would have been preserved.

* * * * *

Bambi Tyree was an Alaskan woman with whom Allen was rumored to have had sex when she was underage and he was in his fifties or sixties. The Report referred to Bambi Tyree as "a juvenile prostitute who had a sexual relationship with Mr. Allen when she was 15 years old." The Schuelke Report stated that in 2004, when an Assistant U.S. Attorney named Frank Russo and an FBI Agent named John Eckstein interviewed her as a witness in a drug and prostitution trial, they questioned her about her relationship with Mr. Allen.

According to Eckstein's interview memo (aka a "302"):

> TYREE had sex with BILL ALLEN when she was 15 years old. TYREE previously signed a sworn affidavit claiming she did not have sex with ALLEN. TRYEE was given the affidavit by

ALLEN'S attorney, and she signed it at ALLEN'S request. TYREE provided false information on the affidavit because she cared for ALLEN and did not want him to get into trouble with the law.

This 302 came to the attention of the prosecutors, some of whom expressed concern that it should be disclosed to defense counsel in cases in which Bill Allen was going to be a witness. However, Marsh made a presentation to the Department of Justice's Professional Responsibility Advisory Office, telling them that the 302 was "ambiguous" and "inconclusive" as to whether Allen had suborned perjury.

Of course, there was nothing at all "ambiguous" or "inconclusive" about it. Tyree told the government that Allen asked her to make a false statement under oath (to keep him out of jail for having sex with a 15 year old). Evidence that the government's star witness has suborned perjury from his statutory rape victim is clearly information that must be disclosed to the defense under *Brady v. Maryland*. But based on the false information that Marsh gave them, his advisors at the Department of Justice concluded the Eckstein interview memo did not need to be disclosed to the defense.

As I read what happened, I became infuriated. In its letter before trial purporting to disclose *Brady* information, the government had represented that there was a rumor that Bill Allen had suborned perjury, but it had been thoroughly investigated and there was "no evidence" that he had done so.

No evidence? Hardly. There was strong evidence, but Nick Marsh buried it.

I also learned from reading the Report that the government had written briefs with an eye toward "smoking out" whether we, the defense, knew about the Tyree episode. We did not. We had relied on the government's representations.

Near the end of the trial, Bill Welch, head of the Public Integrity Section, learned about the Tyree 302. I learned from the Schuelke

278

Report that, to his credit, Welch said to Marsh, "What is f*#@ing ambiguous about this?" and then directed that it be turned over.

We received it—a few days before closing—with over 500 other pages of documents and a cryptic cover letter. We did not realize its value until after trial. We learned from the Schuelke Report that the government had Allen standing by in case we discovered it and they needed to fly him back to try to explain it. Here is how the Schuelke Report wrapped up the long section on Bambi Tyree:

> These astonishing misstatements concealed the existence of documents and information in Mr. Marsh's, Mr. Bottini's and Mr. Goeke's possession and well known to them since at least October 2007, namely, Agent Eckstein's 302 . . . which un-equivocally documented Ms. Tyree's admission that she lied under oath at Mr. Allen's request. The government had every reason to want to avoid any cross-examination of Bill Allen on these issues. Before the trial, Mr. Allen's lawyer, Robert Bundy, told the prosecutors that if Mr. Allen was questioned about Ms. Tyree, he would assert his Fifth Amendment privilege and re-fuse to answer. Agent Kepner told DOJ investigators in 2009, that "Allen would become unglued whenever an article would appear involving allegations related to the [Anchorage Police Department] sexual investigation."

If the jury had known that Bill Allen had asked a juvenile prostitute to lie under oath to keep Allen out of trouble with the law, no juror would have believed a word Allen said. If the jury had known that Allen became "unglued" whenever an article appeared involving him in allegations relating to a child sexual abuse investigation, they would have understood the incredible pressure he was under to please the government. Under those conditions, no jury would have found Ted Stevens guilty.

* * * * *

And, finally, what did the Schuelke Report have to say about other sex abuse allegations against Bill Allen? It reported that about a month before trial the government prosecutors learned there was a new investigation by state investigators and that not only did that investigation have "merit," but also that the police "will be submitting the case to prosecutors in the near future." It reported that Assistant U.S. Attorney Bottini contacted Allen's lawyer and informed him of these new developments.

* * * * *

Reading the Schuelke Report provided one more reason for me to be extremely upset. During the later stages of the trial, I had sat by helplessly as the government prosecutors repeatedly mocked, ridiculed and browbeat Ted and Catherine Stevens for having the audacity to testify that they believed that the time for all workers had been included on the contractors' bills.

Schuelke learned that Rocky Williams, whom the prosecutors sent back to Alaska as opening statements were taking place, had told the government the very same thing shortly before trial. He told them he understood that all of his time was included on the bills. Even more importantly, Rocky Williams told government prosecutors that he had told Ted Stevens that all of his time was on the bills. This completely corroborated the Stevens' testimony that they thought that all his time was included in the bills they paid.

Was this information memorialized in an interview memorandum and provided to the defense? No. Special Agent Chad Joy, the whistleblower, told investigators that either Bottini or Goeke—he could not remember which one—had dictated a memorandum to him that left out this crucial information that would have been helpful to the defense. Instead, Joy was asked only to record a few things that prosecutors thought were harmful to the defense.

That 302, by the way, was never provided to the defense. Not that it would have helped us if it was, because the government only wrote down what was helpful to the government. The government concealed what was helpful to the defense. Don't write it down and it doesn't exist. Talk about an unlevel playing field.

This was brand new information, uncovered for the first time by the Schuelke-Shields investigation, and as I again thought back to the utter contempt with which the government had treated Senator and Mrs. Stevens, I got so angry I had to stop reading and put the Report down for a while. I did, however, think to myself that I wished Senator Stevens and Bill Phillips were around to read it.

* * * * *

The Schuelke Report concluded that Bottini and Goeke intentionally withheld information favorable to the defense regarding Rocky Williams and Bambi Tyree, information that was constitutionally required to be disclosed.

The Report also found that Bottini "withheld significant impeachment information by his intentional failure to correct materially false information given Mr. Allen during his cross-examination, which Mr. Bottini knew at the time was false."

The Schuelke Report made no findings regarding Nicholas Marsh.

It noted that Bill Welch was largely removed from the prosecution team once Morris was appointed the lead.

It accepted Brenda Morris's statement that she did not supervise the team. She was not involved because she was busy making herself as small as possible.

It concluded that Ed Sullivan, the youngest lawyer on the team, had not acted intentionally.

Schuelke's mandate was to determine whether any of the prosecutors should be prosecuted for criminal contempt. To be guilty of criminal contempt, one must intentionally violate a clear and unambiguous court order. Ultimately, Schuelke concluded that Judge Sullivan did not issue a clear and unambiguous order to produce *Brady* information to the defense. He did not issue a clear order because the *Stevens* prosecution team assured Judge Sullivan that it was not necessary, because they were going to fulfill their constitutional duty to disclose evidence of innocence without an order.

Schuelke added, "It should go without saying that neither Judge Sullivan nor any District Judge should have to order the Government to comply with its constitutional obligations." That's exactly right. No judge should have to order a prosecutor to follow the law. But because Judge Sullivan did not issue such an order, criminal contempt charges were not appropriate.

So, the Schuelke Report found intentional misconduct by some prosecutors and "systematic concealment" of evidence of innocence from the defense. But it found it could not recommend prosecution for criminal contempt of court, the only crime Schuelke was authorized to investigate. That meant we would have to wait for the Department of Justice itself to determine whether or not to prosecute its own prosecutors.

* * * * *

Media reaction to the Schuelke report was immediate and widespread. *The New York Times* and the *Washington Post* used the same word to describe the report—"blistering." The headline in the *Wall Street Journal* read: "Report Excoriates Stevens Prosecutors." The *Journal* article quoted the same sentence from the Report as practically every other newspaper: the prosecution was "permeated by the systematic concealment of significant exculpatory evidence which would have independently corroborated Senator Stevens' defense and his testimony and seriously damaged the credibility of the government's key witness."

I felt vindicated by the excellent work that Hank Schuelke and Bill Shields had done. More importantly, I thought the Senator was vindicated. Again, I wished that he and Bill Phillips were alive to read it.

One voice that expressed what I believe the Senator and Bill would have expressed had they still been alive when the Report came out was that of Jim Morhard, who, like Bill Phillips, had worked for Senator Stevens in the past and remained close. When Jim Morhard learned that the Schuelke Report had not recommended criminal contempt charges, he wrote an op-ed for the *Wall Street Journal* entitled "Are Prosecutors Above the Law?"

The Supreme Court said in 1963 (*Brady v. Maryland*) that prosecutors have a constitutional duty to reveal evidence favorable to defendants. Yet the Schuelke report made no recommendation that the prosecutors be charged with criminal contempt of court for failing to reveal such evidence—because Judge Sullivan never gave the prosecutors a "clear and unambiguous" order that they "follow the law."

Well, those of us who were in the court room during the trial watched Judge Sullivan continually direct the prosecution to reveal exculpatory evidence to the defense after they had been caught repeatedly not doing so. Most of it became public only after the trial was over (one widely reported episode involved moving a witness from D.C. to Alaska). The evidence was persuasive enough for the U.S. Attorney General to recommend throwing out the convictions. It most likely would have exonerated Stevens during the trial.

The first duty of a prosecutor, as an officer of the court, is to uphold the rule of law. By withholding exculpatory evidence, these prosecutors failed to do so. A judge should not have to give a prosecutor an order to follow the law. Perhaps it will be argued that charging these prosecutors with criminal contempt of court could have a chilling effect on future federal prosecutors. A reasonable person might respond that charging them might have a chilling effect only on future prosecutors who think they are above the law.

The Stevens prosecutors—by what the report called "significant, widespread, and at times intentional misconduct"—intentionally destroyed the career of an iconic man who had flown the China-Burma "hump" during World War II and served 40 years in the U.S. Senate. Failure to punish them will set a terrible precedent.

Mr. Morhard was the chief of staff of the Senate Appropriations Committee from 2003 to 2005. He was one of four survivors of the plane crash that killed Ted Stevens.

* * * * *

I agreed with Jim—whom I had met and knew to be a wonderful individual with a strong emotional attachment to the Senator—but I understood that Schuelke and Shields had a limited mandate. However, the DOJ's own report would be coming out soon, and surely the Department would punish those prosecutors. And so we continued to wait for justice.

* * * * *

The Department of Justice released its report late in the afternoon on the Thursday before Memorial Day, May 24, 2012. (It is a Washington tradition for government agencies to issue bad news right before holiday weekends to minimize press coverage.) Actually, DOJ did not release it to the public at all. The Department provided the report to the Senate Judiciary Committee—which had been demanding it for quite some time—and it was the Committee that released the DOJ Report to the public.

The factual investigation was thorough (671 pages worth) and professional, and it covered even more ground than the Schuelke Report.

For me, the highlights were the same three failures to disclose evidence favorable to the defense discussed in Schuelke. It determined that the government violated ethics rules and the Constitution by not providing *Brady* information regarding Allen's "covering his ass" testimony, the value of the renovations, Allen's suborning of perjury from Bambi Tyree, and Rocky Williams' belief and statements to Ted Stevens that his time was included in the bills.

The Department of Justice Report concluded that Bill Welch and Ed Sullivan did not engage in misconduct. It concluded that Brenda Morris showed poor judgment by not supervising the prosecution. And, like the Schuelke Report, it declined to make findings as to

Nicholas Marsh. As for Bottini and Goeke, it found that they had engaged in "reckless [not intentional] misconduct."

As for punishment, it recommended a 40 day suspension for Bottini and a 15 day suspension for Goeke. That was it. Both Bottini and Goeke continue to prosecute defendants as federal prosecutors in Alaska and Washington. Mary Beth Kepner continues to work as an FBI agent without any public reprimand.

When the report was released by the Senate, I was in LaGuardia Airport waiting for a long-delayed flight. Fortunately I had my laptop with me, and was able to read large portions of the Report downloaded from the internet. I couldn't believe what I was reading. The Report essentially described the same conduct as the Schuelke Report, but then concluded that the prosecutors were merely "reckless." According to DOJ, they had not acted intentionally at all. And the punishment was almost non-existent. How were things ever going to get better when that was all the Department of Justice was going to do in a case like this?

After Brendan, Simon, and I spoke on the phone, Simon put together a quick statement that he emailed to reporters while I flew back from New York. Here it is:

> Today the Department of Justice demonstrated conclusively that it is not capable of disciplining its prosecutors. Apparently, prosecutors can violate the Constitution, deny the defendant exculpatory evidence demonstrating innocence, and introduce perjured testimony without any fear that they will be punished. Prosecutors orchestrated a miscarriage of justice in Senator Stevens' case that caused the Attorney General of the United States to order the case dismissed. Trial Judge Emmet Sullivan declared the misconduct the worst he had encountered in 25 years on the bench. The misconduct caused a jury to render an illegal verdict, which in turn resulted in the loss of Senator Stevens' re-election bid. And, the balance of power shifted in the United States Senate. The punishment imposed is laughable. It is pathetic. No reasonable person could conclude that a mere suspension of 40 and 15 days for two of the prosecu-

tors is sufficient punishment for the wrongdoing found in the report.

The Report appeared to be comprehensive. But as our statement said, the disconnect between the wrongdoing described in the report and the so-called punishment was a mile wide.

* * * * *

On the one-year anniversary of Ted Stevens' death, there was still no tombstone marking his grave because Catherine Stevens was struggling to decide what to put on it. Of course, a description of his military service belonged on the tombstone, and that would be especially appropriate at a military cemetery like Arlington. But, how do you capture, on a single piece of stone, a life as full as that of Senator Ted Stevens?

During the months since the Senator had died, we had stayed in nearly daily contact with Catherine, and she had repeatedly shared her dilemma—what to put on the tombstone. One day when she came by for lunch she mentioned it again. This time, she was quite serious.

"Okay," Brendan said, "if you really want my opinion, here is what it should say." He grabbed a piece of paper and without pausing wrote: "A life of service to country, state, and family."

Those words, which perfectly describe the Senator's life, are now etched on his tombstone. For him, it was all about service. Reasonable people may have disagreed with where he stood on policy issues, but his Senate colleagues, Democrats and Republicans alike, never questioned his deep commitment to public service. Senator Harry Reid, the opposition leader, said, "Public service was more than a career for Senator Stevens; it was his life's calling."

* * * * *

The Senator started his adult life fighting for his country. At age 84, he fought the government and won; the Department of Justice lost. A select team of experienced prosecutors made the judgment to indict a sitting Senator, and once that decision was made, they had to win "by any means necessary," as Judge Sullivan put it.

As it turned out, their win at all cost mentality doomed the case, disgraced the prosecutors, and enveloped the Department of Justice in what may be its biggest scandal of this generation.

Only with the passage of time and leadership that demonstrates intolerance for prosecutorial abuse will the Department's reputation be restored. Unfortunately, the misconduct of a few can cause us to forget that most Department of Justice lawyers serve honorably and effectively, and should not be tainted by the wrongdoing of some. Civilized society could not exist without prosecutors faithfully enforcing our laws. Senator Stevens—himself a federal prosecutor in the Territory of Alaska—knew, and I know, that the overwhelming majority of prosecutors are honest, conscientious, and hard-working public servants. I always encourage young lawyers to become prosecutors because being a good prosecutor can be government service at its finest.

By the same token, however, if we don't learn from the miscarriage of justice in the case of Senator Ted Stevens, we are bound to repeat it. If what happened to Ted Stevens can happen to a United States Senator in Washington, D.C., four blocks from the U.S. Capitol and six blocks from the Supreme Court, it can happen to any citizen in any courtroom in America.

Chapter
24

Guidance

On January 4, 2010, roughly eight months after the dismissal of the Stevens case, the Department of Justice published a series of memos addressing concerns about the Department's discovery practices and emphasizing that federal prosecutors would receive increased training. The memos established "guidelines" for prosecutors on how to fulfill their discovery obligations, suggesting to them where they should look for discoverable information and what they should look for. The guidelines encouraged them to provide more than the law required and to make a record of what they disclosed so there'd be no question about what had been provided to the defense.

The guidelines suggested that prosecutors should provide favorable evidence to the defense regardless of whether the prosecutor personally believed that the information would actually make a difference in the case. In *United States v. Stevens*, we heard the argument over and over again that clearly favorable evidence did not really need to be disclosed under the Constitution, because it was not material (i.e., in the prosecutor's opinion, it would not have actually made a difference in the outcome of the case). Of course, in the end, there was no conceivable argument that the hidden evidence in the Stevens case was not material to the outcome But the guidelines suggested that prosecutors should not use the tired excuse of "no harm, no foul," that the withheld evidence could not be "material" to the outcome.

The Attorney General himself issued a statement addressing increased training of prosecutors instituted by the Department and the new guidelines: "Along with the increased training for prosecutors we have already instituted, these new guidelines will ensure that we strive to meet that standard every day and in every case." The Attorney General also stressed the importance of doing justice: "The Department of Justice's responsibility is not just to win cases, but to do justice."

* * * * *

While I believed that these efforts were undertaken in good faith by leaders in the Department and applauded them as a step in the right direction, I was disturbed by some of what I heard and read. First, I was disturbed by the fact the Department had concluded in one of its memos that "incidents of discovery failures are rare in comparison to the number of cases prosecuted."

There was no data to support that assertion. The Department did not conduct an empirical study of its past case files to see whether they contained information that should have been disclosed, but was not. The truth is that there is no way to know if there have been discovery failures without looking to see what might have been undisclosed.

Defense lawyers do not have x-ray vision. Almost all discovery failures are uncovered by a combination of aggressive defense challenges and luck. That's what happened in the Stevens case. If we had not pushed and pushed and pushed for discovery, if an FBI whistleblower had not come forward, and if the original prosecutors had not been held in contempt, we never would have learned that Bill Allen had originally told prosecutors exactly the opposite of what he said on the stand, under oath, at trial.

And in fact there were discovery failures by the Department of Justice in other cases in 2009, the same year that *United States v. Stevens* was dismissed. I knew of four others:

- A new trial was ordered in a federal case in California when the prosecution failed to inform the defense of benefits provided to jailhouse "snitch" witnesses. Law enforcement officials had offered cash and freedom to the witnesses in exchange for their testimony, but did not disclose the existence of those rewards to the defense.

- In Montana, federal prosecutors withheld evidence reflecting poorly on the credibility of their main witness. The judge described this withholding of evidence as an "inexcusable dereliction of duty."

- In a case in federal court in Miami, prosecutors failed to turn over evidence that reflected favorably on the defendant and poorly on the credibility of government witnesses.

- And in Massachusetts, the chief federal judge, the Honorable Mark Wolf, discovered a prior inconsistent statement of a government witness when he insisted on reviewing the prosecutors' notes himself. Judge Wolf concluded that there was a "long pattern of inadvertent failures to produce material exculpatory information, and cases of intentional misconduct as well" in the U.S. Attorney's Office for Massachusetts.

I don't know how many discovery failures there have been, but more to the point, the Department of Justice does not know either. I do know that in 2009 there were at least five, the Stevens case and the four described above, which is five too many. And to believe that there were only five is the height of naiveté.

* * * * *

I was also disturbed by the Department's insistence that its new "guidance" did not carry the force of law. One of the memos contained the legalistic disclaimer that this memorandum "provides prospective guidance only and is not intended to have the force of law or to create or confer any rights, privileges, or benefits." In other words, defendants in criminal cases cannot use the guidelines in court to insist on discovery.

What kind of a reform is that? Whether discovery obligations are fulfilled should not rely entirely on the good faith of the prosecutor. It should be a matter of rules.

This was especially offensive to me because there had been a previous movement led by the American College of Trial Lawyers (many of whom are former prosecutors), the pre-eminent group of lawyers who actually try cases, to change the rules to provide more meaningful discovery to the defense. Former U.S. Attorney for the Southern District of New York Robert Fiske was one of the lawyers who spearheaded the effort.

The Department of Justice fought tooth and nail in opposition to this proposed rule change, insisting that they could deal with defense concerns about discovery by amending their internal rules. To beat back the reform movement, the Department amended an internal policy manual to require greater disclosure. But the internal policy manual—like its new "guidance"—stated that it provided no rights or remedies to defendants, and that only the Department of Justice could enforce its own manual.

That was two years before they charged Ted Stevens. The amendments to the Manual were supposed to level the field, but they did not give Ted Stevens a fair trial. Nor did they prevent the other four violations that occurred in 2009.

Now, history was repeating itself: the once-warned Department of Justice was responding to concerns about its discovery practices merely by issuing "guidance."

I was disturbed because until we have tougher rules, rules that could be enforced by defendants, history will surely repeat itself—over and over again.

I wasn't the only person who yearned for reform. Judge Sullivan wrote a thoughtful public letter respectfully suggesting that broader discovery was needed. His efforts were opposed by the Justice Department.

Senator Lisa Murkowski introduced a bill in the Senate that would have required prosecutors to disclose all favorable evidence to the defense except in cases where witness safety or national security was at issue. Her legislation would also have imposed meaningful sanctions for discovery failures in appropriate circumstances. The Department of Justice opposed her efforts.

Editorial pages across the country disagreed with the Justice Department. The *Los Angeles Times* endorsed model legislation proposed by the National Association of Criminal Defense Lawyers that would "require prosecutors to disclose information that is 'favorable to the defendant' even if it's not considered admissible. Prosecutors also would have to disclose material sought by the defense 'without delay.' "

An editorial from *The New York Times* entitled "Justice and Open Files" made several excellent points:

> Prosecutors have a constitutional duty to disclose significant evidence favorable to a criminal defendant. But too often that duty, as laid out by the 1963 Supreme Court decision *Brady v. Maryland,* is violated.

> To help ensure compliance, some prosecutors, criminal defense lawyers and legal scholars have sensibly concluded that prosecutors' files, as a general rule, should be made open to defendants. In cases where turning over evidence might endanger a witness, for example, a judge could allow an exception.

> A small number of state and local governments have adopted open-file policies that require prosecutors to make available well before trial all information favorable to the defense, without regard to whether such information is likely to affect the outcome of the case. North Carolina and Ohio and places like Milwaukee have found that such policies make prosecutions fairer and convictions less prone to error. The Justice Department should join this movement and set a national example. But instead, it continues to take half-measures in response to its own failures to meet disclosure requirements.

It responded to several cases of *Brady* violations by its attorneys—including egregious misconduct in the case of the late Senator Ted Stevens—by providing more training and by directing each United States Attorney's office to set forth clearly its version of the department's *Brady* policy, which is to turn over favorable evidence only if it is "material," meaning likely to make a difference in the case's outcome.

Those changes are not sufficient because the *Brady* rule is too easily skirted. It allows prosecutors to withhold favorable evidence that they deem not to be material, leaving defense lawyers unaware of evidence that may be owed them. Ninety-six percent of federal criminal cases are resolved by plea bargains, so the rule puts defendants at a disadvantage in negotiation: without access to information in the government's files, they don't know the evidence they face and can't assess their odds at trial.

This weakness in the *Brady* rule also means there is no way of knowing how many violations are buried by plea bargains. The few that become known, through trials or post-trial challenges, are no index of the problem's true dimensions, but they can show how deeply rooted it is.

After the Justice Department dropped the case against Senator Stevens in 2009 because of prosecutorial misconduct, including the withholding of exculpatory evidence, Judge Emmet Sullivan of the Federal District Court in Washington, D.C., chose to appoint outside counsel to investigate what went wrong rather than trust the Justice Department to do it.

In 2009, Judge Mark Wolf in Boston likewise found that the long-standing problem eroded his trust in federal prosecutors. "In the District of Massachusetts," he wrote, "the government has had enduring difficulty in discharging its duty to disclose material exculpatory information to defendants in a timely manner."

In both the federal and state court systems, it is essential that rules about disclosing evidence be followed in ways that promote justice. An open-files policy would come closer to meeting this important standard.

* * * * *

Other well-qualified parties have looked at the problems raised by the *Stevens* case. One is the Constitution Project, a think tank founded in 1997 to "bring together policy experts and legal practitioners from across the political spectrum to foster consensus-based solutions to the most difficult constitutional challenges of our time." It emphasizes a bi-partisan approach.

The Constitution Project put together, in letter form, "A Call for Congress to Reform Federal Criminal Discovery." Signed by a bipartisan group of "current and former judges, prosecutors, law enforcement officers, defense lawyers, and others" calling for greater discovery rights for criminal defendants, it cited the *Stevens* case as the "most notable" example of the problem. The letter was signed by more than 100 former federal prosecutors, all alumni of the Department of Justice, who believed that reform of criminal discovery was vitally necessary.

The American Bar Association is the leading organization of American lawyers. Its House of Delegates adopted a resolution proposed by the Council of the Criminal Justice Section which consists of an equal number of prosecutors, defense lawyers and law professors. The resolution called on all federal and state governments to ". . . adopt rules requiring the prosecution to seek from its agents and to timely disclose to the defense before the commencement of trial all information known to the prosecution that tends to negate the guilt of the accused, mitigate the offense charged or sentence, or impeach the prosecution's witnesses or evidence, except when relieved of this responsibility by a protective order."

I heard from a number of people that the Department was taking its post-Stevens training very seriously. I even heard that there were slide presentations that began with a photograph of my friend Ted Stevens. That was gratifying. But the Department's refusal to consider new rules and laws belies its commitment to reforms.

We are a nation of laws, not a nation of guidelines. And while I believed in the good faith of the Justice Department leaders who were promoting the new training and guidelines, I believed that new rules would be a lasting legacy. With exceptions for those rare cases where witness safety or national security is an issue, providing information to a citizen seeking to defend himself should be a fundamental right of all American citizens. No citizen is a match for the information gathering-powers of the United States government. Justice demands that the government share that information with a defendant on trial for his freedom.

Chapter
25

Leveling the Field

It's worth repeating that wrongly-accused citizens themselves have few tools with which to fight injustice. Of course there is the requirement that you cannot be convicted of a crime in America unless a unanimous jury of 12 citizens finds you guilty beyond a reasonable doubt. Sometimes the defense gets to strike more potential jurors than the government. And there's the Fifth Amendment privilege against self-incrimination: no American citizen can be compelled to be a witness against herself.

But those are the only advantages the criminal defendant has. The typical defendant in a criminal case has little chance of success when pitted against public condemnation of the accused, the government's greater ability to gather information, the government's authority to "incentivize" witnesses to testify and the government's far greater resources throughout the investigation and prosecution. Even when you're defending a wealthy citizen, as I have sometimes done, defense counsel is always outmatched by the government's greater resources.

Some will tell you that isn't so. The government lacks resources, they claim. But in truth, nobody has more resources than the government. The government always has virtually unlimited resources which no citizen can match.

Prosecutors have all sorts of ways to gather evidence. As I mentioned earlier, they can execute search warrants, wiretap phones, and seize computer records. And the government can subpoena witnesses to testify before a grand jury. What's more, the law allows the government to lie to witnesses to convince them to talk. Prosecutors can offer them cash. And they can offer witnesses—and their families—freedom. The defense, on the other hand, cannot do any of these things. Witnesses, whether they have been expressly threatened or not, are usually extremely intimidated by the government, and as a result are too scared to talk to defense lawyers.

How do we level the playing field so that the truth is more likely to emerge from a criminal trial? Above and beyond enacting legislation requiring the disclosure of *all* favorable information to the defense, Congress should enact a law making *all* of the government's investigative files open to the defense. Witnesses should be identified and their statements produced in advance of trial.

In those rare cases in which witness safety or national security is an issue, adjustments can be made under court supervision. There already are many mechanisms in effect to insure witness safety and preservation of national security secrets. Courts can issue orders requiring that, when necessary, disclosures be limited to protect witnesses. And a law passed in 1980 known as the Classified Information Procedures Act requires judges to balance a defendant's need for information to defend himself with national security concerns. Concerns about witness safety and national security should not stand in the way of fairness to any defendant, especially those whose trials (like that of Senator Stevens) have nothing to do with witness safety or national security.

I spend much of my professional life representing clients in civil cases. In a civil lawsuit, the parties are required to exchange all relevant information in advance of trial. If that is the best way to find the truth in a civil case where mere money is at issue, why isn't it also the best way to find the truth in a criminal case where human liberty hangs in the balance?

* * * * *

It is also critical that the information a defendant needs be preserved and available without alteration by the government. For

297

this reason, statements by witnesses should be recorded. We should have had a tape recording of the April 15, 2006, interview of Bill Allen during which prosecutors asked him about the most important evidence in the case. We should have had a recording of the September 14, 2008 interview in which he first told the government about the "covering his ass" testimony he invented. We should have had recordings of *all* of Allen's statements so we could track how the testimony of such a well-rewarded witness evolved.

The FBI should have prepared a memo of these two interviews, but did not. Even if it had prepared a memo of the interviews, what is more likely to be complete and accurate: a memo prepared by an FBI agent based on notes and memory or an actual recording? And what is less expensive for the government: paying an FBI agent to type a memo after-the-fact or simply hitting the record button and storing the recording in an electronic data base?

When the Department of Justice Office of Professional Responsibility came to interview me about the Stevens case, they pulled out a recorder and announced that it was office policy that all witness interviews be recorded. If that's the process used when prosecutors are investigating their own, why shouldn't that same process be used when they investigate the rest of us?

It is especially important to record interviews when a witness is testifying in exchange for benefits—such as his freedom or the freedom of his children, and thus has a powerful motive to change his story over time to please the government. The accused, his lawyers, and the jury, deserve to know how the cooperator's story may have changed over time.

* * * * *

Some readers may have wondered why Bill Allen's alleged recollection of what Bob Persons said to him—"Ted's just covering his ass"—was admitted into evidence by Judge Sullivan in the first place. Wasn't that hearsay (defined as "an out-of-court statement offered for its truth")? That's a good question, but, unfortunately, the answer is not as good, certainly not from a defense standpoint.

Allen was allowed to tell the jury what Persons had, allegedly, told him because of an exception to the hearsay rule known as the co-conspirator exception. Bill Allen and Ted Stevens were, the government had alleged, co-conspirators. When offered by the government, the statement that one (alleged) co-conspirator (allegedly) makes to another is almost always admitted into evidence. Appellate courts have held that the conspiracy need not even be illegal for the government to use it.

There is no principled reason for this rule. Its ultimate rationale is to make it easier for the government to win. The co-conspirator exception to the hearsay rule should be eliminated.

* * * * *

If a witness doesn't provide the testimony the government wants to hear, prosecutors often threaten family members with criminal charges. I have seen them do it over and over again. In the case against Senator Stevens, the government threatened to prosecute Bill Allen's children. It's highly likely that the majority of parents would lie to protect their children. How can these sorts of threats possibly be consistent with learning the truth? The laws and rules of ethics should be amended to prohibit this practice.

* * * * *

The practice of rewarding "cooperators" for their testimony is a traditional tool of law enforcement. But it can cross the line. The benefits conferred on Bill Allen were beyond the pale. We need to examine skeptically the practice of giving extravagant benefits to "cooperators." We ought to consider whether conferring any benefits on witnesses is a legitimate tool of law enforcement in the first place.

At the least, the Department of Justice should establish an independent unit that must sign off on benefits provided to witnesses. Such a unit would consider whether the benefits being conferred are likely to corrupt the truth-finding process and whether the testimony of the witness receiving benefits can be independently corroborated. The unit should also ensure that a procedure is in place to make sure that the defense will be provided with accurate information regarding the extent of the benefits being provided and how the so-called cooperator's story has changed over time.

* * * * *

We had 12 lawyers fighting to vindicate Senator Stevens' right to a fair trial. Most American citizens have one overburdened public defender who also has hundreds of other cases going on at the same time. That must change. We must find a way to get lawyers for indigent citizens the resources they need. The Stevens case and hundreds of others listed on the website of the Innocence Project prove that we cannot count on prosecutors to give defendants a fair trial. As Judge Sullivan said, "Thank goodness we don't have to count on the United States to give him a fair trial."

And we also need to insure that judges get the resources they need to vindicate defendants' rights. Congress has not approved a pay increase for federal judges in decades. Clerks for judges routinely make more in the private sector in their first year after clerking than the judges they worked for—even justices of the Supreme Court. That is absurd. Judges with lifetime appointment enforce the Constitution and are the last firewall against executive branch tyranny. They should be paid better than they are.

* * * * *

Prosecutors, being human, are not infallible. Some make honest mistakes. And some lie and cheat.

When prosecutors make honest mistakes that lead to unfair trials, cases need to be dismissed without regard to the political ramifications. And when prosecutors lie and cheat, they need to be disciplined. Sternly.

When prosecutors, who have taken an oath to uphold the law, break their vow and become criminals themselves, they should be prosecuted and metted punishment at least as severe as the punishment they sought for those they prosecuted. I take no joy in saying that. I have devoted much of my career to defending citizens, not trying to put them in jail. But the only way to deter prosecutors from cheating is to punish them severely when they get caught.

In 1940, then-Attorney General and later Supreme Court Justice Robert H. Jackson said, "The prosecutor has more control over life, liberty, and reputation than any other person in America." What Attorney General Jackson said in 1940 is equally true today. Democracy requires that we have very powerful checks on prosecutorial power.

An attitude that prosecutors can do no wrong is very dangerous. Punishment of prosecutors to deter future wrongdoing needs to be taken very seriously. Congress should establish an independent commission—outside the Department of Justice—to investigate and prosecute good faith claims of unethical behavior by federal prosecutors.

* * * * *

Given the gravity of what they did, the tap-on-the-wrist punishment of two of the Senator's prosecutors was pathetic. They disregarded Judge Sullivan's admonitions and ignored the Constitution. The *Stevens* prosecutors rallied together to carry out a prosecution that *had* to be successful.

In *United States v. Stevens,* we had a very smart federal judge who had been on the bench for 25 years, and I believe he sensed, early on, that what was happening was wrong. He kept warning and warning and warning the government. It finally got to the point where he found government lawyers in contempt of court and that triggered the removal of the original prosecution team from the case, post-verdict. When new, honest lawyers entered the case for the government, they quickly found evidence of the initial trial team's wrongdoing.

The fact remains, however, that if this can happen to a U.S. Senator in our Nation's Capital then it can happen to any citizen anywhere in the United States. The fact that we caught them was certainly a product of experience, skill, and aggressive defense work—but it also required luck. And that's the most frightening thing. If you need luck to ensure justice, then we don't have much of a system at all.

Since the dismissal, I have received many insightful observations about what took place and what it means for our system of justice. One that ought to be thought-provoking to any citizen came from Professor James E. Coleman, Professor and Co-Director of the Wrongful Convictions Clinic at Duke Law School.

He wrote: "Many of the people who will praise Mr. Holder for dropping the charges against Mr. Stevens will not care that the same kind of misconduct routinely taints the trials of those who are not rich, or famous, or well-connected, or well-regarded. Nor will they likely step back and learn from what happened to Mr. Stevens."

* * * * *

We think we have a wonderful system; we say it's the best in the world. But in reality we have a flawed system. While it has some protections for the defendant, it also has severe flaws, many of which we don't even recognize.

The system failed Ted Stevens. First, the case never should have been brought in the first place. Junior lawyers were out of control and senior lawyers declined to do the right thing and stop the case. After it was brought, government lawyers hid favorable information. There's no doubt in my mind that if we had had the information the government had concealed, the verdict would have been not guilty. The verdict had to be not guilty. The Government's case could not have survived had, as the law requires, the truth been provided. How many of our citizens are in prison after trials in which the truth was never provided?

* * * * *

On the day the government's ill-conceived and illegally-prosecuted case against the Senator was dismissed, Judge Sullivan asked him if he had anything he would like to say. Ted Stevens rose, and—

302

magnanimously—said, "Until recently, my faith in the criminal system, particularly the judicial system was unwavering, but what some members of the prosecution team did nearly destroyed that faith. Their conduct has consequences for me that they will never realize and can never be reversed. But today, Your Honor, through your leadership and persistence and commitment to the rule of law, my faith has been restored, and I really can never thank you enough. . .

"Your actions gave me new hope that others may be spared from similar miscarriages of justice, and it is my hope that when the dust settles I may be able to encourage the enactment of legislation to reform the laws relating to the responsibilities and duties of those entrusted with the solemn task of enforcing criminal laws."

Tragically, when the dust finally settled, Ted Stevens was unable to fulfill that task because he was no longer alive. Ted Stevens wanted legislation enacted "to reform the laws relating to the responsibilities and duties of those entrusted with the solemn task of enforcing criminal laws." He wanted others to be spared the anguish he had endured. That was his last wish. It is the duty of those who admired and loved him to grant that wish.

Source Notes

In the following source notes, transcripts from *United States v. Stevens* are identified by date and page number. Court filings from *United States v. Stevens* are identified by "Document Number" or "Doc. No." Exhibit are identified as "Government Exhibit" or "Defense Exhibit" followed by the exhibit number.

Judge Sullivan Quote

"Thank goodness we don't have to rely upon the United States . . . .": Transcript, Oct. 2, 2008 at 25 (am)

Chapter 1

"The courtroom clerk asked Ted Stevens . . . .": Transcript, July 31, 2008 at 2-3

"Acting Assistant Attorney General Matthew Friederich . . . .": www.youtube.com/watch?v=g7fTq9wWjIU (last visited May 28, 2014)

"How realistic is it . . . .": Transcript, July 31, 2008 at 7-8

"Usually we don't mind . . . .": Transcript, July 31, 2008 at 13

"The government is prepared . . . .": Transcript, July 31, 2008 at 20

Brady v. Maryland, 373 U.S. 83 (1963)

"The bulk of it . . . .": Transcript, July 31, 2008 at 20

Chapter 2

"the newspapers were reporting . . . .": E.g., *Anchorage Daily News,* "FBI Raids Legislative Offices," Sept. 1, 2006

"The Alaska press was reporting . . . ." *id.*

"'Operation Polar Pen' was the FBI's code name . . . .": A. Coyne & T. Hopfinger, *Crude Awakening* at 123 (Nation Books 2011)

"the press was reporting . . . .": *Anchorage Daily News*, "FBI Wanted to Know About VECO," Sept. 6, 2006

"Allen had dropped out of high school . . . .": Transcript, Sept. 30, 2008 at 56 (pm)

"After stints in Texas . . .": Transcript, Sept. 30, 2008 at 58-60 (pm)

"A good welder, young Bill Allen caught the eye . . . .:" Transcript, Sept. 30, 2008 at 61 (pm)

"Allen and a man named William Veltrie . . . .": Transcript, Sept. 30, 2008 at 63 (pm); *International Directory of Company Histories*, Vol. 7 at 558 (St. James 1993)

"They started with about a dozen . . . .": Transcript, Sept. 30, 2008 at 63 (pm)

"Not long afer they renamed the company . . . .": *International Directory of Company Histories*, Vol. 7 at 558 (St. James 1993)

"By the time the pipeline was completed . . . .": Transcript, Sept. 30, 2008 at 66 (pm)

"In the 1980s VECO's business . . . .": *International Directory of Company Histories*, Vol. 7 at 558 (St. James 1993)

"By the year 2000, VECO had 4000 employees.": Transcript, Sept. 30, 2008 at 69 (pm)

"Video surveillance conducted as part of Operation Polar Pen revealed . . . .": www.youtube.com/watch?v=ajh9yco8EjQ (last visited May 28, 2014); www.youtube.com/watch?v=xyW3YS6lvYA (last visited May 28, 2014)

"The FBI confronted Allen . . . .": Transcript of Allen Sentencing, Oct. 28, 2009 at 55

"Allen later admitted . . . .": Transcript, Oct. 1, 2008 at 98-99 (am).

"Bill Allen and Mark Allen had been overheard . . . .": Office of Professional Responsibility Report: Investigation of Allegations of Prosecutorial Misconduct in *United States v. Theodore F. Stevens,* Crim. No. 08-231 (D.D.C. 2009) (EGS) at 435

"But if Allen provided 'cooperation' . . . .": Transcript, Oct. 6, 2008 at 67- 68 (pm)

"Allen was given time to sell . . . .": *id.* at 68 (pm)

"In fact, thanks to his 'cooperation' . . . .": Transcript, Oct. 7, 2008 at 49-50

"Allen's cooperation would be considered the same as VECO's . . . .": Defendant's Exh. 3372

"CH2M Hill negotiated a special provision . . . .": Defendant's Exh. 3491, Transcript, Oct. 7, 2008 at 52-59 (pm)

"prosecutors advised a federal judge . . . .": Transcript of Allen Sentencing at 26

"Under the guidelines . . . .": Defendant's Exh. 3372

"Allen received a sentence . . . .": Transcript of Allen Sentencing at 61

"Mark Allen, one of Bill Allen's sons, used some of his wealth . . . .": *Anchorage Daily News,* "Derby Winner's Owner Has Ties to Alaska Bribery Scandal", May 2, 2009

"After Allen began cooperating . . . .": *Alaska Dispatch*, "Full Disclosure, Jan. 31, 2008; *Alaska Dispatch,* "Another Sexual Abuse Claims Threaten to Taint Star Witness in Stevens Trial", Sept. 18, 2008

"Without any public explanation . . . .": *Anchorage Daily News*, "Federal Officials Won't Prosecute Bill Allen on Sex Charges," Aug. 22, 2010

"One of the most famous examples is Scooter Libby . . . .": *Washington Post,* "Libby Found Guilty in CIA Leak Case," Mar. 7, 2007

"Another well-known example is . . . .": *Wall Street Journal,* "Martha Stewart Is Found Guilty of All Charges," Mar. 7, 2004

"The Andersen conviction . . . .": *Arthur Andersen LLP v. United States,* 544 U.S. 696 (2005)

Chapter 3

"a city with roughly ten times as many Democrats . . . .": District of Columbia Board of Elections and Ethics Monthly Report of Voter Registration Statistics for the Period Ending February 28, 2007

"Alaska. . .has more Republicans than Democrats . . . .": Alaska Voter Registration by Age as of 5/3/2006

"He had served more than 40 years . . . .": *The New York Times,* "Ted Stevens, Longtime Alaska Senator, Dies at 86," Aug. 11, 2010

"From 2003-2007, Ted Stevens served as President Pro Tem . . . .": *PRO TEM: Presidents Pro Tempore of the United States Senate Since 1789* at 111 (Senate Historical Office 2009)

"Senator Inouye, a rather formal speaker . . . .": *Time,* "Ted Stevens," Dec. 16, 2010

"Stevens, a Republican, campaigned for Inouye . . . .": *Roll Call,* "Inouye Decries Partisan Fighting," Oct. 4, 2011

"His motto was, "To hell with politics . . . .": Cong. Record, Nov. 20, 2008, S10688

"First, 62 percent of the land . . . .": Congressional Research Service, "Federal Land Ownership and Data," Feb. 8, 2012

"there are still parts of Alaska that lack basics . . . .": *Anchorage Daily News,* "Northern Exposure; Obama's Team Sees Difficulties, Unique to the Bush," Aug. 12, 2009

"in 2000, the state legislature named him . . . .": *id.* at 79

"According to the *Almanac of American Politics* . . . .": The *Almanac of American Politics* at 76 (National Journal Group 2006)

"I never lose my temper. I always know . . . .": *The New York*

Times, "Ted Stevens, Longtime Alaska Senator, Dies at 86," Aug. 11, 2010

"He was born in 1923 . . . .": Transcript, Oct. 16, 2008 at 94 (pm)

"his parents divorced . . . .": *id.* at 95 (pm)

"When his grandfather died, young Ted and his grandmother . . . .": *id.* at 96 (pm)

"Ted Stevens worked multiple jobs . . . .": *id.* at 97 (pm)

"Ted Stevens attempted to enlist . . . .": *id.* at 97-98 (pm)

"After two months of these exercises, he tried . . . .": *id.* at 98 (pm)

"Soon he was flying C-46 and C-47 supply planes . . . .": *id.* at 100-01 (pm)

"All told, he flew 228 combat missions." Military Record and Report of Separation, Certificate of Service for Theodore F. Stevens

"The Army awarded him two Distinguished Flying Crosses . . . .": *id.*

"Ted Stevens finished college at UCLA and then enrolled at Harvard Law . . . .": *id.* at 101-02 (pm)

"worked for a few years . . . at Northcutt Ely . . . .": *id.* at 103 (pm)

"He met Ann Cherrington . . . .": *id.* at 104

"That same year, Ted Stevens got a job practicing law in Fairbanks . . . .": *id.* at 104-05 (pm)

"Ted Stevens . . . was asked to be the top federal prosecutor . . . .": *id.* at 105 (pm)

"Ted Stevens was appointed to be a lawyer at the U.S. Department of the Interior . . . .": *id.* at 106

"President Eisenhower opposed statehood . . . .": *Anchorage Daily News*, "Eisenhower Was Reluctant Supporter of Alaska Statehood," July 6, 2008

"Ted Stevens' nickname . . . .": *Alaska Dispatch*, "Ted Stevens: The Long Goodbye," Aug. 18, 2010

". . .Ted Stevens worked on the legislation . . . .": Transcript, Oct. 16, 2008 at 106-107 (pm)

"Ted Stevens moved back to private practice . . . .": Transcript, Oct. 16, 2008 at 108 (pm)

"One of the first cases he worked on . . . .": S. Haycox & A. Mc-Clanahan, *Alaska Scrapbook* at 177-78 (CIRI Foundation 2007)

"In 1964, Ted Stevens ran for, and won . . . .": Transcript, Oct. 16, 2008 at 108 (pm)

"In the next term, he was elected Majority Leader . . . .": S. Doc. 111-16, "Ted Stevens: Memorial Addresses and Other Tributes" at, (Government Printing Office 2012)

"Later that year when Bob Bartlett, the Senator holding the other Alaska seat . . . died in office . . . .": Transcript, Oct. 16, 2008 at 109 (pm)

"was re-elected six times . . . .": *Almanac of American Politics* at 76 (National Journal Group 2006)

"During his forty years in the Senate, Ted Stevens was instrumental . . . .": *The New York Times*, "Ted Stevens, Longtime Alaska Senator, Dies at 86," Aug. 11, 2010

"Ted Stevens had been an outspoken critic of President Carter's boycott . . . .": www.teamusa.org/HOF-Class-of-2012-Home/HOF-class-of-2012-TedStevens (last visited May 28, 2012)

"Donna de Varona, the Olympic gold medal swimmer . . . .": *We-News*, "Ted Stevens Was Guardian Angel of Women in Sports," Aug. 18, 2010

"as chair of the Senate subcommittee responsible for civil service issues, he was a key player . . . .": *Washington Post*, "Ted Stevens, Former Senator from Alaska, Was a Champion of Federal Workers," Aug. 12, 2010

"Watergate prosecutor Jim Neal . . . .": *The New York Times*, "Jim Neal, Litigated Historic Cases, Dies at 81", Oct 23, 2010

"Two weeks later . . . .": georgebush-whitehouse.archives.gov/news/releases/2007/05/images/20070523-4_p052307sc-0481-772v.html (last visited May 28, 2014)

"The FBI 'raid' of the Stevens" cabin . . . .": E.g. *Washington Post* "Alaska Senator's Home is Raided", July 31, 2007; http://transcripts.cnn.com/TRANSCRIPTS/0707/31/sitroom.01.html (last visited May 28, 2014)

"The note read . . . .": Government Exh. 495

"At his confirmation hearing . . . .": S. Hrg 110-478, "Confirmation Hearing on the Nomination of Michael B. Mukasey to Be Attorney General of the United States," at 99, Oct. 17 & 18, 2007

"The Office of Inspector General . . . eventually found . . . .": U.S. Department of Justice, "An Investigation into the Removal of Nine U.S. Attorneys in 2006," Sept. 2008

"The Inspector General did find . . . .": U.S. Department of Justice, An Investigation of Allegations of Politicized Hiring and other Improper Personnel Actions in the Civil Rights Division, July 2, 2008

"What appeared to be the final straw . . . .": U.S. Department of Justice, "An Investigation of Allegations of Politicized Hiring by Monica Goodling and Other Staff in the Office of the Attorney General," July 28, 2008

"The next day, the *Washington Post* ran a front page story . . . .": *Washington Post*, "Internal Justice Dept. Report Cites Illegal Hiring Practices," July 29, 2008

Chapter 4

"The next day, the story of . . . .": *Washington Post,* "Sen. Stevens Indicted on 7 Corruption Courts," July 30, 2008

"The 28 pages indictment . . . .": Docket No. 1

"based on her own experience in being cleared . . . .": *The New York Times*, "The Ill-Timed Trial of Senator Stevens of Alaska," by Carl Hulse, Sept. 19, 2008

"Three years before I joined . . . .": *United States v. Omni International Corp.*, 634 F. Supp.1414 (D. Md. 1986)

"The process of being assigned to a judge . . . .": *The New York Times* "Spin of Wheel May Determine Judge in 9/11 Case," Nov. 27, 2009

"The federal court in the District of Columbia . . . now uses a computer . . . .": Local Rule 40.3(a) of the Legal Rules for the U.S. District for the District of Columbia

"Judge Sullivan was born and raised . . . .": Official Biography of the Honorable Emmet G. Sullivan

Chapter 5

"First, . . . the government is required to provide . . . .": Rule 16 of the Federal Rules of Criminal Procedure

"Second, under a Supreme Court decision . . .": 353 U.S. 657, (1957); 18 U.S.C. 3500; Rule 26.2 of the Federal Rules of Criminal Procedure.

"Third, and finally, under the case of *Brady* . . .": 373 U.S. 83 (1963)

"The government's been investigating . . . .": Transcript, July 31, 2008 at 4

"Deputy Chief Morris responded . . . .": *id.* at 6

"The next day, I followed up with a letter . . . .": Doc. 60-2

"Once the government has provided the discovery it is obligated to provide, then the rules . . . .": Rule 16 of Federal Rules of Criminal Procedure.

"We asked Judge Sullivan to order the prosecutors . . . .": Transcript, Aug. 13, 2008 at 9-10

"The hard drive also contained pages and pages . . . .": *id.* at 4-8

"The Federal Rules of Evidence provide that evidence of other crimes, wrongs or acts . . . .": Rule 404 of the Federal Rules of Evidence,

"Among the facts they wanted to use . . . .": Doc. Nos. 33, 45 & 49, Transcript, Oct. 19, 2008 at 108-16

"We had to go to Judge Sullivan, who ordered them to provide us with copies . . . .": Transcript, Sept. 16, 2008 at 23

"We understand our obligations . . . .": Doc. No. 130-4

"The letter purported to summarize . . . .": Doc. No. 130-6

"When I was arguing for access to the interviews . . . .": Transcript, Sept. 12, 2008 at 30-41; *Anchorage Daily News*, "Judge Orders That Stevens' Lawyers Get Pile of Paper Data," Sept. 13, 2008

Chapter 6

"The law allows a federal case to be transferred . . . .": Federal Rule of Criminal Procedure 21(b)

"I wrote a short letter . . . .": Doc. No. 4-2

"Here was his response . . . .": Doc. No. 4-1

"We estimated that over 90 percent . . . .": Doc. No. 4

"The prosecution team argued . . . .": Doc. No. 9; Transcript, Aug. 20, 2008 at 26-39

"In order to illustrate . . . .": Transcript, Aug. 20, 2008 at 2-25

"The Assistant Attorney General answered . . . .": www.youtube.com/watch?v=g7fTq9wWjIU (last visited May 28, 2014)

"We filed a motion . . . .",: Doc. No. 13

"I argued to Judge Sullivan . . . .": Transcript, Sept. 10, 2008 at 18-22

"At one point, prosecutor Joseph Bottini . . . .": *id.* at 22-27

"In the end, Judge Sullivan ruled . . . .": *id.* at 27-31

"We filed a motion saying that the Department of Justice had no constitutional basis . . . .": Doc. No. 15

"Judge Sullivan denied our motion . . . .": Transcript, Sept. 10, 2008 at 78-79

"Prosecutors filed a motion seeking to prevent us from cross-examining government witnesses . . . .": Report to Hon. Emmet G. Sullivan of Investigation Conducted Pursuant to the Court's Order Dated April 7, 2009 at 270-86

"Typically, the government had posted its notice about an irrelevant real estate . . . .": Doc. No. 20

"The government argued that we were off-base. They also stated . . . .": Report to Hon. Emmet G. Sullivan of Investigation Conducted Pursuant to Court's Order dated April 7, 2009 at 289-351

"Judge Sullivan ruled that we could cross-examine . . . .": id. at 284-85

"The prosecution opposed this standard motion, saying . . . .": Doc. No. 32

"Judge Sullivan disagreed with the government . . . .": Transcript, Sept. 10, 2008 at 4

Chapter 7

"The government hired . . . .": Transcript, Sept. 23, 2008 at 10-12 (am)

"I only recall . . . .": *id.* at 65-75 (am)

"There was another potential juror whom I recall quite clearly . . . .": id. at 144-51 (pm)

"Here is how Matt Apuzzo . . . .": Associated Press, "Stevens Jury Shows Senator He's Far From Alaska", Sept. 24, 2008 (reprinted with permission of the Associated Press)

Chapter 8

"The following article appeared . . . .": From *The New York Times*, Sept. 19, 2008 © 2008 The New York Times. All rights reserved. Used by permission and protected by the Copyright Laws of the United States. The printing, copying, redistribution, or retransmission of this Content without express written permission is prohibited.

"This is a simple case . . . .": Transcript, Sept. 25, 2008, at 27 (am)

"He took away the public's right . . . .": *id.* at 28 (am)

"Ladies and gentlemen . . . .": *id.* at 28-30 (am)

"The defendant is a career politician . . . .": *id.* at 30-31 (am)

"Morris referred to Senator Stevens as 'the defendant' . . . .": *id.* at 27-52 (am)

"At the conclusion of this case . . . .": *id.* at 52 (am)

"He began by thanking the jurors . . . .": *id.* at 55 (am)

"At the end of the day . . . .": *id.* at 56 (am)

"the Torricelli note . . . .": *id.* at 73 (am)

"At the end of the case I'm going to come back here . . . ." *id.* at 82-83 (am)

"Hess testified that the purpose of the renovation was to create some space . . . .": *id.* at 98 (am)

"and that Catherine Stevens was the driver . . . .": *id.* at 50 (pm)

"Hess also testified that local restaurateur Bob Persons was going to be involved, because the Senator himself was too busy.": *id.* 105-06 (am) and 51 (pm)

"Hess futher told the jury that the Senator had sent him a note after lunch . . . .": *id.* at 23-24 (pm)

"Mr. Hess testified further that he believed the note . . . .": *id.* at 24 (pm)

"The Senator, for his part . . . .": Transcript, Oct. 17, 2008 at 27-32 (am)

"One was employed by the contractor . . . .": Transcript, Sept. 26, 2008 at 70-96 (am)

"Not one of these workers ever met . . . .": Transcript, Sept. 25, 2008 at 8 through Sept. 26, 2008 at 96 (am)

"The government's seventh and next witness was a woman named Cheryl Boomershine . . . .": Transcript, Sept 26, 2008 at 6:51 (pm)

"According to the records, one of the workers . . . .": Gov't Exh. 177

"The law allows for the use . . . .": Rule 803 (6) of The Federal Rules of Evidence

"Hearsay is defined . . . .": Rule 801 of the Federal Rules of Evidence

"I pointed out . . . .": Transcript, Sept. 26, 2008 at 54 (pm)

"Rocky told us . . . .": Doc. No. 103-4

"Our motion . . . began like this . . . .": Doc. No. 103

"disturbed about the contents . . . .": Transcript, Sept. 29, 2008 at 3 (am)

"Marsh explained . . . .": *id.* at 4-6 (am)

"It doesn't matter if these costs . . . .": *id.* at 7 (am)

"I responded for the defense . . . .: *id.* at 12-13 (am)

"They put on testimony, the last witness . . . .": *id.* 32 (am)

"a very different conception . . . .": *id.* at 18 (am)

"We're distressed that we're being accused of this . . . .": *id.* at 21 (am)

"They filed papers accusing us . . . .": Doc. No. 105

"It would have been better if . . . .": Transcript, Sept. 29, 2008 at 33-34 (am)

"We never tried to hide him." . . . .": *id.* at 35 (am)

"What gave the government authority . . . .": *id.* at 35-38 (am)

"I established . . . .": Transcript, Sep. 29, 2008 at 49-73 (am)

"Prosecutors called several more workers . . . .": Transcript, Sept. 29, 2008 at 74 (am) through Sept. 30, 2008 at 88 (am)

"Under Bottini's questioning . . . .":Transcript, Sept. 30, 2008 at 52 (pm) through Oct. 1, 2008 at 102 (am)

Chapter 9

"Dear Mr. Cary . . . .": Doc No. 126-2

"One said that Bill Allen had . . . .": Doc. No. 126-2

"The second memo said that Allen had told the government . . . .": Doc. No. 126-2

"Here's what the government's September 9th letter said . . . .": Doc. No. 126-3

"I have been a member of this court . . . .": Transcript, Oct. 2, 2008 at 4-6 (am)

"I've been talking about *Brady* . . . .": *id.* at 8-10 (am)

"Brenda Morris responded for the government . . . .": *id.* at 10-22 (am)

"Brendan replied . . . .": *id.* at 23-24 (am)

"Brenda Morris quickly shot back . . . .": *id.* at 24 (am)

"The judge interjected . . . .": *id.* at 24 (am)

"Morris argued . . . .": *id.* at 24 (am)

"Judge Sullivan erupted . . . .": *id.* at 24-25 (am)

"Judge Sullivan then posed a question . . . .": *id.* at 25 (am)

"The ensuing dialogue . . . .": *id.* at 25-27 (am)

"Before trial, it began . . . .": Doc. No. 126

"The government responded . . . .": Doc. No. 127

"Through nobody's fault . . . .": Transcript, Oct. 2, 2008 at 3-5 (pm)

"Now, coincidentally . . . .": *id.* at 8-9 (pm)

"Morris responded, No. No . . . .": *id.* at 9 (pm)

"She even submitted an affidavit . . . .": Doc. No. 128

"Judge Sullivan interjected . . . .": Transcript, Oct. 2, 2008 at 13 (pm)

"I argued that would not work . . . .": *id.* at 11-13 (pm)

"Yes, I responded . . . .": *id.* at 13 (pm)

"Judge Sullivan asked, Why? . . . .": *id.* at 13 (pm)

"Because that was *Brady* information . . . .": *id.* at 13-14 (pm)

"It's fundamental . . . .": *id.* at 24-25

"What about that *Brady* information" . . . .": *id.* at 26-29 (pm)

"How does the Court . . . .": *id.* at 29 (pm)

"Brenda Morris, to my surprise, agreed . . . .": *id.* at 29 (pm)

"How do I have that confidence? It's about integrity. It's about officers . . . .": *id.* at 29-30 (pm)

"But, Judge, please understand . . . .": *id.* at 30 (pm)

"Judge Sullivan said . . . I don't know if the government . . . .": *id.* at 30 (pm)

"No, Your Honor, we are . . . .": *id.* at 30-34 (pm)

"Anything else . . . .": *id.* at 34 (pm)

"I responded, yes . . . .": *id.* at 34-35

"And . . . Judge Sullivan had one of his decisions reversed . . . .": *United States v. Oruche*, 484 F.3d, 590 (D.C. Cir. 2007)

"Judge Sullivan decided not to dismiss . . . .": *id.* at 51-53(pm)

Chapter 10

"Until today, defense counsel have refrained . . . .": Doc. No. 130

"The government's response accused us . . . .": Doc No. 134

"Judge Sullivan held another hearing . . . .": Transcript, Oct. 8, 2008 at 32-44 (pm)

"Judge Sullivan pointed out . . . .": *id.* at 52-55 (pm)

"Marsh, responding for the government, ...": *id.* at 55 (pm)

"Judge Sullivan was upset anew . . . .": *id.* at 56-68 (pm)

"Marsh responded . . . .": *id.* at 82 (pm)

"I don't' believe we heard anything from the government . . . .": *id.* at 82 (pm)

"What prompted it . . . .": *id.* at 84 (pm)

"Morris replied . . . .": *id.* at 84-86 (pm)

"It's very troubling . . . .": *id.* at 89-90 (pm)

"The first tape . . . .": Government Exh. 650

"The second . . . .": Government Exh. 651

"The third . . . .": Government Exh. 652

"Brendan's cross-examination of Allen . . . .": Transcript, Oct. 6, 2008 at 55 (pm) through Oct. 7, 2008 at 79 (am)

"The Supreme Court has repeated . . . .": *Ford v. Wainwright*, 477 U.S. 399 (1986); *Crawford v. Washington*, 541 U.S. 36 (2004)

". . . an FBI agent who read emails into the record . . . .": Transcript, Oct. 8, 2008 at 22-114 (am)

"Another worker who repaired a boiler . . . .": *id.* at 29-55 (pm)

"And three recordings of calls . . . .": Government Exhs. 659, 660 and 662

"On the stand, Anderson . . . .": Transcript, Oct. 9, 2008 at 23-82 (am)

"According to Tony Hopfinger . . . .": *Alaska Dispatch* "Bill and Ted's Excellent Adventure," Aug. 13, 2008

"He said that he did a lot of work . . . .": Transcript, Oct. 9, 2009 at 23-82 (am)

Chapter 11

"Former Secretary of State Colin Powell . . . .": Transcript, Oct. 10, 2008 at 5-15 (pm)

"Republican Senator Orin Hatch . . . .": Transcript, Oct. 10, 2008 at 6-12 (am)

"Donna de Verona, an Olympic swimmer . . . .": Transcript, Oct. 14, 2008 at 51-62 (pm)

"And Gwendolyn Sykes, then Chief Financial Officer . . . .": Transcript, Oct. 14, 2008 at 25-32 (am)

"The late Senator Daniel Inouye . . . .": Transcript, Oct. 14, 2008 at 64-79 (pm)

"The first of our witnesses . . . was a neighbor names Keith Tryck . . . .": Transcript, Oct. 14, 2008 at 33-44 (am)

"Bob Persons estimated that the renovations would cost $87,000 . . . .": Government Exh. 2003; Defendant's Exh. 431

"According to Randall . . . .": Transcript, Oct. 10, 2008 at 34-56 (am); Defendant's Exh. 30

"The assessors testified . . . .": *id.* at 29-81 (pm); Defendant's Exh. 632-34

"Bob and Jean Redmond testified . . . .": Transcript, Oct. 14, 2008 at 83-111 (am)

"Hannah testified . . . .": *id.* at 57-82 (am)

"He testified consistently with . . . .": *id.* at 90-94 (am)

"In court, he testifed . . . .": Transcript, Oct. 14, 2008 at 95-112 (am) & 12-50 (pm)

"In total, the money she spent was . . . .": Defendant's Exhs.10, 137, 182, 187, 192, 197, 224, 292, 303, 306, 308, 313, 316, 318, 323, 328, 331, 336, 341, 348, 363, 378, 380, 381, 391, 393, 406, 434, 437, 02, 560, 570, 590, 631, 966 and 967

"They said that he needed to be advised . . . .": Transcript, Oct. 14, 2008 at 43-46 (am)

"As Persons told it . . . .": Transcript, Oct. 14, 2008 at 6 (pm) through Oct. 15, 2008 at 41 (am)

"I asked Catherine at trial . . . .": Transcript, Oct. 14, 2008 at 43 (am) & 8 (pm)

"Brenda Morris's cross-examination of Catherine . . . .": *id.* at 8 - 78 (pm)

Chapter 12

"One alleged gift not related to the chalet was actually specified in the indictment: a car swap with Bill Allen . . . .": Doc. No. 1

"Judge Sullivan effectively dismissed . . . .": Transcript, Oct. 8, 2008 at 90 (pm)

"Jeanne Penny—a friend of Catherine's . . . .": Transcript, Oct. 14, 2008 at 75-89 (am); Oct 16, 2007 at 97-99 (am)

"For his part, Ted Stevens could not have cared less . . . .": Government Exh. 454

"The Stevens prosecutors suggested . . . .": Transcript, Oct. 21, 2008 at 29-30 (am)

"According to the disclosure form, ...": Government Exh. 884

"That did not keep Stevens' prosecutor Bottini . . . .": Transcript, Oct. 21, 2008 at 29-30 (am)

"It was also upsetting to Catherine Stevens . . . .": Transcript, Oct. 16, 2008 at 103 (am)

"When the Senator testified . . . .": Transcript, Oct. 21, 2008 at 49-51 (am)

"Bob Persons thought . . . .": Transcript, Oct. 15, 2008 at 45-47 (am)

"Ted Stevens, who did not know . . . .": Transcript, Oct. 17, 2008 at 93 -101 (am)

"The Senator and Mrs. Stevens were furious . . . .": Transcript, Oct. 16, 2008 at 99-100 (am)

"The government prosecutors claimed to have caught . . . .": Transcript, Oct. 20, 2008 at 29-30 (am)

"One was Jim Vargos, ...": Transcript, Oct. 9, 2008 at 91-98 (pm)

"Osmar himself testified . . . .": Transcript, Oct. 9, 2008 at 80-90 (pm)

"Monson testified . . . .": Transcript, Oct. 9, 2008 at 99-111 (pm)

"One of our witnesses was Orie Williams . . . .": Transcript, Oct. 14, 1008 at 60-64 (am)

"Heldi Sandvik was a similar witness . . . .": Transcript, Oct. 14, 2008 at 45-59 (am)

"We also called Julie Kitka . . . .": Transcript, Oct. 10, 2008 at 28-37 (pm)

"Louise Johnson . . . .": Transcript, Oct. 10, 2008 at 16-29 (pm)

"Pro-Stevens witness Mano Frey . . . .": Transcript, Oct. 10, 2008 at 81-90 (pm)

"Sampson . . . testified . . . .": Transcript, Oct. 10, 2008 at 90-93 (pm)

"Howell testified . . . .": Transcript, Oct. 10, 2008 at 94-110 (pm)

"Joe Terry asked her, "In connection with your job . . . .": Transcript, Oct. 10, 2008 at 94-97 (am)

Chapter 13

"the press had reported that the government's case had many

problems . . . .": *The New York Times*, "Judge Berates Prosecutors in Trial of Senator," Oct. 3, 2008; *Huffington Post*, "Ted Stevens Trial Winds Down for Prosecutors," Oct. 8, 2008; *CNNPolitics.com*, "Judge Denies Motions to End Stevens Trial," Oct. 8, 2008

"What's more, he had promised . . . .": *Juneau Empire,* "Sen. Stevens Says He Plans to Testify at Corruption Trial," Sept. 21, 2008

"Ted Stevens' testimony began with . . . .": Transcript, Oct. 16, 2008 at 94 (pm)

"The Senator then gave the jury . . . .": *id.* at 94-111 (pm)

"The Senator next testified . . . .": Transcript, Oct. 16, 2008 at 9-59 (am); Oct. 17, 2008 at 4-9 (am)

"And the Senator testified about the heart of the defense . . . .": Transcript, Oct. 16, 2008 at 59-61 (am); Government Exh. 495

"Brenda Morris' cross-examination . . . .": Transcript, Oct. 16, 2008 at 50 (pm) through Oct. 20, 2008 at 97 (am)

Chapter 14

"On the intervening Saturday, the 18th of October, Judge Sullivan held a hearing . . . .": Transcript, Oct. 18, 2008 at

"We asked for a jury instruction . . . .": Doc. No. 213

"The government fought us . . . and Judge Sullivan did not give . . . .": Transcript, Oct. 16, 2007 at 27; Doc. No. 224

"Prosecutor Joseph Bottini, who gave the government's first closing, began by arguing . . . .": Transcript, Oct. 21, 2008 at 9-59 (am)

"they filed a motion . . . .": Doc. No. 206

"Judge Sullivan, of course, denied that motion.. . .": Transcript, Oct. 20, 2008 at 10 (pm)

"Brendan began . . . .": Transcript, Oct. 21, 2008 at 60 (am) through 44 (pm)

"What?" Screamed Brenda Morris . . . .: *id.* at 44-74 (pm)

Chapter 15

"The jury got the case . . . .": Transcript, Oct. 22, 2008 at 62-65

"At 3:55 pm, the jury sent a note . . .": Doc. No. 226

"Judge Sullivan, of course, ...": Transcript, October 22, 2008 at 67-68

"At 11:30 the next day, the jury sent another note . . . .": Doc. No. 230

"At noon, they sent another note . . . .": Doc. No.230 (page 2 of 4)

"Twenty-three minutes later, they sent . . . .": Doc. No. 230

"As for the note about Juror No. 9, ...": Transcript, Oct. 23, 2008 at 25-26 (daytime version)

"At 4:45 p.m. that day, the jury sent a fourth and final note . . . .": Doc. No. 230

"That evening, everybody was thrown a curveball . . . .": Transcript, Oct. 23, 2008 (evening version)

"Judge Sullivan asked some standard questions . . . .": Transcript, Oct 24, 2008,

"On that Sunday evening, the judge replaced . . . .": Transcript, Oct. 26, 2008

"At 3:15 that afternoon, the jury sent a note . . . .": Doc. No. 234 (page 2 of 2)

"The jury entered the room . . . .": Transcript, Oct. 27, 2008 at 20-23

"Brendan and the Senator were on the front page . . . .": *Washington Post*, Oct. 28, 2008

"While we left the courthouse . . . .": www.c-span.org/video/?282050-3/senator-stevens-verdict-news-conference (last visited May 28, 2014)

Chapter 16

"Hundreds of Alaskans were waiting . . . .": *Anchorage Daily News*, "Anchorage Rally Welcomes Stevens," Oct. 30, 2008: http://www.youtube.com/watch?v=NMWml8vmuL4 (last visited May 28, 2010)

"Another emphasized how much Ted Stevens had meant . . . .": www.youtube.com/watch?v=WqGudtuWS0Y

"My favorite ad showed a lumberjack . . . .": www.youtube.com/watch?v=2EhcbohEiVE (last visited May 28, 2014)

"Judge Sullivan issued an order . . . .": Doc No. 240

"The hearing was held . . . .": Transcript, Nov. 3, 2008

"As Juror No. 7 walked to the subway . . . .": *Associated Press*, "Missing Juror Lied About Father's death," Nov. 3, 2008

"The Senator himself addressed the State of Alaska . . . .": http://www.youtube.com/watch?v=YBavRguoDOU (last visited May 28, 2014)

"Senator Stevens conceded . . . .": *Politico,* "Ted Stevens Concedes," Nov. 18, 2008

"Two days later, the Senator gave his last speech on the floor . . . .": 110 Cong. Record S10688 (Nov. 20, 2008)

"The Senators . . . and staffers . . . gave him . . . .": Associated Press, "Stevens Gives Last Speech as Staffers Weep," Nov. 20, 2008

"the Democratic Senate passed . . . .": U.S. Senate: Legislation and Records, http://www.senate.gov/legislative/LIS/roll_call_lists/roll_call_vote_cfm.cfm?congress=111 & Session=1&vote=00396 (last visited May 28, 2013)

"At 4:47 a.m. on November 15th . . . .": Doc. No. 241

"We also made a motion to Judge Sullivan . . . .": Doc. No. 241

"We complained harshly about this tactic . . . .": Doc. No. 245

"We filed a brief that began: 'This country . . . .' ": Doc. No. 308

"Judge Sullivan ruled . . . .": Doc. No. 255

"Their most important argument . . . .": Doc. No. 302

"On December 23, 2008, we filed a motion for a new trial.": Doc. No. 257.

Chapter 17

"So we had a hearing before Judge Sullivan . . . .": Transcript, Jan. 14, 2009

"Late in the next day, the government filed a motion to reconsider . . . .": Doc. No. 264

"The government never wanted the public . . . .": Doc. No. 265

"he denied the government's motion . . . .": Doc. No. 268

"The government's next move . . . .": Doc. No. 266

"Judge Sullivan issued an order . . . .": Doc. No. 274

"We submitted a motion . . . .": Doc. No. 287

"At a hearing on February 14 . . . .": Transcript, Feb. 14, 2009

Chapter 18

"Two days after Judge Sullivan held . . . .": Doc. No. 317-19

"a chain of emails . . . .": Report to the Honorable Emmet G. Sullivan of Investigation Pursuant to Court Order of April 7, 2008 at 372-74

"This is what Assistant U.S. Attorney Goeke . . . .": *id.* at 365

"notes of prosecutor Ed Sullivan . . . .": *id.* at 364

"A bit later, the government filed a motion . . . .": Doc. No. 324

"Some people were saying . . . .": National Public Radio, "Justice Department Seeks to Void Stevens' Conviction," April 1, 2009

Chapter 19

"For nearly 25 years . . . .": Transcript, Apr. 7, 2009 at 3-10

"Paul O'Brien, for the government spoke . . . .": *id.* at 10-13

"First off, let me say . . . .": *id.* at 16-37

"Thank you very much, Your Honor, for the privilege . . . .": *id.* at 39-41

"On October 28, the day after the verdict . . . .": *id.* at 41-42

"This Court has repeatedly been told . . . .": *id.* at 45-48

"I recognize the circumstances were . . . .": *id.* at 50

"There was never a judgment of conviction . . . .": Doc. No. 372

Chapter 20

"Among the multitudes who issed statements were . . . .": *Washington Post*, "Ted Stevens' Death: Washington Reacts," Oct. 10, 2010

"Senator Lisa Murkowski . . . .": *id.*

"Senator Patrick Leahey . . . .": *id.*

"Senator Murkowski . . . .": S. Doc. 111-16, "Ted Stevens: Memorial Addresses and Other Tributes" at 91-92

"The first eulogist was Joe Biden . . . .": *id.* at 93-97

"Senator Daniel Inouye . . . also eulogized the Senator . . . .": *id.* at 99-101

"Reverend Normal Elliott. . .was one of the last to speak . . . .": *id.* at 103-106

"David Rubinstein . . . .": *id.* at 120-25

"Alaska's Governor, Sean Parnell . . . .": *id.* at 137-41

Chapter 21

"A Yale-educated lawyer transplanted from Kansas . . . .": *Washington Post*, "How Joe Miller Caught Lisa Murkowski by Surprise," Aug. 25, 2010

"McAdams issued a statement . . . .": *Alaska Dispatch*, "How Murkowski Fumbled in GOP Primary," Aug. 31, 2010

"Miller promptly took a trip . . . .": *Alaska Dispatch*, "Alaska's Lisa Murkowski Declares Victory, Makes History," Nov. 17, 2010

"In it, Mayor McAdams is seen trying on ties . . . .": www.youtube.com/watch?v=K4aL-GNjPas (last visited May 28, 2014)

"The ad begins with one of Senator Stevens' daughters . . . .": www.youtube.com/watch?v=20mlkvPJZrK (last visited May 28, 2014)

"The front page of the next day's *Anchorage Daily News* showed . . . .": *Anchorage Daily News*, "Murkowski's Write-In Bid Makes Modern History," Nov. 18, 2010

"I think everybody [in rural Alaska] . . . .": *Alaska Dispatch*, "Alaska's Lisa Mukrowski Declares Victory, Makes History," Nov.17, 2010

Chapter 22

"One day after the dismissal of the Stevens case, Attorney General Holder attended . . . .": *Associated Press*, "Attorney General Holder Tells Prosecutors to 'Do the Right Thing' ", Apr. 9, 2009

"Attorney General Holder took another significant step . . . .": *Washington Post*, "Holder Opts for Experience Over Political Connections in Personal Changes at Justice Department," Apr. 9, 2009

"At a speech during her first month . . . .": *Main Justice*, 'Over-Zealous,' 'Under-Zealous' and 'Uninformed' Prosecutors Prone to Trouble," May 6, 2009

"Bill Welch, the Chief of the Public Integrity Section, returned to . . . .": *Washington Post*, "William Welch, Head of Justice Department's Anti-corruption Unit, to Leave Post." Apr. 29, 2009

"He would later leave . . . .": *The Blog of the Legal Times*, "Stevens Prosecutor William Welch II Leaving DOJ," Apr. 16, 2012

"Welch was replaced by Jack Smith . . . .": *Main Justice*, "DOJ Picks New Head of Public Integrity Section," Mar. 11, 2010

"Lead courtroom lawyer Brenda Morris . . . .": *Main Justice*, "Life After Stevens," Apr. 15, 2010

"Later, she turned up in Alabama . . . .": *Harpers Magazine*, "The Justice Department Rolls Snake Eyes in Alabama Gaming Trial", Aug. 15, 2011

"Nicholas Marsh and Edward Sullivan of the Public Integrity Section were transferred . . . .": *Main Justice*, "Welch Removed from Abramoff-Related Case", Jun. 18, 2008

"Two Assistant U.S Attorneys from Alaska . . . .": *The Blog of Legal Times*, "Two Prosecutors in Stevens Case Appeal Disciplinary Action", Jun. 27, 2012

"FBI agent Mary Beth Kepner . . . .": *Alaska Dispatch*, "Why Is Lead FBI Agent in Botched Ted Stevens Case Still Employed?" June 6, 2012

"A federal judge in Alaska sentenced him . . . .": FBI Press Release, Oct. 28, 2009

"But an article in the *Anchorage Daily News* . . . .": *Anchorage Daily News*, "Corruption Figures Allen, Smith Begin Federal Prison Term,", Jan. 13, 2010

"But on August 22, 2010 . . . .": *Anchorage Daily News*, "Federal Officials Won't Prosecute Bill Allen on Sex Charges," Aug. 22, 2010

"On December 13, 2010, an editorial in the Anchorage Daily News . . . .": *Anchorage Daily News*, "Our View: A Matter of Justice", Dec. 13, 2010 (reprinted with permission of the *Alaska Dispatch*, which has acquired the *Anchorage Daily News*)

"Bill Allen was released . . . .": Bureau of Prisons Inmate Locator; *Anchorage Daily News*, "Bill Allen Scheduled for Release Next Week", Nov. 15, 2011

Chapter 23

"Its first sentence almost said it all . . . .": Report to Hon. Emmet G. Sullivan of Investigation Conducted Pursuant to Court's Order dated April 7, 2009 at 1

"Schuelke and Shields had learned . . . .": *id.* at 39-46

"Schuelke and Shields interviewed a government technology specialist . . . .": *id.* at 103-05

"one trial observer, Cliff Groh, a former Alaska Prosecutor . . . .": http://alaskacorruption.blogspot.com (last visited May 28, 2014)

"We learned from the Report the government was very concerned about the Toricelli note . . . .": *id.* at 356-60

"The court-appointed investigations described the birth of the "covering his ass" testimony . . . .":*id.* at 424-62

"Brendan had asked Allen on cross-examination . . . .': *id.* at 469-96

"Memory failure . . . .": *id.* at 21

"The Report referred to Bambi Tyree as 'a juvenile prostitute' " . . . .": *id.* at 198-350

"What did the Schuelke Report have to say about . . . .": *id.* at 9

"Schuelke learned that Rocky Williams . . . .": *id.* at 106-97

"The Schuelke Report concluded that Bottini and Goeke intentionally withheld . . . .": *id.* at 513

"The Report also found that Bottini . . . .": *id.* at 513

"The Schuelke Report made no findings regarding Nicholas Marsh . . . .": *id.* at 513 n.74

"It noted that Bill Welch was largely removed . . . .": *id.* at 506

"It accepted Brenda Morris's statement . . . .": *id.* at 506

"It concluded that Ed Sullivan, ...": *id.* at 507

Schuelke added, 'It should go without saying' . . . .": *id.* at 513

"*The New York Times* and the *Washington Post . . . .*": *The New York Times,* "Inner Workings of Senator's Troubled Trial Detailed," Mar. 15, 2012, *Washington Post,* "Prosecutors Concealed Evidence in Ted Stevens Case, Report Finds," Mar.15, 2012

"The headline in the *Wall Street Journal* read . . . .": *Wall Street Journal,* Mar. 15, 2012

"When Jim Morhard learned that the Schuelke Report had not recommended criminal contempt charges, he wrote . . . .": *Wall Street Journal,* "Are Prosecutors Above the Law?" Dec. 3, 2011 (reprinted with permission of the author)

"It determined that the government violated ethics rules and the Constitution . . . .": *id.* at 666-68

"The Department of Justice Report concluded that Bill Welch and Ed Sullivan did not . . . .": *id.* at 670

"It concluded that Brenda Morris showed . . . .": *id.* at 670

"As for Bottini and Goeke, it found . . . .": *id.* at 670-72

"Senator Henry Reid, the opposition leader, said "Public service . . . .": S. Doc. 111-16, "Ted Stevens: Memorial Addresses & Other Tributes" at 66

"by any means necessary . . . .": Transcript Oct. 2, 2008 at 8-10 (am)

Chapter 24

"On January 4, 2010, roughly eight months after the dismissal of the Stevens case, the Department of Justice published a series of memos . . . .": http://www.justice.gov/dag/dag-memo.html; http://www.justice.gov/dag/discovery-guidance.html; http://www.justice.gov/dag/dag-to-usas-component-heads.html (last visited May 28, 2014)

"The Attorney General himself issued a statement . . . .": http://blogs.justice.gov/main/archives/493 (last visited May 28, 2014)

"A new trial was ordered in a federal case in California . . . .":

United States v. Torres-Ramos, Case No. 2:06-cr-00656-SVW, Doc. No. 997

"In Montana, federal prosecutors withheld . . . .": Falling from Grace: How the Failed Prosecution of W.R. Grace Shows Why Rule 16 Needs Revision, www.omm.com/files/upload/ Bloomberg_Federal_Practice_Dec2009.pdf (last visited May 28,, 2014)

"In a case in federal court in Miami, prosecutors failed . . . .": *United States v. Shaygan,* 661 F.Supp. 2d 1289 (S.D. Fl. 2009), rev'd on other grounds, 652 F.3d 1927 (11th Cir. 2011)

"And in Massachusetts, the chief federal judge, ...": *United States v. Jones,* 620 F.Supp. 2d 163 (D. Mass. 2009)

". . .there had been a previous movement led by the American College of Trial Lawyers . . . .": 41 American Criminal Law Review 93 (2004)

"Judge Sullivan wrote a thoughtful letter . . . .": Doc No. 414

"Senator Lisa Murkowski introduced a bill in the Senate . . . .": S. Bill 2197

"The *Los Angeles Times* endorsed model legislation . . . .": *Los Angeles Times*, "Defending the Brady Rule," Nov. 21, 2011

"An editorial in *The New York Times* entitled 'Justice and Open Files' made . . . .": From *The New York Times*, Feb. 27, 2012 © 2012 The New York Times. All rights reserved. Used by permission and protected by the Copyright Laws of the United States. The printing, copying, redistribution, or retransmission of this Content without express written permission is prohibited.

"One is the Constitution Project, a think tank founded in 1997 to 'bring together' . . . .": www.constitutionproject.org (last visited May 28, 2014)

"Its House of Delegates adopted a resolution . . . .": American Bar Association Resolution 105 D, Aug. 8-9, 2011

Chapter 25

"And a law passed in 1980 known as the Classified Information Procedures Act . . . .": 18 U.S.C. App. III. 1-16

"When offered by the government, the statement that one (alleged) co-conspirator . . . .": Federal Rule of Evidence 801(d)(2)(E)

"Appellate courts have held . . . .": *United States v. Layton*, 855 F.2d 1388 (9th Cir. 1988); *United States v. Weisz*, 718 F.2d 413 (D.C. Cir. 1983)

"listed on the website of the Innocence Project . . . .": www.innocenceproject.org (last visited May 28, 2014)

"As Judge Sullivan said, "Thank goodness . . . .": Transcript, Oct. 2, 2008 at 25 (am)

"Congress has not approved a pay increase for federal judges . . . .": *Bloomberg News*, "Federal Judges in Cost-of-Living Suit Collect a 14 Percent Raise After Years of Legal Battles," Jan. 13, 2014

"In 1940, then-Attorney General . . . .": www.roberthjackson/the man/speeches—articles/files/the-federal-prosecutor.pdf (last visited May 28, 2014)

"He wrote, 'Many of the people who will praise Mr. Holder . . . .": *Huffington Post*, "One System, Two Realities," April 3, 2009

"Ted Stevens rose . . . .": Transcript, April 7, 2009 at 39-41

Acknowledgments

Senator Stevens encouraged me to write this book, but he died before I completed it. When he died, his family encouraged me to finish what I had started. I thank them for their encouragement. I also thank them for sharing their husband, father and grandfather with our nation for so many years.

Bill Phillips first brought Ted Stevens to Williams & Connolly. During the course of the pre-trial investigation, the trial itself and the post-trial battles, Bill was a source of strength to the Senator, the Senator's family and to our legal team. He always did the right thing, and he wanted this story told. Like Ted Stevens, Bill was a great man. One of his legacies is the truth coming out about what our government did to Ted Stevens. Another of Bill's legacies is his family. I am grateful to Bill's family for sharing Bill with the Senator and with our legal team.

Bill Phillips was not the only former Stevens staffer to stand by the Senator in his time of need. Some former staffers were witnesses at trial. Many came to court to show their support. They shed tears on the day of the illegal verdict, and again on the day the Senator was exonerated. They loved their boss, and their boss loved them. Like Senator Stevens and Bill Phillips, they served the public with honor. I appreciate their integrity and their loyalty.

The lawyers on the Stevens defense team grew to become like brothers and sisters. Each is mentioned by name in the body of this book. They know how much they mean to me, and they know much they meant to Senator Stevens. I thank the lawyers on the Stevens team for their tireless and unselfish work on behalf of Senator Stevens. Brendan Sullivan stands out. As Ted Stevens used to say, "When

God made Brendan, he threw away the mold." Brendan inspired our team every day of the case and continues to inspire us.

I could not imagine a better group of people with whom to practice law than my partners at Williams & Connolly. They have provided me with the finest professional examples of how to advocate ethically and aggressively. I consider all of my more senior partners mentors, and I consider all of my partners family. Our firm is a one-of-a-kind place, and I am blessed to be a part of it. That said, the opinions expressed are my own.

In addition to the lawyers who worked on the case, there were many others who contributed greatly to the Senator's ultimate victory in court. David Gerkin, Margaret Havinga, John Holton, Alton Jackson, Patrick Markey, Rhonda Meadows, Tom Paschalis, Moses Sterling and Diane Yeager provided instrumental assistance. Liz Montgomery not only provided excellent support during the litigation, but she typed many drafts of this book. I thank all of them for their efforts.

I was blessed to have had a number of exceptionally bright and diligent interns and research assistants throughout the years I spent writing this book. Carter Scott, Robert Thorpe, Michael Kawi, Austin Yancey, Casey Dennis, Annie Cary and Annie Graham provided excellent research, proofreading and advice. Each has a bright future ahead of them, and I am grateful for their help.

John Greenya is a gifted writer who helped me turn my lawyerly writing into a narrative worthy of publication. I thank him for sharing his talent with me, for the enthusiasm with which he undertook this project and for his friendship.

I am grateful to the following people who read and commented upon drafts of this book: Norman Reimer, Jim Morhard, Judith Richards Hope, Lynda Schuler, Tim McKeever, and Lily Stevens Becker. I hope that I have done justice to their suggestions.

The National Association of Criminal Defense Lawyers has worked hard to make sure that our criminal justice system is fair and that the public learns the truth about what happened to Ted Stevens.

Norman Reimer, Ivan Dominquez and James Bergmann in particular have been instrumental in getting this story published. I thank them and their colleagues for their steadfast work on behalf of fairness and the truth.

Aaron Micheau, an experienced trial lawyer himself, has been a terrific editor. I am grateful to him and Joe Kubes and the remainder of the team at Thomson Reuters for getting this book over the finish line. I am also thankful for the professionalism and hard work of Bill Hamilton and Sarah Christiano at Fenton Communications.

Trials and other professional obligations have taken away from the time I have been able to spend with my family. My wife, Mary Kate, who is the most talented person I know, and my daughters Annie and Gracie give me great joy. I thank them for tolerating my professional obsessions. I hope they know that I love them more than anything else in the world. I also hope that my daughters and other young people who read this book will come to understand that injustice often dwells in unexpected places.